PROPERTY IN WORK

Studies in Modern Law and Policy

Series Editor: Ralf Rogowski

The series provides a forum for the discussion of new fields and new theoretical analyses of law. It seeks to publish research which is located at the interface of law and policy. It is devoted to the contextual analysis of law. Context is understood as meaning both the political and social context as well as the international context of law. Accordingly the series comprises international, European and comparative as well as interdisciplinary approaches to the study of law. A special emphasis lies on socio-legal studies of general legal trends.

Also in the Series

Rulemaking, Participation and the Limits of Public Law in the USA and Europe
Theodora Th. Ziamou
ISBN 978-0-7546-2179-9

Labour Law in the Post-Industrial Era
Lord Wedderburn, Max G. Rood, Gérard Lyon-Caen, Paul van der Heijden and Wolfgang Däubler
ISBN 978-1-85521-644-0

Global Law Without a State
Gunther Teubner
ISBN 978-1-85521-879-6

Contract and Control in the Entertainment Industry
Steve Greenfield and Guy Osborn
ISBN 978-1-85521-561-0

Making Foreign People Pay
Ali Cem Budak
ISBN 978-1-84014-436-9

Property in Work
The Employment Relationship in the Anglo-American Firm

WANJIRU NJOYA
University of Oxford, UK

ASHGATE

Published by
Ashgate Publishing Limited
Gower House
Croft Road
Aldershot
Hampshire GU11 3HR
England

Ashgate Publishing Company
Suite 420
101 Cherry Street
Burlington, VT 05401-4405
USA

Ashgate website: http://www.ashgate.com

British Library Cataloguing in Publication Data
Njoya, Wanjiru
Property in work : the employment relationship in the Anglo-American firm. - (Studies in modern law and policy)
1. Labor Laws and legislation - Great Britain 2. Labor laws and legislation - United States 3. Industrial relations - Great Britain 4. Industrial relations - United States
I. Title
344.4'101

Library of Congress Cataloging-in-Publication Data
Njoya, Wanjiru.
Property in work : the employment relationship in the Anglo-American firm / by Wanjiru Njoya.
p. cm. -- (Studies in modern law and policy)
Includes bibliographical references and index.
ISBN-13: 978-0-7546-4587-0 1. Employee rights--England. 2. Right of property--England. I. Title.

KD3009.N55 2007
344.4201--dc22

2006031582

ISBN-13: 978-0-7546-4587-0

Printed and bound in Great Britain by Antony Rowe Ltd, Chippenham, Wiltshire.

Contents

Table of Cases

UK Cases

US Cases

European Cases

Commonwealth Cases

Table of Statutes

UK Statutes and Statutory Instruments

US Statutes

European Directives

Preface

Since the early 1960s when Simon Rottenburg's article entitled 'Property in Work' appeared in the *Industrial & Labor Relations Review*, followed shortly afterwards by Frederic Meyers's monograph *Ownership of Jobs*, the debate about workers' property rights has been dormant. Yet the idea that there is a link between work and property rights remains compelling. Today most workers in the Anglo-American economies are employed by large publicly-traded firms, and in the debate over corporate ownership and control the idea of property in work has been advanced by various commentators to explain workers' relationship with the firm. The fact that this idea has not become established as a matter of doctrinal law does not in itself outweigh its analytical value in clarifying the nature of the employment relationship in the firm, nor detract from its practical value in encompassing both employee and shareholder interests. The idea of property in work, then, provides a framework for reconciling job security with flexibility, competitiveness and profitability.

In this study the concepts of ownership and property are understood not in the general sense in which one might assert absolute rights to items of personal property, but as a 'bundle of rights' which may be shared, or held concurrently, by different stakeholders in the firm. Critics of property rights theories of the firm often fail to appreciate the sophistication and flexibility of property, overlooking the fact that proprietary entitlements are more often relative than absolute. It is precisely these qualities that make property such a helpful concept in analyzing social and economic institutions. While it is customary to explain the network of relationships in the firm by reference to the concept of contract there is no reason to restrict the analysis to a single conceptual perspective. In view of the limitations of contract in protecting the legitimate expectation of employment security, defining workers' rights as proprietary may offer a useful safeguard for jobs put at risk by 'downsizing', 'offshoring', 'outsourcing', and other forms of corporate restructuring. The aim is to strike a more socially desirable balance between job security and economic efficiency.

This study is the outcome of research undertaken at the University of Cambridge, supervised by Simon Deakin. The intellectual debt owed to Simon Deakin is evident from the citations in the book, but no bibliography could ever fully reflect the true extent of his generosity, including all the time spent discussing these ideas and offering this project his unstinting support. St Edmund's College Cambridge was a congenial home away from home while conducting this research. The University of Kent, and later St John's College Oxford, provided vital research facilities without which the book could not have been written. Mark Freedland and Simon Whittaker at St John's have been very supportive colleagues in the final stages of the book, particularly Mark Freedland in reading part of it and offering valuable comments. Michael Hurst read the entire manuscript and offered helpful criticism and ideas. John Keown read the entire manuscript at a formative stage and offered helpful suggestions on the structure. Kena Njoya, Martin Ernst and Frank Fellenberg also took time out of their busy schedules to read parts of earlier drafts. Alison Kirk and her team at Ashgate have been a great pleasure to work with in publishing the book. And finally, an acknowledgement of my students, whose readiness to offer their views about 'property in work' has been a real inspiration.

Wanjiru Njoya
St John's College, Oxford
10th January 2007

Introduction

Corporations, Workers and Property

The Complexity and Relativity of Property

The title of this book, *Property in Work*, may provoke two preconceptions about the nature of property rights which it is as well to clarify at the outset. The first preconception is that workers cannot have such a proprietary interest because they cannot buy or sell their jobs. However it does not follow that because one owns property one can therefore sell it, or that what cannot be sold is not property: there may be all sorts of legal restrictions on what owners can do with their property, and not all proprietary interests can be bought and sold. So the fact that workers cannot alienate their jobs does not in itself counter the idea of property in work. The second preconception is the far more significant one that if the law were to declare that workers have such a proprietary interest it would imply that all workers hold their jobs 'for life' making it impossible for employers to lay anybody off no matter how incompetent they turned out to be. This line of argument yields too readily to an overly simplistic understanding of property. Proprietary interests come in different 'bundles of rights', making the concept of ownership in Anglo-American law extremely versatile. There is no legal presumption that an 'owner' can never be divested of any rights in property, though there is certainly a presumption that the owner is entitled to compensation for loss of these rights. The idea of property in work does not, then, rely on an unrealistic expectation of 'jobs for life'. Just as the 'owner' of a house may find it compulsorily purchased (or, more commonly, lose it to a mortgagee) so too the 'owner' of a job could find it involuntarily terminated or lost for failure to keep up with various terms and conditions on which it is held. These preconceptions about the nature of property therefore cannot sustain a case against defining workers' rights as property. What they reflect is an objection to any claim to job ownership as immunity from dismissal, a claim which this book nowhere defends.

Preconceptions about property, and the standard objections raised to the idea of property in work, overlook the complexity inherent in property rights. The sanctity of private property does not, contrary to popular belief, imply that because one owns property one can do whatever one wants with it. Therefore even outside the context of dismissal the idea of property in work does not imply that the employer would lose all power to make unilateral decisions in relation to the performance of work; it is not suggested that management should no longer have any control or decision-making authority. Instead the property-based proposals of the stakeholder theory of the firm, which this books advances, seek to identify guiding principles concerning the measure of employment security to which the law ought to aspire. The point was made by Otto Kahn-Freund that the essence of property rights in work is not immunity from dismissal but the aspirations of 'social ethics'. In his words:

> There is something in the analogy between ownership of tangible assets and tenure of employment. For the large majority of people their job is their principle asset. They have invested their skill and their strength in the job. Just as the Government may, in virtue of its right of eminent domain or compulsory acquisition, for the public good, deprive a person of land and other property so it may be in the public interest that a person may have to sacrifice his job. But in both cases a rule of social ethics requires that he who sacrifices an asset should receive a fair amount of compensation.[1]

Property as Relative Entitlement

It is not argued in this book that one's job should be deemed an indefeasible or *inalienable* entitlement. There is a crucial distinction between property rules and rules about inalienability.[2] A discussion of property rules governing the employment relationship is not to be conflated with rules about inalienability, which would imply that once the employment relationship had begun the employee could neither quit nor be fired. The discussion in this book emphasizes that the concept of property is one of *relative* rather than *absolute* entitlement. The main reason for using the language of ownership is not to imply that property in work is held absolutely but to clarify the 'normative significance' and 'value-laden assumptions' which society associates with any resource in which a property right is claimed.[3] As Joseph Singer has argued, the courts' reluctance to accept that jobs may in certain circumstances give rise to property rights is attributable to their underlying value assumptions regarding the workers' sense of entitlement, rather than any doctrinal difficulties posed by recognizing property rights emanating from long-term employment relationships.[4] This point will be addressed more fully as the argument in this book progresses, but it should be clear at the outset that the absolutist notions which represent the popular understanding of property do not stand in the way of formulating a theory of property in work. As will be seen in the course of the discussion in this book, ideas of property in work are concerned with shifting the focus from purely *procedural* rights and the

1 *Labour Law: Old Traditions and New Developments* (Toronto: Clarke, Irwin & Co, 1968) at 38 (cited in Jo Carby-Hall, 'Redundancy' (2000) 42 *Managerial Law* 1–127 at 8).

2 Guido Calabresi and Douglas A. Melamed, 'Property Rules, Liability Rules, and Inalienability: One View of the Cathedral' (1972) 85 *Harvard Law Review* 1089–1128.

3 James W. Harris, *Property and Justice* (Oxford: Oxford University Press, 1996) at 64. Harris makes a persuasive case for the utility and value of the language of ownership; see particularly Chapter 5, 'Ownership as an Organizing Idea'.

4 Jack M. Beermann and Joseph W. Singer, 'Baseline Questions in Legal Reasoning: The Example of Property in Jobs' (1989) 23 *Georgia Law Review* 911–95.

prevailing assumption that fairness in dismissal is satisfied by technical adherence to procedural requirements (in particular giving 'reasonable notice' of dismissal) and formulating a *substantive* notion of job security based on a stakeholder theory of the firm. The aim of the book is to investigate how rights of property in work might be defined in the modern economy so as to balance workers' substantive entitlement to job security against the requirements of flexibility and competitiveness in the context of corporate restructuring in the large, publicly-held firm.

Definition and Context

The concepts of 'property' and 'ownership' are multidimensional and resist clear-cut definition. Much depends on the context in which the terms are used, which may make property rights in one resource different from property rights in another. The difficulty in defining ownership and property has prompted suggestions that these concepts serve no useful function in understanding modern institutions.[5] Yet in spite of, or perhaps because of, this lack of fixed or immutable meaning these concepts are central to various areas of law. Focusing on the interface between corporate law and labour law this book sets itself the limited task of suggesting how the concepts of ownership and property can, by complementing the notion of contract, help to advance our understanding of the role and interests of workers in the firm. The selected context is that of a topical and important problem: workers being summarily laid off to boost the firm's short-term share value. Because the meaning of property is highly context-specific the book does not attempt to make any broad generalizations about property in work outside this context, and in particular does not consider the context of the *individual* employment relationship as contrasted with the employment relationship between workers as a stakeholder group and the firm as employing entity.[6] The reason for selecting this context for study is that economic dismissals during corporate restructuring geared towards boosting short-term share value impose significant social costs on workers and their communities, a problem which merits study in its own right. The question whether lessons from

5 These claims are addressed by Jeremy Waldron in *The Right to Private Property* (Oxford: Clarendon Press, 1988) at 30–31.

6 This distinction (discussed more fully below) is based on the terminology of Mark Freedland, *The Personal Employment Contract* (Oxford: Oxford University Press, 2003). Research into the notion of property in work as it relates to the individual employment relationship would require a different methodology from that adopted in this book; in particular it would require a more detailed analysis of doctrinal rules of law, rather than the interdisciplinary conceptual analysis of this book. A good starting point from the perspective of legal doctrine in both the UK and US would be Paul Davies and Mark Freedland, *Labour Law: Texts and Materials* (2nd ed.) (London: Weidenfeld and Nicolson, 1984); Phil J. White, 'Unfair Dismissal Legislation and Property Rights: Some Reflections' (1985) 16 *Industrial Relations Journal* 98–105; Donald H.J. Hermann and Yvonne S. Sor, 'Property Rights in One's Job: The Case for Limiting Employment-At-Will' (1982) 24 *Arizona Law Review* 763–820; Beermann and Singer.

this context have application elsewhere is put aside for another occasion.[7] Before addressing further the social costs of economic dismissals a brief statement of the book's main argument will be given.

The Central Argument

The main aim of this book is to reassert the value of ownership and property as analytical tools in examining the nature of the employment relationship in the large publicly-traded firm. Large firms employ more workers than any other employer in the modern economy, and because this relationship is today understood as contractual it is widely assumed that this concept of contract has always explained the employment relationship in the common law tradition. In the corporate governance debates the dominant presumption is that the corporation is owned by its shareholders and the workers' interests are fully defined and protected by their employment contracts. This is depicted as the Anglo-American norm. It is then assumed that the stakeholder model, which suggests that the interests of employees are just as central to the firm as those of shareholders, is foreign to the Anglo-American tradition in which freedom of contract and respect for private property point exclusively to the primacy of shareholder interests. The assumption is that there is no basis within the common law framework, other than contract, for defining stakeholder interests in the firm.

This book argues that these assumptions are unfounded. The historical development of the employment relationship in English and American law reveals a more complex picture, in which freedom of contract and respect for private property have not traditionally been associated *exclusively* with the rights or status of the employer. The modern tendency to associate these values with shareholder primacy, and to see stakeholder theory as a challenge to these fundamental freedoms, is therefore not borne out by the historical record. That record reveals a consistent theme of rights at work running through the law, conceptualized as inherent in the nature of work and independent of contract. In some situations they are understood as rights of property, not as absolute claims to immunity from dismissal or power to alienate the job, but as an entitlement to legal protection from arbitrary or unilateral dispossession by the employer. Notions of individual liberty and respect for private property have long been invoked to support the rights of *workers* as well as the rights of *employers*. If that theme is traced from the Middle Ages to the present day it can be seen that at key stages in its historical development the employment relationship was at least partly explained by rights of property.

Modern corporate law associates property rights in the firm with managerial prerogative exercized on behalf of shareholder-owners to the exclusion of employee interests. This is justified on the ground of efficiency in the allocation of ownership and control of the firm. The book assesses the shareholder primacy norm against the

7 Further delineation of the boundaries and scope of the book are considered in the course of discussion in subsequent chapters, particularly Chapter 2 which considers the analytical value of ownership.

background of property rights in work and concludes that there is far less evidence to support the efficiency of exclusive shareholder ownership than is currently supposed. This has important implications for employment security and the stakeholder theory of the firm. Far from constituting a novel approach which is incompatible with the modern economy, or irreconcilable with the ideals and principles that undergird the common law, stakeholder ideas about property rights in work reflect values deeply embedded within the Anglo-American common law tradition and supportive of economic progress.

Economic Dismissals and Job Security

> A profession or a job is frequently far more valuable than a house or bank account, for a new house can be bought, and a new bank account created, once a profession or job is secure.[8]

The need to reconsider the nature of the employment relationship in the firm is imperative in the ongoing debate over how to balance job security with flexibility, competitiveness and profitability. It is understood that there cannot be an absolute right to job security, but at the same time the social cost of dismissing thousands of workers en masse points to the need to strike a better balance between jobs and profits. This difficult question is in turn informed by the respective roles of workers and shareholders in the firm. This part of the discussion therefore explains the meaning of job security, how this is understood within the context of the large publicly traded firm, and how it is related to the concepts of ownership and property rights within the Anglo-American context.

Regulating Economic Dismissals

Large firms regularly undertake organizational restructuring during which a single decision to lay off workers may result in hundreds or even thousands losing their jobs with significant social, economic and political implications. When firms 'downsize' and lay off their employees for economic reasons, often referred to as 'economic dismissals', there is an apparent legitimacy to the employer's action as it seems indisputable that the firm's economic success must take priority over job security. This perspective is reflected in the law governing the termination of employment, which provides relatively weak protection for workers in this context. Indeed it has been said that 'in these cases the law scarcely makes any attempt to prevent or deter dismissal'.[9] In advocating job security the International Labour Organization (ILO) acknowledges that the 'operational requirements of the undertaking' may justify termination of employment. Although the exhortation of the ILO is that employers

---

8 Charles A. Reich, 'The New Property' (1964) 73 *Yale Law Journal* 734–87 at 738.

9 Hugh Collins, 'The Meaning of Job Security' (1991) 20 *Industrial Law Journal* 227–39 at 233.

should only resort to dismissal where there is no alternative, it takes the view that this should be 'without prejudice to the efficient operation of the undertaking'.[10] This balance is reflected in UK legislation which allows dismissal for 'economic, technical or organizational reasons' as a defence to an unfair dismissal claim,[11] and at common law where, in the words of Lord Hoffmann: 'Employment law requires a balancing of the interests of employers and employees, with proper regard not only to the individual dignity and worth of the employees but also to the general economic interest.'[12] Similarly although American law declares an employer's refusal to bargain with a relevant union before organizational restructuring to be an unfair labour practice, the employer's decision to proceed with unilateral changes may be justified on grounds of 'business necessity'.[13] This study therefore takes account of the balance that must be struck in corporate restructuring between job security on the one hand, and operational efficiency on the other.

The Meaning of Job Security

The meaning of job security may be analyzed from a number of viewpoints.[14] One perspective is based on the notion of fundamental human rights, the idea that economic considerations do not justify violation of fundamental rights at work.[15] In this sense job security could be framed as a fundamental right of all citizens, granting them rights of different kinds along a spectrum ranging from assistance in securing alternative employment, to recognition that the workers ought not to be deprived of their jobs in the first place, or at least not in a manner which is arbitrary or unjust. Related to this is the conceptualization of job security as the workers' right to be treated with dignity and respect.[16] This is reflected in notions of 'good faith' and 'mutual trust and confidence' which the employer should observe in the period

10 ILO Recommendation No 119 of 1963, Art 2(1) and Art 12.

11 Article 4(1) of the European Acquired Rights Directive No 2001/23 provides that 'The transfer of the undertaking, business or part of the undertaking or business shall not in itself constitute grounds for dismissal by the transferor or the transferee. This provision shall not stand in the way of dismissals that may take place for economic, technical or organizational reasons entailing changes in the workforce.'

12 In *Johnson v Unisys* [2003] 1 A.C. 518 at par. 37.

13 Under the National Labour Relations Act, 29 U.S.C. §§ 151–169 (1935); Jeffrey Chicoine, 'The Business Necessity Defense to Unilateral Changes in Working Conditions Under the Duty to Bargain in Good Faith' (1992) 8 *Labor Lawyer* 297–312.

14 Anne Davies, *Perspectives on Labour Law* (Cambridge: Cambridge University Press, 2004).

15 Bob Hepple, *Rights At Work: Global, European and British Perspectives* (London: Sweet & Maxwell, 2005).

16 Hugh Collins, *Justice in Dismissal: The Law of Termination of Employment* (Oxford: Clarendon Press, 1992).

leading up to, and possibly in the context of, dismissal.[17] Another perspective is based on industrial democracy, which focuses on the political arena and the role of trade unions and other forms of collective representation in protecting and promoting the interests of workers.[18] Like the 'workers' dignity' approach, this focuses on procedural controls such as employees' rights of information and consultation prior to dismissal. Job security could also be defined in terms of the remedies available for unfair or wrongful dismissal, ranging from monetary compensation or damages (the dominant approach at common law) to the invalidation of a dismissal based on wrongful or unfair grounds. Job security may therefore be defined in different ways. According to Simon Deakin and Gillian Morris 'the key to the meaning of employment security is the existence of some form of regulatory intervention designed to protect workers against arbitrary managerial decision-making'.[19] The choice made within a particular economy or legal system as to how job security is best conceptualized, especially in the context of economic dismissals, is a complex choice influenced by many different factors.

The current trend in understanding job security in market economies is geared largely towards workers' likelihood of finding alternative work if they are laid off, rather than their likelihood of retaining the jobs which they in fact have. The focus has shifted from preventing job losses towards creating new job opportunities. Even in continental Europe, traditionally seen as more protective of workers' interests than the UK or the US, employment policy no longer emphasizes holding jobs for life, or indeed for the long-term. Attention is turning from job security to job flexibility or, in a merger of the two, 'flexicurity'.[20] Policy documents from the European Commission reflect this shift. The Commission's earlier concern with full employment is giving way to concepts such as adaptability and employability, with flexibility on the workers' side depicted as the workers' capacity to anticipate change and move readily from one type of job to another.[21] With job losses now viewed as an inevitable concomitant of corporate restructuring, European employment policy emphasizes the creation of 'more and better jobs' to ensure that workers who lose their jobs will find alternative opportunities within a dynamic and vibrant economy. This attempt to balance 'job security' with 'job creation' is reflected in the 2006 Organization for Economic Co-operation and Development (OECD) *Employment Outlook*, which notes that employment protection legislation may impede job

---

17 *Johnson v Unisys* [2003] 1 A.C. 518; *Eastwood v Magnox Electric Plc* [2004] I.R.L.R. 733.

18 The classic work is Sidney Webb and Beatrice Webb, *Industrial Democracy* (Edinburgh: R & R Clark Limited, 1898).

19 Simon Deakin and Gillian Morris, *Labour Law* (4th ed.) (Oxford: Hart Publishing, 2005) at 388.

20 See Sandra Fredman, 'Women at Work: The Broken Promise of Flexicurity' (2004) 33 *Industrial Law Journal* 299–319.

21 See for example *Restructuring and Employment – Anticipating and Accompanying Restructuring in order to Develop Employment: The Role of the European Union* COM (2005) 120 final (30th March 2005).

creation. By regulating economic dismissals such legislation potentially 'increases the costs for the employer of adjusting their workforce and can create a barrier to hiring'. The report concludes that 'The key issue for policy is how to reconcile the employers' need for flexibility in hiring and firing with that of workers for employment security'.[22]

This concern with 'flexicurity' filters through into the legislation governing termination of employment. For example the legislation governing redundancies which appears at first sight to be concerned with institutionalizing disincentives designed to discourage managers from laying off workers, by imposing on them the cost of paying compensation to redundant workers, in fact has the overriding goal of easing the transition period and thereby supporting economic change and growth.[23] Deakin and Morris suggest that this concern with flexibility and worker mobility reflects not so much a concern with employment *security* but more with employment *stability*, in other words the expectation of continued or alternative employment which depends on 'economic circumstances' which ensure stable employment.[24] The apprehension is that job security for the employed would allow them to become entrenched in their positions regardless of their individual productivity, and thus deny new entrants into the market the chance to try their hand at the job. This would not improve the lot of workers as a whole but would simply result in 'the protection of incumbents against others'.[25] At this level job security is understood as a concern with the availability of jobs in the economy as a whole.

The concern that job security may result in rigidity of the labour market leading to rising levels of unemployment, cannot be dismissed out of hand. However recent empirical studies published by the OECD provide some assurance that this fear may be unwarranted: they 'generally have not found robust evidence for a significant direct effect of [employment protection legislation] on unemployment'.[26] It therefore seems likely that there is no direct link between employment protection legislation and rising or persistent levels of unemployment. The OECD found that evidence of *indirect* effects on job creation remains ambiguous. The risks of adverse effects on opportunities for the unemployed appear to arise only when job protection is

22 *Employment Outlook: Boosting Jobs and Incomes* (OECD: Paris, 2006) at par. 3.3.

23 Hence Deakin and Morris observe that 'the main aim of the Redundancy Payments Act was not, as it might seem, to recognize a kind of property right in jobs, but to ensure that employees displaced from declining industries were given incentives to abandon resistance to technical change, and to enhance job mobility by granting displaced workers a form of compensation which would assist them in the job search': *Labour Law* at 391 (referring to the Redundancy Payments Act, 1965).

24 Deakin and Morris, at 387.

25 Simon Rottenburg, 'Property in Work' (1961–62) 15 *Industrial & Labor Relations Review* 402–5 at 403.

26 *Boosting Jobs and Incomes*, at par. 3.3. Studies cited include Andrea Bassanini and Romain Duval, 'Employment Patterns in OECD Countries: Reassessing the Role of Policies and Institutions' OECD Social, Employment and Migration Working Paper, No. 35, and OECD Economics Department Working Paper, No. 486 (Paris: OECD, 2006).

'too strict', and not simply from the mere existence of job protection.[27] Job security understood as a concern with availability of jobs in the market therefore requires not eschewing employment protection legislation altogether, but conducting a careful assessment of the appropriate degree of protective legislation. The OECD recommends that in order to be successful the implementation of such legislation should be 'quick, predictable and distort labour turnover as little as possible', and 'should be carefully coordinated with reforms to the unemployment benefits system ... so as to reconcile so far as is possible labour market flexibility with security for workers'.[28]

The OECD focus is, necessarily, on job opportunities in the wider economy, often described as a *general* right to work vested in all citizens. This book takes a different approach, focusing on employment security in the precise jobs which employees have in a particular firm. The premise of this focus is that while the effects of employment protection on the *unemployed* must be taken into account, particularly where disadvantaged groups in society are systematically marginalized or excluded from the labour market, the solution does not lie in abandoning security of employment for the *employed*. This study therefore emphasizes and builds upon the crucial point made by Deakin and Morris that 'a secure job is still an essential aspect, for most individuals, of their long-term economic security', in the traditional sense in which job security is understood.[29] This explains why the European Commission's recent shift in emphasis from job security to flexibility and competitiveness has evoked a mixed response from employee representatives, illustrated by the European Metalworkers' Federation (EMF) caution that 'You will never persuade anyone to be happy about losing his/her job by saying that he/she is contributing to the competitive strength of the EU. Developing a positive approach to corporate restructuring will only be possible if the traumatic experience of unemployment can be avoided'.[30] Employment security must indeed incorporate a concern with the implications for the *availability* of jobs but this book argues that ways should be found of doing so while retaining safeguards in respect of *existing* jobs. This concern with employees' loss of their long-held jobs continues to influence core aspects of the law governing the termination of the employment relationship and should not be overlooked in the preoccupation with flexibility and competitiveness.

---

27 *Boosting Jobs and Incomes*, at par. 3.3.

28 Ibid.

29 *Labour Law* at 569. They note that employment protection legislation 'rarely goes to the lengths of granting a worker absolute protection in relation to a specific job classification; but nor is it concerned simply with individuals' opportunities in the labour market. It focuses instead on employees' positions within employing organizations, and operates on the disciplinary and managerial powers of employers in relation to those who are employees, and not in relation to those who are job seekers or applicants for employment': *Labour Law* at 387–88.

30 100th EMF Executive Committee Meeting, Luxembourg, 7th and 8th June 2005. EMF Comment on the EU Commission Communication COM (2005) 120 final.

Ownership of the Firm

Regulating economic dismissals associated with corporate restructuring directly raises questions of ownership and control in the firm by encroaching upon the traditional preserve of managerial prerogatives.[31] A vital tension arises between the notion that corporations in market economies are the shareholders' property and managers must therefore make decisions with the sole aim of maximizing shareholder value; and the contention, on the other hand, that the firm 'belongs' no more to the shareholders than it does to its workers. The solution to this conundrum has direct implications for economic dismissals, that is, dismissals which have nothing to do with the employee's capability or competence and are prompted entirely by the decision to reorganize the company. The changing notions of ownership and property rights have contributed to the conceptual underpinning of the law governing the termination of employment in this context, and can be seen as an essential part of its theoretical structure. In exploring this issue the stakeholder model offers a framework for adopting the language of ownership and property in the corporate governance debates.

The association of property rights in the firm with the shareholder-owners has so far limited the utility of property rights as a conceptual basis for explaining the employment relationship in the firm. The underlying assumption at common law is that the entitlement of the employer as 'owner' to control access and use of his property is incompatible with job security.[32] Yet the concept of property retains its analytical value in explaining the relationship of a firm with its workers. Owing to the controversy and indeterminacy that surrounds the meaning of property and ownership when applied to large corporations, this part of the discussion gives an indication of the sense in which these terms are used in this book and the aims which the book sets out to accomplish in adopting this approach.

The Relevance of Ownership

From a conceptual perspective it could be argued that it is problematic to define *any* interest in the firm as proprietary and that the analysis of shareholder and employee interests in the firm would benefit by declaring once and for all that *nobody* owns the firm. It could further be argued that if viewing the firm as shareholders' exclusive property poses such difficulty then the language of ownership should be eschewed altogether and that, in any case, the separation of ownership and control makes the whole concept of ownership irrelevant in the context of the modern firm.[33] For proponents of employee participation in corporate governance this position seems

31 Deakin and Morris, at 532.

32 Steven Anderman, 'Termination of Employment: Whose Property Rights?' in Catherine Barnard, Simon Deakin and Gillian Morris (eds.), *The Future of Labour Law: Liber Amicorum Sir Bob Hepple QC* (Oxford: Hart Publishing, 2004).

33 This argument is put succinctly by John Kay and Aubrey Silberston, 'Corporate Governance' (1995) 153 *National Institute Economic Review* 84–95; Eugene Fama, 'Agency Problems and the Theory of the Firm' (1980) 88 *Journal of Political Economy* 288–307.

attractive at first glance. Without the concept of property in the firm it would be easier to argue that corporate law should allocate decision-making rights to employees and indeed other non-shareholder stakeholders who wish to make claims on the firm. This was recognized by Adolf Berle and Gardiner Means, who argued that the 'traditional logic of private property' no longer applies to the modern firm. They suggested that ownership of the firm has ceased to be important, which implies that 'it remains only for the claims of the community to be put forward with clarity and force'.[34] They wrote:

> the owners of passive property, by surrendering control and responsibility over the active property, have surrendered the right that the corporation should be operated in their sole interest – they have released the community from the obligation to protect them to the full extent implied in the doctrine of strict property rights.[35]

The call to abandon property as a basis for explaining conflicting interests in the firm has its attractions, but it does not fully appreciate the fact that the so-called 'myth of shareholder ownership' remains pervasive and enjoys enduring appeal in Anglo-American society.[36] This book, rather than taking up the critics' call, joins the debate from a perspective which recognizes, and attempts to harness, the analytical value of 'ownership'. The book therefore counters exclusive notions of shareholder ownership not as part of a general assault on the concept of ownership but as a query about the way ownership is understood within the firm. Therefore as a starting point it accepts the analytical and functional value of ownership and property rights in the firm.[37]

The Normative Appeal of Property

Critics of stakeholder theory, in arguing that the firm is shareholders' property, focus on 'the role of property in providing a source of security against a range of interfering forces in society at large'.[38] In this sense property serves as a basis for those seeking to protect corporate enterprise from external regulation and from non-shareholder

---

34 Adolf A. Berle and Gardiner C. Means, *The Modern Corporation and Private Property* (New York: Harcourt, Brace & World, 1932) at 312.

35 At 355. See the classic debate: Adolf Berle, 'Corporate Powers as Powers in Trust' (1931) 44 *Harvard Law Review* 1049–74; E. Merrick Dodd, 'For Whom Are Corporate Managers Trustees?' (1932) 45 *Harvard Law Review* 1145–63; Berle, 'For Whom Corporate Managers Are Trustees: A Note' (1932) 45 *Harvard Law Review* 1365–72.

36 Paddy Ireland, 'Company Law and the Myth of Shareholder Ownership' (1999) 62 *Modern Law Review* 32–57; Sarah Worthington, 'Shares and Shareholders: Property, Power and Entitlement' (2001) 22 *The Company Lawyer* 258–66; 307–14; Ross Grantham, 'The Doctrinal Basis of the Rights of Company Shareholders' (1998) 57 *Cambridge Law Journal* 554–88.

37 On the functional value of ownership see Thomas Merrill and Henry Smith, 'What Happened to Property in Law and Economics?' (2001) 111 *Yale Law Journal* 357–98 at 363.

38 Merrill and Smith, at 364.

interest groups (such as employees) making claims upon its profits. As such the view that the corporation belongs to its shareholders remains quite deeply entrenched. Such perspectives admittedly rely largely on what Joan Williams terms 'the intuitive image of property', but this is itself an important characteristic of property that continues to cast its shadow on the law.[39] This intuitive image of property is reflected in Blackstone's famous assertion, still often cited today, that property is 'that sole and despotic dominion which one man claims and exercises over the external things of the world, in total exclusion of the right of any other individual in the universe'.[40] This assertion is often depicted as a failure to understand or accept the inherent limitations of property rights, but this critique has not detracted from its normative appeal. Modern reliance on Blackstone's words should not be dismissed out of hand as symptomatic of a limited grasp of the true nature of property or inapplicable to modern society, but rather acknowledged as an illustration of the many dimensions of the concept of property, including its intuitive image.[41] One significant illustration of this image is the assumption that property rights grant the owner exclusive control over the resource and that 'any attempt by the public to exercise simultaneous rights in privately owned property constitutes "regulation",' an interference with rights of property.[42] This perspective has been used to support the allocation of exclusive control of the firm to shareholders.

As Williams argues, the legal formulation and protection of property rights depends to an important extent on the intuitive appeal of these rights, which in turn reflects the moral choices of society and carries considerable philosophical and ideological weight. The debate about the conflicting claims of shareholders and employees in the modern firm therefore cannot be settled simply by saying that ownership of the firm is irrelevant or meaningless. Nor does saying that corporate wealth is owned by the corporation itself and not by its shareholders detract from the dominant influence of shareholder-primacy or simplify the debate, because it leads to even more esoteric debates as to whether an artificial legal person can have goals, such as profit maximization, and whether the firm is capable of having an interest 'in itself'.[43] Far better, it seems, to accept that the law has been influenced by a deeply ingrained vision of what property is, which now lies at the foundation of

---

39 Joan Williams, 'The Rhetoric of Property' (1998) 83 *Iowa Law Review* 277–361.

40 *Commentaries on the Laws of England* (16th ed.) (London: J. Butterworth & Son, 1825) Book 2 at 1, cited in Harris, at 30.

41 For an interpretation of Blackstone's comments on property see Harris, at 29–30 noting (at 30) that Blackstone, 'perfectly familiar' with the limitations inherent in the exercise of property rights, 'summarizes the political culture which he considered owed its legitimacy to conventional acceptance of the common law, by speaking of the "absolute" right to property "inherent in every Englishman"'.

42 Williams, at 295.

43 Gunther Teubner, 'Company Interest: The Public Interest of the Enterprise "In Itself"' in Ralf Rogowski and Ton Wilthagen (eds.), *Reflexive Labour Law* (Deventer: Kluwer, 1994).

most institutions in the market economy. For an institution of such great importance as the corporation this aspect of property should not be overlooked.

A Pluralist View of Property

In terms of analytical clarity there may be much to be said in support of the narrower and more technical view of property which makes it inapplicable to the modern corporation. However this would be of limited use in a study concerned with the social and economic significance of prevailing notions of ownership and control in the firm. It is appreciated within legal philosophy that there is value in taking this kind of broad perspective when the problem under investigation transcends doctrinal categories and boundaries.[44] The implications of property rights in regulating the respective interests of shareholders and employees in the large firm cannot be fully understood from a single perspective. Hence this book prefers a 'pluralist' view of property such as that formulated by Stephen Munzer. Munzer recognizes that critics may view the pluralist approach as 'the academic lawyer's penchant for ransacking every available cupboard for a multi-course banquet of arguments, with little thought given to the integrity of the meal'.[45] Nevertheless he argues convincingly that different perspectives brought together may shed more light on the nature of property than any single perspective taken on its own: 'too many theorists attempt to reduce too much to a single perspective … Each of these thinkers, through the intensity of his partial vision, contributes much to thinking about property, but at the same time obscures the validity of other perspectives'.[46] While Munzer's theory of property selects three main principles and shows how these principles are related, this book explores the links between different analyses of ownership and property rights in different disciplines concerned with the structure of the firm, seeking to extract lessons from diverse perspectives about employees' rights as property.

Attention is also paid to Edward Freeman's caution that in developing stakeholder theory undue technicality in the analysis of property rights would be unhelpful in attaining the primary goal of changing the way large corporations are managed: 'we need to avoid isolated theorizing that is unconnected and unconnectable to the practice of value creation and trade. We need to avoid philosophical distinctions that, for the most part, don't make a difference.'[47] This book is therefore an investigation

44 For instance Waldron argues that 'Conceptual definition is a complicated business and the idea that it always involves the precise specification of necessary and sufficient conditions must be regarded as naïve and outdated. A term which cannot be given a watertight definition in analytical jurisprudence may nevertheless be useful and important for social and political theory; we must not assume in advance that the imprecision or indeterminacy which frustrates the legal technician is fatal to the concept in every context in which it is deployed' (at 31).

45 Stephen Munzer, *A Theory of Property* (Cambridge: Cambridge University Press, 1990) at 9.

46 Munzer, at 7.

47 Edward Freeman, 'Business Ethics at the Millennium' (2000) 10 *Business Ethics Quarterly* 169–80 at 178.

not of technical rules and abstract conceptual constructs, but of prevailing notions and 'background assumptions about property rights'.[48] Rather than join the largely unsuccessful attempts to downgrade the importance of ownership and property in the firm, stakeholder theory joins in the efforts to develop a shared notion of ownership, reconceptualizing ownership of the firm as an interest shared between shareholders and other participants in corporate activity. This seems a useful way forward. As Freeman argues, it enables stakeholder theory 'to join the mainstream conversation about business and capitalism'.[49] Rather than introducing new analytical constructs it proposes that it may be worth utilizing the familiar conceptual tools of ownership and property rights to explore alternative ways of understanding the nature of rights and interests in the firm.

An Interdisciplinary Method

This study is interdisciplinary, drawing from the perspectives of law, economics and management science.[50] These disciplines are all indispensable in understanding the ownership and control of the firm, and share in common the recognition that the role of labour is essential in the corporate governance debates. The study does not of course claim expertise in all these fields, but seeks to combine their insights in order to highlight the fact that the governance of large corporations cannot be fully understood without taking into account disciplinary perspectives that reflect the broad range of factors influencing their operation and management. To facilitate this diverse approach the study adopts the broad definition of corporate governance formulated by Margaret Blair: 'the whole set of legal, cultural, and institutional arrangements that determine what publicly traded corporations can do, who controls them, how that control is exercised, and how the risks and returns from the activities they undertake are allocated'.[51]

In using a proprietary framework to draw together different approaches to employee participation in corporate governance the book does recognize that different disciplines adopt different definitions of ownership and property rights, which certainly poses difficulty for the coherence of any debate about property.[52]

48 Merrill and Smith, at 367.

49 At 174.

50 Other possible approaches include social theory: 'Social theorists of our day insist that welfare entitlements and jobs are in some sense "property"': Harris, at 7; and philosophy: Christopher M. Coope, 'Justice and Jobs: Three Sceptical Thoughts about Rights in Employment' (1994) 11 *Journal of Applied Philosophy* 71–7; however these possibilities are not explored in this book.

51 Margaret M. Blair, *Ownership and Control: Rethinking Corporate Governance for the Twenty-First Century* (Washington D.C.: Brookings Institute, 1995) at 3.

52 As James Harris puts it (at 6–7): 'Property is ubiquitous and complex, socially important and controversial. Yet any general notion of property is notoriously elusive. Political philosophers who have dealt with it are not obviously discussing the same thing, and what lawyers mean by it seems to be something different again ... Is there anything in the

These difficulties have prompted some commentators to question the utility of 'property' as a conceptual tool, arguing that it ought 'to be regarded as ambiguous or confused and certainly as analytically unhelpful'.[53] Yet despite significant disparities in the conceptual parameters of different disciplines property continues to be viewed as an important legal, social and economic institution.[54] This recognition is the basic starting point of this book. The shared appreciation, amongst different disciplines, of the continued relevance and value of property in understanding and explaining the nature of corporate enterprise, is a sufficient premise for the limited purposes of a book which proceeds *within* a property rights theory of the firm. As this is not a philosophical study it is only necessary to establish as a starting point that the property rights view is of analytical value, a task which is tackled in subsequent chapters. It is not necessary for this purpose to ensure that every insight regarding property rights meets the requirements of internal coherence within the theoretical specifications of each and every discipline, and no attempt is made to do so. Nor is there any attempt to directly compare or contrast the ways in which different disciplines use these concepts, a task which would be difficult if not futile.[55] Nevertheless the discussion is not oblivious to the fact that on occasion the definition of property derived from one discipline would not be considered accurate within another. It is not assumed that the different disciplines share the same normative goals in relation to the protection of workers' interests, and care is therefore taken to identify the normative argument of each perspective where such exists. This applies with particular force to the economic 'property rights theory of the firm' which uses the term 'property' in a different sense from the law. If it were intended to show that the proprietary perspectives are superior to other perspectives by contrasting the analytical cogency of the property rights theories with other theories, then these difficulties might have needed to be addressed. However this study proceeds within the framework of the property rights perspectives, saying nothing about whether these perspectives are better or worse than other perspectives of the nature of the firm. The aim is not to distinguish between the selected disciplinary approaches, but simply to suggest various ways of thinking about property in work. Therefore the book does not attempt a general defence of 'property rights' against critics who assert

---

term 'property' which makes all these expressions branches of a common conceptual tree? ... Is there anything, could there be anything, which constitutes an essence of propertiness underlying all these uses?'

53 Waldron, at 30.

54 Harris opens his *Property and Justice* with the statement that 'Property is a legal and social institution governing the use of most things and the allocation of some items of social wealth' (at 3). Reich notes that 'property is not a natural right but a deliberate construction by society' (at 771).

55 Any attempt to satisfy the requirements of every discipline in defining ownership and property would be highly ambitious: 'All attempts in the history of theorizing about property to provide a univocal explication of the concept of ownership, applicable within all societies and to all resources, have failed': Harris, at 5.

at a general level that property is meaningless as a theoretical construct.[56] However, it *does* engage with critics who question the value of property in the context of work and the firm. In doing so it aims to demonstrate that there is much to be learned from the discourse of various disciplines about the proprietary nature of the employment relationship in the firm. While care is taken to identify the disciplinary context of each argument as the discussion proceeds, all references to ownership and property rights are taken on their own terms in so far as the different uses of these terms have the same common aim: that of investigating and describing the entitlement of the participants in corporate enterprise.

This is a somewhat eclectic and wide-ranging theoretical approach whose usefulness can only be judged at the end of the book, but a few remarks will now be made to give an indication of the links between the different theoretical perspectives. Beginning with management science, this discipline may be credited most directly with the proprietary stakeholder model of the firm. It is within this framework that attempts were first made to define a coherent stakeholder theory of the firm. There are various stakeholder theories, not all of which are founded on property rights. The proprietary stakeholder model is itself most fully developed by Thomas Donaldson and Lee Preston, and this book is largely an attempt to apply their ideas within a legal framework.[57] Turning to legal philosophy, this operates as an overarching framework for all the different perspectives as applied in this book. This is the arena which has seen the most detailed and wide-ranging investigation of the concepts of ownership and property rights. In this study particular reliance is placed on the ideas of Jeremy Waldron, whose analysis of the institutions of private property includes a helpful discussion of the corporation.[58] Regarding the legal concept of property rights, this in many ways, and for sound reasons, exhibits the most technical and narrow use of 'property' in its application to doctrinal rules. It is sometimes argued that on a strict interpretation of property in law it has no application to the company.[59] Yet the underlying assumptions which shape the common law rules of company law are heavily influenced by concepts of ownership and property. The concern in this

56 The charge is that '"property" means nothing in particular and those who seek to justify or condemn it, or to decry or applaud any particular distribution of it, engage in sound and fury signifying nothing': Harris, at 8. Waldron and Harris respond compellingly to these critiques.

57 Thomas Donaldson and Lee Preston, 'The Stakeholder Theory of the Corporation: Concepts, Evidence, and Implications' (1995) 20 *Academy of Management Review* 65–91.

58 Waldron sees 'corporate property rather as a mutation of private property than as a distinct form of property in its own right'. He considers it to remain private property because it 'was brought about as a result of private initiatives and for the purposes of the particular private individuals (and their successors in the arrangement) who were involved' (at 57).

59 See, arguing that shares in the company are not property, Arianna Pretto-Sakmann, *Shares and Sub-Shares: The Boundaries of Personal Property* (Oxford: Hart Publishing, 2005); reviewed by John McGee, (2006) 122 *Law Quarterly Review* 525–28; Wanjiru Njoya, (2006) 17 *Kings College Law Journal* 182–88.

book is with these underlying assumptions and not simply with the doctrinal rules of law, although doctrine does serve a crucial illustrative function.

The neoclassical economic theory of the firm defines the firm as a 'nexus of contracts', but at the same time there is an influential property rights approach in economics which focuses on the proprietary structure of the firm.[60] When the economic theories refer to property rights they are generally concerned only with maximizing utility and efficiency by means of the optimal allocation of ownership. They are concerned not with *rights* but with incentives. For instance ownership rights are allocated to shareholders not on grounds that they are *entitled* to be owners, but because it is said that they would otherwise have no incentive to continue to invest capital in the firm. Despite this different focus the economic theories have greatly influenced the legal analyses of rights and entitlements because achieving efficient outcomes is seen as one of the goals of the law in defining property rights. Indeed facilitating efficient outcomes is thought to constitute the overriding function of law. According to Richard Posner 'common law rules and decisions are best explained on the "as if" assumption, not intended to be realistic, that judges are consciously trying to promote efficient resource allocation, where efficiency is defined as wealth maximization'.[61] The theory is that wealth maximization 'should guide common law adjudication' at the very least, and at most 'should guide public policy in all spheres'.[62] In the context of this discussion the implication is that the common law should (and in fact does) 'mimic the market' by allocating ownership and control in the firm in a way that will ensure the maximization of profit.[63] Related to this is the

60 Armen Alchian and Harold Demsetz, 'Production, Information Costs, and Economic Organization' (1972) 62 *American Economic Review* 777–95; Ronald Coase, 'The Nature of the Firm' (1937) 4 *Economica* 386—405; Coase, *The Firm, the Market, and the Law* (Chicago: University of Chicago Press, 1988); Harold Demsetz, 'Toward a Theory of Property Rights' (1967) 57 *American Economic Review* 347–59; Oliver Hart and John Moore, 'Property Rights and the Nature of the Firm' (1990) 98 *Journal of Political Economy* 1119–58.

61 Richard A. Posner, 'A Reply to Some Recent Criticisms of the Efficiency Theory of the Common Law' (1980-81) 9 *Hofstra Law Review* 775–94 at 775. These assumptions will become highly relevant in the discussion in Chapter 2 of 'who owns the firm'. Posner's premise is that economic models are not intended to be 'realistic' and indeed would not be useful analytical tools if they were complex enough to include all aspects of reality. He argues (at 781): 'The more complicated a model is, the less likely it is to yield empirically refutable implications; and a model that is not refutable cannot tell us anything about the world'. But as Coase points out in *The Firm, the Market, and the Law*, this very caution must apply as well to the ideas of efficiency and wealth maximization: 'There is no reason to suppose that most human beings are engaged in maximizing anything unless it be unhappiness, and even this with incomplete success' (at 4). Note however, that although a realistic set of assumptions tends not to be manageable 'there may well be branches of theory where assumptions are both manageable and realistic' (at 33).

62 Posner, at 778.

63 Posner, at 788: 'The common law's proper role is to "mimic" the market (in cases where the costs of market transactions are prohibitive), that is, to try to bring about the same allocation of resources that the market would bring about if it could be made to work'.

view that any statutory interventions aimed at reallocating rights from shareholders to employees would constitute an interference with the efficient equilibrium which evolved spontaneously at common law, as judge-made law, founded on protection of shareholders' property and the freedom of contract, is innately superior to legislative imposition. The conventional view in the discipline of 'law and economics' is that regulatory intervention cannot improve upon the efficient equilibrium arrived at by the common law.

The result of these assumptions is, as Steven Anderman points out, that legislative measures designed to enhance job security are 'implicitly assumed to be a burden on business'; it is feared that 'if they are given too purposive an interpretation they will interfere with the efficient running of a business' and society will be worse off as a result.[64] It is said that an efficient equilibrium will result if the legal framework simply allows market forces to run their course. The law should therefore allow corporate activity to be governed as far as possible by the customary norms which develop in the private interactions between market participants.[65] Simon Deakin and Frank Wilkinson have presented a persuasive argument against this view of the relationship between the law and the market.[66] They illustrate various ways in which, owing to market failures, regulation may support and enhance the efficient working of the market. Therefore they argue that while the existence of market failures does not necessarily mean that some form of legislative intervention is required, such intervention should not invariably be assumed to introduce restrictions or rigidities into the market. They join Ronald Coase in drawing attention to 'the role which regulation may play in widening the market' by reducing transaction costs of operating in those markets as well as ensuring full participation of all who are capable of making a contribution to the labour market.[67] This results in positive outcomes for both employees and employers.[68]

---

64 Anderman, 'Termination of Employment' at 103–4.

65 Avery Katz, 'Taking Private Ordering Seriously' (1996) 144 *University of Pennsylvania Law Review* 1745–63; Melvin A. Eisenberg, 'The Corporation as a Nexus of Contracts and the Dual Nature of the Firm' (1999) 24 *Journal of Corporate Law* 1253–92.

66 Simon Deakin and Frank Wilkinson, *The Law of the Labour Market* (Oxford: Oxford University Press, 2005).

67 Coase, *The Firm, the Market, and the Law* at 9. Coase recognizes that 'the mere existence of "externalities" [adverse effects on the society at large] does not, of itself, provide any reason for governmental intervention … The fact that governmental intervention also has its costs makes it very likely that most "externalities" should be allowed to continue if the value of production is to be maximised' (at 26).

68 The firm also benefits from the protection of stakeholder interests: 'regulations which further the public interest will not necessarily impose net private costs on firms. In particular, regulations that seek to correct a market failure may, if they work effectively, result in a net benefit to firms that comply': John Armour, 'Who Should Make Corporate Law? EC Legislation Versus Regulatory Competition' ESRC Centre for Business Research, University of Cambridge, Working Paper No. 307 June 2005 at 7.

Although it is interdisciplinary, the book does not analyze the law purely from these external perspectives. It adopts an interdisciplinary methodology which respects the autonomy of each discipline, and it gives pride of place to the law. A few remarks are necessary to explain this apparent reversal of the interdisciplinary claims made earlier. The methodological approach adopted here, taking inspiration from that propounded by Gunther Teubner, is based on the idea of systems theory that the legal system is 'open to the environment and adaptive'.[69] Teubner argues that if the legal system is environmentally open then the social, political and economic environment will certainly exert an influence on its rules and norms, but crucially systems can be environmentally open in this sense without losing their autonomy. They continue to seek their 'unity and identity ... in themselves', and not in terms of their adjustment to external environmental conditions.[70] Law can be both influenced by and independent of related disciplines. This theory offers a useful starting point in embarking upon an interdisciplinary investigation. Teubner argues that law, like other 'self-producing' systems, is 'self-referential', meaning that it is only with reference to itself that the legal system can continue to organize itself and reproduce in such a way that it remains 'differentiated' from its environment. But crucially, the legal system is autonomous without being *closed* to external influence. This theory promotes an understanding of the complex 'interdependencies' between different disciplines.[71] The interaction between these disciplines is one of exchange allowing fresh insights to be gained from external sources without the autonomy of each discipline being lost. This methodology allows both a consideration of perspectives external to the law, as well as a critical inquiry of the law from an internal perspective, 'trying to make sense of legal thinking and discourse in their own terms'.[72] This enables an analysis of the broader picture of social, political and economic context, as well as a detailed analysis of the law.

The Anglo-American Firm

This study is based on English law, with American law used to provide a contrast where such comparison illuminates the conceptual structure of the common law.[73]

---

69 Gunther Teubner, *Law as An Autopoietic System* (Oxford: Blackwell Publishers, 1993) at 13.

70 At 15.

71 'It is in this sense that the legal system and the wider institutions of the economy and society become "fitted" to one another through co-evolution': Simon Deakin, 'Evolution for our Time: A Theory of Legal Memetics' ESRC Centre for Business Research, University of Cambridge, Working Paper No 242, September 2002 at 23 (published in (2002) 55 *Current Legal Problems*1–42).

72 Ernest J. Weinrib, *The Idea of Private Law* (London: Harvard University Press, 1995) at 3.

73 Reference may also be made to Australian law, which is understood as part of the same common law tradition. See for instance a Research Report by Richard Mitchell,

A comparative study of the legal systems of England and America is particularly instructive because of their emergence from a common root; lessons about the evolution of systems are most compelling where similar systems diverge, at points where they would have been expected to follow the same evolutionary path. The context of the study is the 'Anglo-American firm', a term used in the corporate governance debates to describe the large publicly-held firms with fragmented shareholder-ownership which dominate the UK and US economies, and the economies of other countries whose legal systems are based to varying degrees on the English common law. These firms have widely dispersed shareholders, who have an 'outsider' relationship with the company and usually view themselves purely as investors, not as hands-on owners.[74] The publicly-held firm, characterized in this way by the separation of ownership and control, is therefore often referred to as the 'Berle and Means' corporation after the authors of the first definitive study of this phenomenon.

Despite evidence that global competition is leading to convergence of corporate organizational structures around the world it remains the case that European firms, by contrast to Anglo-American firms, are dominated by closely-held firms within which shareholder-owners are often concentrated in significant blocks, usually along family lines.[75] Corporate governance understood as a study of the separation of ownership and control and the mechanisms by which managers are held accountable to dispersed outsider shareholders is therefore largely an Anglo-American concern. Indeed there is a debate as to whether the common law is itself responsible for, and a necessary part of, the fragmented shareholding that is thought to be an essential component of a vibrant securities market.[76] The debate over employees' relationship with the firm, as contrasted with that of shareholders, therefore exhibits attributes peculiar to the common law world.

Furthermore, as evidenced by the 2006 OECD measure of the 'strictness' of employment protection legislation, it is possible to identify a common approach to

---

Anthony O'Donnell and Ian Ramsay, *Shareholder Value and Employee Interests: Intersections Between Corporate Governance, Corporate Law and Labour Law* (Melbourne: University of Melbourne, 2005).

74 Brian R. Cheffins, 'Does Law Matter? The Separation of Ownership and Control in the United Kingdom' (2001b) 30 *Journal of Legal Studies* 459–84.

75 Armour observes that 'Unlike their Anglo-American counterparts, public companies in continental Europe typically have concentrated share ownership, with control being exercised by a single large blockholder or a coalition of blocks' (at 11). Similarly John Coffee has described the continental European system as a 'concentrated ownership system, characterized by controlling blockholders [and] weak securities markets': 'The Rise of Dispersed Ownership: The Roles of Law and the State in the Separation of Ownership and Control' (2001) 111 *Yale Law Journal* 1–82. For a description of how Japanese firms differ see Sanford Jacoby, *The Embedded Corporation: Corporate Governance and Employment Relations in Japan and the United States* (Princeton: Princeton University Press, 2004).

76 Rafael La Porta, Florencio Lopez-de-Silanes and Andrei Shleifer, 'Corporate Ownership Around the World' (1999) 54 *Journal of Finance* 471–517.

employment protection legislation amongst 'English-speaking countries', with the US and the UK leading in the preference of these countries for limited legislative intervention.[77] The starting point of the discussion is, therefore, that the corporate governance systems of the UK and the US are similar in material respects and have developed a common approach to understanding the interaction between shareholder and employee interests in the firm. At the same time the dangers of over-generalization are borne in mind. It is recognized that despite similar trends at the general level of ownership structures, the operation of the law with regard to employee interests in the company is quite different in the UK from that in the US. The different social and economic environments, as well as different legal and political institutions, inevitably influence the law in both countries.[78] The book therefore draws attention to differences which reveal how the employment relationship is understood within both jurisdictions. Although the main interest is in Anglo-American law the book refocuses its comparative lens before it concludes, to consider the influence of European law and social policy on English law.

Outline of the Book

The overall aim of the book is to explain how the concepts of ownership and property as conceptualized within the common law influenced the resultant rules that now regulate job security during corporate restructuring. The current legal framework is therefore depicted as an emanation of its historical antecedents. Chapter 1 explores the links between work, property and liberty in the common law tradition. Property and liberty have always gone hand in hand, and this chapter demonstrates the influence of 'individual liberty' and the 'protection of private property' on the legal regulation of the employment relationship in English and American law. Both legal systems emerged out of the Master and Servant Acts, the operation of which rested on the idea that the master had property in his servant's labour and was therefore entitled to exercise control over the servant. The two legal systems subsequently diverged, eventually settling on different formulations of the notion of 'employment at will'. This is true of both English and American law, despite the existence of the 'notice rule' in England. Both jurisdictions reveal an early concern with employment

---

77 *Boosting Jobs and Incomes*, at par. 3.3. Based on data from 2003, countries are ranked on a scale from 0 to 6, in ascending order of levels of employment protection legislation. The US has the lowest score at just over 0.5, and the UK follows at just over 1.0. Canada, New Zealand, Ireland and Australia (1.5) closely approximate the UK score. Italy and Germany rank at 2.5; France, Greece and Spain at 3.0 and Portugal and Turkey have the highest scores at 3.5.

78 See Michael Whincop, *An Economic And Jurisprudential Genealogy Of Corporate Law* (Aldershot: Ashgate/Dartmouth, 2001) discussing the implications of these differences for corporate governance. These differences are often more of *form* than of *function*, particularly as the competence and structure of the British parliament differs markedly from the state legislatures of the US which usually have competence over employment matters.

security but in the end the overriding view was that the liberty of *both* master and servant was best protected by a freedom to hire and fire at will. The chapter illustrates that this was thought to be justified not only on grounds of protecting the employer's rights of property, but also to protect the employee's right to exercise freedom and autonomy over his own labour. A paradox therefore emerged in which fundamental rights and freedoms appeared to point more in the direction of employment at will than of employment security.

Nevertheless the underlying tensions in the case law, with powerful dissenting opinions in the House of Lords and the US Supreme Court supporting employment security, indicate that the common law tradition encompassed both interpretations. Although employment at will was eventually established as the 'rule' it did not by any means enjoy unanimous support from the courts through which it was formed. Indeed there is an argument that the modern at-will rule did not emerge and develop at common law in the usual way but 'sprang full-blown from the busy and perhaps careless pen of an American treatise writer', Horace Gray Wood, in 1886; he appears to have considered the idea of employment at will more in keeping with the 'zeitgeist of an emerging industrial nation' than the English annual hiring rule.[79] Described as a 'prolific' writer who was something of 'an enigma', the impression may be drawn that Wood simply made up the at-will rule ('with us the rule is inflexible, that a general or indefinite hiring is *prima facie* a hiring at will'[80]) attributing it to a doubtful line of cases, and nobody questioned his statement of the rule until it was far too late as several courts including the New York Supreme Court had validated the rule in reliance on his treatise.[81] This allegation is disputed, and in fairness it must be stated that Wood had 'an excellent reputation as a learned, accurate and original law author … a man of genius',[82] but the reason why his treatise is mentioned here is to make the point that the uncertainty about the pedigree of the at-will rule reflects the ambiguity of the common law on the conceptual nature of the employment relationship.[83] Illustrating this ambiguity is central to the task in the first chapter.

---

79 Theodore J. St. Antoine, 'You're Fired!' (1982) 10 *Human Rights* 32–7 and 53–4 at 33; contested by Andrew P. Morriss, 'Exploding Myths: An Empirical and Economic Reassessment of the Rise of Employment at-Will' (1994) 59 *Missouri Law Review* 679–774 at 681 and Sanford Jacoby, 'The Duration of Indefinite Employment Contracts in The United States and England: A Historical Analysis' (1982) 5 *Comparative Labor Law* 85–128 at 111–16.

80 Horace G. Wood, *A Treatise on the Law of Master and Servant* (2nd ed.) (Albany: John D. Parsons, 1877) (original ed. 1886) cited in Jacoby at 111.

81 Jay M. Feinman, 'The Development of the Employment at Will Rule' (1976) 20 *American Journal of Legal History* 118–135 at 126. See *Watson v Gugino*, 204 N.Y. 535 (1912).

82 Feinman, at 126, note 68.

83 For the debate on Wood's rule see Morriss; Feinman; Deborah A. Ballam, 'The True Origins of the Employment-at-Will Doctrine' (1996) 17 *Berkeley Journal of Employment and Labor Law* 91–130.

The main aim of the first chapter, then, is to develop the argument that while modern notions of property in work do not represent orthodoxy, nevertheless they derive considerable support from within the common law. It becomes evident that the idea of property in work is not as startling as appears at first sight, nor as unsettling as modern libertarians suppose. The concept of property is as central to the basic thought and reasoning of the common law in this area as that of contract, and indeed it was only in the modern era that contract replaced the notion that 'the rights that masters enjoyed – rights to control, to benefit by, and to exclude third parties from their workers' labour – [were] considered property'.[84] In the course of this chapter it will be seen that the courts on occasions intuitively, although less explicitly in England than in America, fall back on the underlying assumptions of ownership and property in explaining the rights of the parties to the employment relationship. This chapter considers what is meant by ownership of jobs and property in work, and explains the implications of the proprietary perspective for job security and the concept of employment as contract. This serves as an essential background to the discussion in Chapter 4 of European law, which does not construe the employment relationship in the firm as 'contract' in quite the same way as Anglo-American law.[85] The chapter finishes by delineating the boundaries of the claims made by stakeholder theory and defines the limits of the argument in this book.

In Chapter 2 the focus shifts from the historical development of the employment relationship to a detailed discussion of ownership of the firm. This part of the study is essential to a treatment of job security where large numbers of employees are dismissed for economic reasons during corporate restructuring. The chapter considers the links between shareholder ownership, profit maximization and stakeholder theory. Stakeholder theory offers a means of linking ideas of property in work to theories of the firm, but the theory has yet to be developed into one capable of delineating stakeholder claims with the necessary precision. The central purpose of this chapter is to illustrate how a modern theory of ownership as a shared and contingent entitlement can be used to define stakeholder claims as proprietary claims in the firm.

It is usually thought that ideas of property in work and stakeholder claims to shared ownership are incompatible with efficiency. Although stakeholder theory is not based on notions of absolute ownership or total control it must nevertheless address the apprehension that any derogation from the shareholder primacy norm and the single-minded pursuit of profit maximization would ultimately make society worse off as unprofitable firms would be forced to close and unemployment would increase. The third chapter addresses this concern. Corporate law and governance is

---

84 Robert J. Steinfeld, *The Invention of Free Labor: The Employment Relation in English and American Law and Culture, 1350–1870* (Chapel Hill: University of North Carolina Press, 1991) at 67.

85 See Mark Freedland, 'Employment Law' in John Bell, Sophie Boyron and Simon Whittaker, *Principles of French Law* (Oxford: Oxford University Press, 1998) discussing differences between English and French employment law.

largely based on the assumption that 'the triumph of the shareholder-oriented model over its principal competitors' reflects its inherent efficiency and optimality.[86] This chapter suggests that this view does not take full account of the complex process of evolution and change in the market and the myriad factors that cause certain institutional forms to be 'weeded out' over time while others proliferate. The chapter considers the examples of takeovers and European worker participation and concludes that efficiency considerations do not point invariably in the direction of *exclusive* shareholder ownership or the *automatic* prioritization of profits over job security.

Chapter 4 analyzes the current legal framework. The common law governing the directors' fiduciary duty to make decisions in the best interests of *the company* is usually interpreted as a duty to act in the best interests of *the shareholders*. However this rule is not as straightforward as might be expected, as directors exercise considerable discretion to promote the interests of other stakeholders, currently described as the principle of 'enlightened shareholder value.' The chapter considers the interpretation of this idea in English law under the Companies Act and in American law under the anti-takeover legislation, and concludes that as a descriptive matter shareholder primacy remains the predominant rule in practice. Nevertheless the predominance of this rule in practice does not mean that this is the legal requirement. The law does not prescribe the mandatory prioritization of shareholder interests. Having argued in Chapter 1 that the historical record does not point exclusively to property rights vesting in the employer, this chapter argues that the same may be said of the legal framework. The chapter then suggests that there is room within the law for further recognition of stakeholder claims within a proprietary model. This suggestion is supported by reference to the law regulating employment rights in the context of transfers of undertakings and the law granting rights of 'information and consultation' to employees. The final chapter then draws a brief conclusion.

86 Henry Hansmann and Reinier Kraakman, 'The End of History for Corporate Law' (2001) 89 *Georgetown Law Journal* 439–68 at 468. More recently published in Jeffrey Gordon and Mark Roe (eds.), *Convergence and Persistence in Corporate Governance* (Cambridge University Press, New York, 2004).

Chapter 1

Work, Property and Liberty

Introduction

This chapter takes a historical perspective, investigating the influence of individual liberty and the protection of private property on the regulation of work in English and American law. The chapter draws from studies of different stages in the development of the employment relationship, which illustrate the effect of the contemporaneous understanding of ownership and property on the rules governing dismissal, and argues that the underlying conceptual structure of the employment relationship in both jurisdictions has been shaped by notions of both contract and property. Particular reliance is placed on studies by Deakin and Wilkinson in the context of English law, and Robert Steinfeld and Christopher Tomlins in the context of America.[1] It is well established that both legal systems were rooted in the Master and Servant Acts and the annual hiring rule, but while English law eventually developed the 'notice rule' American law settled on the doctrine of employment at will. This divergence occurred at the turn of the nineteenth century at a time when security of tenure had increasingly begun to be linked to restrictions on workers' liberty, and job security was deemed by the courts to be irreconcilable with the fundamental rights of liberty and property of *both* master and servant.

The association of employment at will with the employer's property rights is well known; it is an outcome of the early nineteenth century concept that a master purchased the labour of his workers which then became his property over which he had exclusive control.[2] Steinfeld notes that the master and servant laws were understood to be based on 'a kind of property that employers enjoyed in the services of their workers, a legal right to the exclusive use and enjoyment of their workers' energies for the period or purposes specified in the agreement'.[3] This insight is true of both English and American law although judicial reference to rights of 'property' was much more explicit in the US than in England partly because in the US the constitutional protection of property rights formed the backdrop for the early debates about job security. This constitutional theme emerged in the litigation over an employers' right

1 See citations above, notes 66 and 84; Christopher L. Tomlins, *Law, Labor and Ideology in the Early American Republic* (Cambridge: Cambridge University Press, 1993).

2 Thomas Cochran and William Miller, *The Age of Enterprise* (New York: Harper and Row, 1961); Steinfeld at 81.

3 At 4.

to dismiss, with a connection drawn between an employer's property rights and the freedom to dismiss workers at will. Although similar litigation in the English context was usually conducted within the conceptual framework of 'freedom of contract' the same understanding of property rights was implicit in judicial reasoning.[4] This association of property rights with the employer, coupled with the general view of ownership as a unified and one-dimensional construct, did not allow much room for developing the idea of property in work. It was generally, though not unanimously, thought that *any* form of 'right' in work that was not granted and defined by the terms of the employment 'contract' would impose a vague and unenforceable duty on the employer. These developments are significant in understanding the current legal framework of job security as they have set the context for the modern debate about property in work, primarily through the argument that any form of 'ownership of jobs' would run counter to the fundamental values underlying the common law. A better understanding of this legal tradition therefore serves as an essential background to the analysis of the modern debate in subsequent chapters. One of the overall aims of this book is to identify the underlying assumptions that characterize the employment relationship at common law, therefore no reference is made at this stage to the current framework of statutory employment protection.

From Status to Contract

This part of the discussion gives an overview beginning from the time when servants were compelled by law to work on pain of criminal sanctions ranging from fines to imprisonment, to the modern day when the standard work relationship is based on a contract allowing either employer or employee to terminate the relationship at will or by notice. As highlighted by Deakin and Wilkinson, before contract became established as the conceptual basis of the employment relationship the law was based on 'a hierarchical model of service'.[5] Although the relationship was a form of 'contract of service' the master exercised control over the servant's labour on the basis of status-dependent rules governed by the Master and Servant Acts. Because the servant was not free in any real sense to enter into or leave any employment on terms of his choice, this relationship cannot be accurately understood as contractual except in the loosest sense – Steinfeld describes it as 'contractual unfree labor'.[6] By virtue of his *status* the servant had obligations of obedience, loyalty and fidelity to the master, who in turn had obligations of care towards the servant.[7] As these obligations were determined by status the outcome of legal disputes surrounding dismissal

4 For a critical analysis of how implicit values and assumptions influence judicial reasoning in the context of property rights see Beerman and Singer.

5 Deakin and Wilkinson, at 1.

6 At 5.

7 Anderman, 'Termination of Employment' at 105.

depended more on the claimant's 'station in life' than on the law of contract.[8] It will be seen later how this affects the interrelationship between contract and property in the employment context.

The Master and Servant Acts

The regulatory framework of the Master and Servant Acts is the subject of detailed analysis by other commentators; only an overview is given here.[9] Until their repeal in 1875 the Master and Servant Acts constituted the primary framework for the regulation of work in English law. The most important of these Acts were the Statutes of Labourers passed in 1349 and 1350[10] and the Statute of Artificers of 1563,[11] which imposed compulsory labour on defined categories of able-bodied adults and provided for the imprisonment of servants found to be in breach of the duties owed to their masters. The servant was not allowed to leave his work, and in return the master was obliged to look after the servant and not discharge him until the duration of service, typically a year under the 'annual hiring rule', had ended.[12] The master was deemed to have acquired a proprietary entitlement to his servant's labour, and absconding workers were therefore treated as criminals who had misappropriated their master's property; they were hunted down and, when captured, 'put in Prison till they shall finde sufficient Surety well and honestly to serve their Masters, Mistresses or Dames

8 In *Yewens v Noakes* Lord Thesiger defined a 'servant' under the Acts as 'the ordinary menial or domestic servant', that is, 'not in the sense in which any clerk or manager is called the servant of his employer': [1880] 6 Q.B.D. 530 at 538. The Acts did not apply to higher-status workers. It was said of a clerk that 'it would be, indeed, extraordinary, if a party, in his station of life, could be turned off at a month's notice, like a cook or scullion': Best C.J. in *Beeston v Collyer*, where Park J. remarked 'Persons in the situation of the Plaintiff must be supposed to possess superior acquirements, and are entitled to more respect than to be turned off without any reason being assigned': (1827) 4 Bing 309, 130 E.R. 786 (Ct.C.P).

9 For a detailed analysis see Deakin and Wilkinson.

10 23 Edw. 3 (The Ordinance of Labourers) and 25 Edw. 3, St. 1 (the Statute of Labourers), both finally repealed by the Statute Law Revision Act 1863. The Statute of Labourers stated in its preamble that 'Whereas late against the Malice of Servants, which were idle, and not willing to serve after the Pestilence, without taking excessive Wages, it was ordained … That such Manner of Servants, as well Men as Women, should be bound to serve … and that the same Servants refusing to serve in such Manner should be punished by Imprisonment of their Bodies'. The pestilence refers to the Black Death.

11 Statute of Artificers, 5 Eliz. c. 4.

12 Annual hiring extended to many, though not all, servants, based on the classification in the Statute of Artificers: 'Within the rural labour force the term "servant" denoted a worker who was normally unmarried, hired for the year, and paid mainly in kind through food, clothes and lodging, while the term "labourer" denoted one who was hired by the week or the day and paid cash wages': Deakin and Wilkinson, at 45; see also Otto Kahn-Freund, 'Blackstone's Neglected Child: the Contract of Employment' (1977b) 93 *Law Quarterly Review* 508–28.

from whom they so departed or fled, according to the Order of the Law'.[13] Indeed it could be said that in various contexts the law conceived of servants as property.[14]

Until the turn of the nineteenth century the Master and Servant Acts continued to be amended in order to extend the scope of this criminal jurisdiction. It was only with the introduction of the Act of 1867, which limited the scope of imprisonment and the effect of fines, that a retreat from the criminal enforcement of work obligations at last began.[15] This followed representations made before a House of Commons Select Committee on Master and Servant in 1865 against the harsh operation of the Acts, and especially the unequal treatment shown to servants. The servant was usually brought before the court on arrest warrants, 'dragged as a criminal to the bar … [and] while he may be taken there manacled, the employer is taken into court as a gentleman; he is simply summoned there and treated with the respect which is due to mankind generally …'[16] There was an increasing body of opinion that it was inappropriate to use criminal penalties to regulate the relations between master and servant, especially since it was virtually impossible for a servant to enforce any of the civil penalties available against masters. Hence it was argued on behalf of the servant 'classes' that employment should be governed entirely by contract, and not by relative status. It was represented to the Select Committee on behalf of the *Associations of the Working People* that the employment relationship

> is a simple contract of hiring, and that in law is a civil contract, and what they object to is, that criminal consequences should be attached to their non-fulfilment of the contract on the one side of the contract, while it remains a purely civil contract as it affects the masters on the other side.[17]

The Acts were eventually repealed in 1875 by the Conspiracy and Protection of Property Act,[18] but even after this formal repeal they continued to influence the regulation of the employment relationship for most industrial workers.[19] This was because in practice the development of the employment contract terminable on reasonable notice only applied to higher status workers. As Deakin argues, the regulation of the employment relationship was still very much dependent on the *status* of the worker and most industrial workers did not benefit from the 'reasonable notice' protection.[20]

---

13 Statute of Artificers, s. XXXIX, cited in Steinfeld, at 32.

14 Jacoby, 'The Duration of Indefinite Employment Contracts' at 87; Steinfeld, at 66–73, discussing Maitland's statement that a villein 'was merely the chattel of his lord to give and sell at his pleasure' (at 67).

15 30 &31 Vict. c. 141.

16 House of Commons Report, 17 May 1866, par. 13.

17 House of Commons Report, 2 June 1865 par. 3.6.

18 38 & 39 Vict. c. 86.

19 Simon Deakin, 'The Contract of Employment: A Study in Legal Evolution' (2001b) 11 *Historical Studies in Industrial Relations* 1–36 at 24.

20 This reliance on status continued until the adoption of what Deakin describes as 'the "unitary" model of the contract of employment, which by 1945 came to extend to all

Turning to America, Steinfeld observes that at the time when English law made a formal break with the Master and Servant Acts these statutes had long fallen into disuse in America. At the outset the Acts were formally adopted as law in the American colonies, including the Statute of Labourers, the Statute of Artificers and various settlement laws.[21] This was reflected in the early treatises on the law of master and servant, and continued in some states well into the nineteenth century.[22] However, as Steinfeld demonstrates, for various reasons which related to different political environments and different labour market conditions in the two countries, during the period in which the ambit of the Acts was being steadily extended in England with increasingly harsh criminal penalties the American legislatures did not continue to build on this statutory framework. Tomlins attributes the American approach to a 'vibrant popular culture' unwilling to perpetuate the notions of domination and subordination implicit in the concepts of master and servant. The prevailing popular appeal of 'free labour' had sufficient political strength to ensure that no American state would perpetuate a statutory law of employment with penal provisions.[23] By the time English law developed the 'reasonable notice' rule the 'employment at will' rule had become well-established in the States. This divergence is explored further below.

The Annual Hiring Rule

Jacoby's analysis of the employment relationship at common law at the turn of the nineteenth century suggests that before they diverged English and American law were both, to varying degrees, constructed upon the annual hiring rule. In England the presumption of a yearly hiring, as stated in Blackstone in 1765, was that

> If the hiring be general without any particular time limited, the law construes it to be a hiring for a year; upon a principle of natural equity, that the servant shall serve, and the master maintain him, throughout all the revolutions of the respective seasons; as well when there is work to be done as where there is not; ... and no master can put away his servant, or servant leave his master after being so retained; either before or at the end of his term, without a quarter's warning; unless upon reasonable cause to be allowed by a justice of the peace.[24]

---

categories of wage-earners' regardless of status: 'The Contract of Employment' at 31–2.

21 Steinfeld, at 41–54. For a discussion of the settlement laws in the US see Elizabeth G. Brown, 'Poor Relief in a Wisconsin County, 1846-1866: Administration and Recipients' (1976) 20 *American Journal of Legal History* 79–117.

22 Francis B. Sayre, *Cases on Labor Law* (Cambridge: Harvard University Press, 1922) at 3–17. In 1837 Timothy Walker's *Introduction to American Law* describes the common law of master and servant as the basis of the law of employment in America (Philadelphia, 1837; revised ed., by J. Bryant Walker, 1869) at 243. Wood's 1877 treatise was also broadly patterned on the master and servant framework, highlighting variations between American and English law where these existed.

23 At 231–34.

24 Wayne Morrison (ed.), *Blackstone's Commentaries on the Laws of England* (London: Cavendish Publishing, 2001) vol. I par. 425–6. The applicability of this statement to conditions

This rule was cited in both English and American cases as authority for the common law presumption of an annual hiring, which was 'socially and legally the most significant form of wage labour for most of the eighteenth century'.[25] The main concern of this rule was not the servant's security of tenure but rather to ensure that the masters were adequately supplied with labour throughout the year. Any servant subject to the jurisdiction of the Master and Servant Acts who left his service before the year was out would forfeit his wages and be subject to imprisonment and fines. Annual hiring was linked to 'settlement by hiring' and continued to have effect in England until settlement by hiring was repealed in 1834.[26] Similarly, Jacoby notes that in the American colonies 'a servant dismissed without cause during the winter months' was entitled to compensation from his master to prevent him becoming a charge on public funds under the settlement laws.[27] Several colonies followed the English practice under which settlement depended on a servant 'showing that he

---

prevailing at the time of Blackstone's writing is disputed: see *Marrison v Bell* [1939] 2 K.B. 187 where it was observed that 'the great majority of employed persons in this country are employed on terms of a week's or, at any rate, a month's notice – mostly a week's notice'. For a discussion of whether Blackstone misstated this rule see Deakin and Wilkinson, at 50–51.

25 Deakin and Wilkinson, at 45. For the rule in America see cases cited by Jacoby: *Bleeker v Johnson*, 51 How.Pr. 380 (1876): 'the English rule is accepted as the law in this country'; *Davis v Gorton*, 16 N.Y. 255 (1857): 'where services in the management of a farm and household are performed under a general retainer, without any express agreement as to the time or measure of compensation or the term of employment, and such services continue for a series of years, no payments being made, the law will regard the hiring as from year to year, and the wages payable at the same time.' In 1852 Charles M. Smith's *Treatise on the Law of Master and Servant* stated a presumption that a general hiring was a yearly hiring for all servants, unless there was a custom or other evidence to the contrary (London: S. Sweet, 1852).

26 Deakin, 'The Contract of Employment' at 20, discussing the gradual demise of this rule starting in the 1780s; as late as 1919 the rule was still cited in the case law: *Cayme v Allan, Jones and Co* (1919) 35 T.L.R. 453. Settlement by hiring refers to the rule that a labourer's parish of settlement for purposes of the Poor Law was that in which he was hired. The parish would be responsible for his upkeep should he be put out of work. It was no easy matter for a poor person to gain settlement: see Adam Smith *An Inquiry into the Nature and Causes of the Wealth of Nations* (Edwin Cannan, ed.) (5th ed.) (London: Methuen and Co, 1904) (original ed. 1776), Chapter X.

27 Jacoby at 89. The extent to which the annual hiring rule extended throughout the states is debated, though there is clear evidence that it did apply. Ballam argues that it never took root and that 'employment at will' has constituted the norm in American law since the earliest colonial days; see also Michael Bennett, 'Montana's Employment Protection: A Comparative Critique of Montana's Wrongful Discharge from Employment Act in Light of the United Kingdom's Unfair Dismissal Law' (1996) 57 *Montana Law Review* 115–41. Feinman notes that during this period 'American law … exhibited a confusion of principles and rules. Through the middle of the nineteenth century, American courts and lawyers relied heavily on English precedents but often came to different results' (at 122).

had been hired to serve and had served for one year'.[28] It seems clear then that both English and American law developed from the same starting point, an annual hiring under the remit of the criminal jurisdiction of the Master and Servant Acts.[29]

As to subsequent developments there is some uncertainty surrounding the precise reasons which, at the turn of the nineteenth century, caused the legal presumption in America to evolve to employment at will while English law developed to require reasonable notice before dismissal. This puzzle was first brought to attention by Jay Feinman's investigation of the different factors which prompted the emergence of the at-will rule. Feinman's study traces American law back to its roots in English law, investigating the reasons why American law embarked on the at-will rule, and at the same time emphasizing that the differences between the at-will rule and the English rule of dismissal on reasonable notice must not be overstated because the 'notice' required under English law to dismiss certain workers, primarily lower-status workers, was extremely short. In some industries such as coal mining workers could be dismissed on a minute's notice.[30] Lower status servants were often employed virtually at will.[31]

One factor which was highly influential in determining the path taken by both English and American law in developing alternatives to the annual hiring rule, and which shaped their respective formulations of employment at will, was the reliance on notions of individual liberty and property rights in defining the employment relationship.[32] Notions of liberty and property as fundamental rights are by no means the most important factors in explaining the respective paths taken by the law of master and servant, but they are the most informative in the context of this study. Both countries considered liberty and property as fundamental rights highly relevant in delineating the scope of job security, although the link between liberty and property was more readily in evidence in the US than in England primarily because these rights were enshrined in the US constitution and therefore a matter falling within the jurisdictional competence of the US Supreme Court. By contrast

---

28 Jacoby at 91. In *Heidleberg v Lynn* the issue was whether a pauper had gained settlement in an Ohio township; the point was made that 'as our system of poor laws had its origin in that of England, and as many of her statutory provisions were re-enacted here, we must turn to some of them to have a view of the whole ground in contest': 5 Whart. 430 (1840) Gibson, C.J. although Jacoby notes (at 104) that cases such as *Heidleberg v Lynn* were rare as contrasted to the situation in England.

29 Bennett, at 117.

30 The colliers' 'minute contracts' are discussed in the House of Commons' *Report from the Select Committee on Master and Servant; Together with the Proceedings of the Committee, and Minutes of Evidence*, June 1865 to May 1866, at par. 158.

31 'Employment at will was applied *de facto* to casual hirings and to certain industrial employments': Simon Deakin, *Contract, Labour Law and the Developing Employment Relationship* (PhD Thesis: University of Cambridge, 1989) at 138.

32 Herbert Hovenkamp, *Enterprise and American Law: 1836-1937* (Cambridge: Harvard University Press, 1991). Feinman and Jacoby place reliance on other factors in explaining these developments.

master and servant cases in England were usually tried in summary hearings before propertied laymen or magistrates.[33] Disputes concerning job security did not often reach the highest courts, although as will be seen below the House of Lords on occasion invoked notions of individual liberty when called upon to consider the limits of the employer's power of dismissal. Rights of liberty and property were relied upon not just to protect the master, but also to release the servant from the restrictions of the annual hiring rule.

The Strictures of Indefinite Hiring

The requirement of English common law that workers cannot be dismissed without reasonable notice in theory offers protection against at-will dismissal – the longer the period of notice the better protected the worker is. This was the rationale behind the old presumption of an annual hiring. However, in practice the annual hiring caused hardship to a worker who left his employment before the year was out, as he would not be entitled to any wages at all even if he had worked the year almost to a close. A good illustration is *Huttman v Boulnois, The Younger* where the servant left his employment before a full year had passed and brought an action for his wages for the period worked.[34] The question posed to the court on his behalf was, 'suppose a clerk remains with his employer three hundred and sixty four days, and then goes away, does he forfeit the whole of his wages by not stopping the remaining day?' The employer's argument was that 'every species of hiring, where no time is specified, is by law a hiring for a year, and therefore the servant was bound to serve for a year, or show some reason which would justify his leaving earlier, or else he would not be entitled to his wages'.[35] The servant's claim was denied, which was particularly harsh because the servant had been compelled to resign, against his will, by personal difficulties of which his employer was aware. Hence the annual hiring rule provided servants with a measure of employment security at the expense of freedom and fairness.

Later, as Jacoby has shown, when the annual hiring rule was replaced by the reasonable notice rule even minimum notice requirements began to be seen as a hardship by workers who would incur criminal liability for breach of contract by going on strike without giving the requisite notice of intention to terminate the contract.[36] Hence many workers supported the employers' preference for 'freedom to discharge their operatives at a few hours' notice'.[37] Sidney and Beatrice Webb described how workers came together and 'fought hard to get rid of their "yearly

33 Douglas Hay, 'Master and Servant in England: Using the Law in the Eighteenth and Nineteenth centuries' in William Steinmetz (ed.), *Private Law and Social Inequality in the Industrial Age: Comparing Legal Cultures in Britain, France, Germany, and the United States* (Oxford: Oxford University Press, 2000).

34 (1826) 2 Car. & P. 510.

35 At 511.

36 Jacoby, at 98.

37 Webb and Webb, at 431.

bond"', and 'many Trade Unions ... expressly prohibited their members from entering into longer engagements'.[38] The yearly hiring was replaced by weekly and fortnightly engagements, or even hiring by the hour or minute. While this subjected workers to the risk of dismissal at the employer's will, it vitally allowed them to bargain collectively for their terms and conditions of work: annual hiring 'was incompatible with Collective Bargaining.' The Webbs thought that the worker's capacity to leave work at will, 'to throw up his job when he likes', was therefore an essential element of their collective freedom. They concluded that 'The briefest possible term of service, terminable at a day or a week's notice on either side, has accordingly come to be preferred, for different reasons, by both employers and Trade Unionists'.[39]

Similarly Tomlins demonstrates that America's departure from the status-based master and servant laws was linked quite explicitly to notions of liberty and equality.[40] This is reflected in contemporary treatises, an early *Treatise on the Law of Contracts* noting that

> [in England] the relation of master and servant is in many respects regulated by statutory provisions, and upon some points is materially affected by the existing distinction of ranks, and by rules which have come down from periods when this distinction was more marked and operative than at present ... [in America] we have nothing of this kind. With us, a contract for service is construed and governed only by the general principles of the law of contract.[41]

Although as Tomlins points out it is doubtful that contract had indeed completely replaced status in regulating the employment relationship in America by the time this treatise was published in 1853, it seems clear that the reliance on status distinctions in determining the rights and obligations of the employment relationship did not assume the same importance in American as in English law.[42] The contract of employment became established across the states and by 1912 it was held in New

---

38 Webb and Webb, at 431.

39 Webb and Webb, at 432.

40 Tomlins, at 231-4; Jacoby, at 104: 'After the Revolution, the concept of criminal proceedings to enforce the contract was repugnant to the doctrines of personal liberty and equality under the law...'

41 Theophilus Parsons, *A Treatise on the Law of Contracts* (Boston: Little, Brown, 1853) vol. 1 at 86, cited in Tomlins at 269. For an overview of the early treatises see Feinman.

42 Jacoby observes that the annual hiring rule continued to apply in Britain long after its demise in America because it 'helped courts to maintain status distinctions in a much more highly status-conscious society' (at 97). This appears to be borne out by the fact that at the time the at-will rule emerged in America, notice periods in England 'varied according to the status of the worker or employee in question. "Higher-status" workers, such as clerical and managerial employees, benefited from long periods of notice ... By contrast, most industrial workers during the period from 1875 were employed on contracts with short periods of notice-possibly of no more than a day or even an hour': Deakin, 'The Contract of Employment' at 27.

York that 'the rule is settled that unless a definite period is specified in the contract, the hiring is at will and the master has the right to discharge and the servant to leave at any time'.[43] This reciprocity was perceived as an important element of the rule. Hardly ever was the master's power to dismiss at will mentioned without reference to the servant's equal freedom to leave; as Jacoby observes, 'the courts made heavy use of the contractual imagery that both employee and employer had equal liberty to terminate employment at will'.[44]

This is significant emerging as it did out of the criminal jurisdiction of the Master and Servant Acts, with imprisonment of servants who left their service. Unlike the old English settlement laws which did not permit a poor man to simply leave his parish and try to find work in a different parish the at-will rule was associated in popular culture with the ability to find work wherever one pleased with no need to even give notice.[45] Therefore the courts emphasized that the employer's freedom to discharge an employee at will was the same as the employee's right to quit at will. The classic statement of the rule is that of the Tennessee Supreme Court in the 1884 case of *Payne v West Atlantic Railroad*:

> men must be left, without interference to buy and sell where they please, and to discharge or retain employees at will for good cause or for no cause, or even for bad cause without thereby being guilty of an unlawful act *per se*. It is a right which an employee may exercise in the same way, to the same extent, for the same cause or want of cause as the employer.[46]

A similar rule was laid down by the House of Lords in 1898, Lord Davey stating in *Allen v Flood* that 'An employer may discharge a workman (with whom he has no contract), or may refuse to employ one from the most mistaken, capricious, malicious, or morally reprehensible motives that can be conceived, but the workman has no right of action against him.'[47] In this way the classic rule in both English and American law relied on the notion of freedom of contract, with its connotations of equality between the parties. The workers' liberation from the strictures of annual hiring paradoxically constituted the basis for their lack of job security.

Liberty, Property and Due Process

The importance of the at-will rule in the American constitutional litigation over an employer's absolute right to dismiss a worker, to which attention is drawn by Andrew Morriss, relates to the interpretation of the 'substantive due process' clauses of the US constitution, which provide that no person shall be deprived of life, liberty

43 *Watson v Gugino*, 204 N.Y. 535 (1912).

44 At 125.

45 For a discussion of the effect of Poor Law settlement on labour migration see Deakin and Wilkinson, at 115–24.

46 81 Tenn. 507, at 518–19 (1884).

47 [1898] A.C. 1 at 172.

or property without due process of law (the fifth and fourteenth amendments). These provisions were relied on by the Supreme Court to strike down state laws regulating employment, including dismissal, wages, hours, product quality and price, and trade restrictions, on grounds that these laws 'infringed on the freedom of employers and employees to contract at-will'.[48] An overview of how the Supreme Court exercised its constitutional jurisdiction to strike down protective legislation and uphold the at-will rule is given by Lawrence Blades, who explains the key cases as illustrative of the Court's desire to protect the 'inviolable rights of property and uninhibited freedom of contract'.[49] *Adair v United States* concerned the constitutionality of a Federal statute (the Erdman Act) which prohibited railways from dismissing or refusing to hire workers on grounds of union membership.[50] The Act was similar in effect to a number of state statutes which sought to protect union members from discrimination or dismissal. In *Adair* the US Supreme Court ruled that this law violated the Fifth Amendment: it was an interference with 'the right of the purchaser of labor to prescribe the conditions upon which he will accept such labor from the person offering to sell it'.[51] It was therefore 'an arbitrary interference with the liberty of contract which no government can legally justify in a free land'.[52] Similarly in *Coffeyville Vitrified Brick & Tile Co. v Perry* it was held that any legislation which imposed on an employer the obligation of keeping in his service anyone whom, for any reason, he should not desire, would be a denial of his constitutional rights.[53] The business conducted by the company was held to be its property, and the exercise of this ownership was protected by the constitution. This included a right to discharge, without reason, any employee. In *Pitcher v United Oil & Gas Syndicate, Inc* it was held that it was only fair for the employer to have the right to discharge at will as the employee enjoyed the right to quit at will:

> an employee is never presumed to engage his services permanently, thereby cutting himself off from all chances of improving his condition; indeed, in this land of opportunity it would be against public policy and the spirit of our institutions that any man should thus handicap himself; and the law will not presume … that he did so intend. And if the contract of employment be not binding on the employee for the whole term of such employment, then it cannot be binding upon the employer'.[54]

---

48 Morriss, at 686.

49 Lawrence E. Blades, 'Employment at Will vs. Individual Freedom: On Limiting the Abusive Exercise of Employer Power' 67 *Columbia Law Review* 1404–35, at 1417–19.

50 208 U.S. 161 (1908). A review of this and the cases which follow is given by Blades at 1417 et seq and Jacoby at 122 et seq.

51 At 174.

52 At 175.

53 66 Kan. 297 (1904).

54 174 La. 66 (1932) at 69.

Boyer v Western Union Tel. Co. illustrates further how the courts associated the at-will rule with the fundamental freedom of the individual, an explicit part of the American constitutional and political heritage.[55] Here a District Judge held that

> in a free country like ours, every employee, in the absence of contractual relations binding him to work for his employer a given length of time, has the legal right to quit the service of his employer without notice, and either with or without cause, at any time; and in the absence of such contractual relations, any employer may legally discharge his employee with or without notice, at any time.[56]

The point was even more strongly put in *State v Kreutzberg*[57] where the Wisconsin Supreme Court, in reference to a statute similar to that struck down in *Adair*, said:

> as each morning comes, the employee is free to decide not to work, the employer to decide not to receive him, but for this statute. That the Act in question invades the liberty of the employer in an extreme degree, and in a respect entitled to be held sacred, except for the most cogent and countervailing considerations, we have pointed out. Hardly any of the personal civil rights is higher than that of free will in forming and continuing the relation of master and servant.[58]

In *Coppage v Kansas* the Kansas Supreme Court recognized that the *liberty* of both parties does not go hand in hand with the *equality* of both parties.[59] One party, the employee, is in need of special protection. The Kansas court stated that it was a matter of common knowledge that 'employees, as a rule, are not financially able to be as independent in making contracts for the sale of their labor as are employers in making a contract of purchase thereof.'[60] But on appeal the United States Supreme Court was quick to counter this argument, in essence ruling that inequalities of fortune or bargaining power have nothing to do with liberty and freedom of contract:

> no doubt, wherever the right of private property exists, there must and will be inequalities of fortune; and thus it naturally happens that parties negotiating about a contract are not equally unhampered by circumstances … since it is self-evident that, unless all things are held in common, some persons must have more property than others, it is from the nature of things impossible to uphold the freedom of contract and the right of private property without at the same time recognizing as legitimate those inequalities of fortune that are the necessary result of the exercise of those rights.[61]

Justice Day in his dissent endorsed the Kansas view that an equation of the rights of the employer with the rights of the employee was inconsistent with the basic

---

55 124 Fed. 246 (1903).

56 At 248, cited in Jacoby at 123–4.

57 114 Wis. 530 (1903).

58 At 546, cited in Jacoby at 123.

59 (1915) 125 Pac. 8. See discussion of this case in Blades at 1417.

60 125 Pac. 8 at 10.

61 236 U.S. 1 (1915) at 17. Discussed in Blades at 1417.

inequality in the positions of the two: 'the law should be as zealous to protect the constitutional liberty of the employee as it is to guard that of the employer. It should not be necessary to the protection of the liberty of one citizen that the same right in another citizen be abridged or destroyed'.[62] But the majority of the Court maintained that the freedom of the employer to hire or fire whom he pleased was not qualified by a requirement that this freedom be exercised fairly. The issue here was whether an employer was entitled to insist, in flagrant breach of Kansas law, that an employee 'should elect whether to remain in the employ of the company or to retain his membership in the union'.[63] The Supreme Court found that the Kansas law restricting employers from making such rules was an infringement of the employers' constitutional rights.[64] Pitney J stressed that if the company has a legal right to insist upon such an election 'that insistence is not rendered unlawful by the fact that the choice involves a pecuniary sacrifice' to the employee.[65] Further, if the right is 'founded on a constitutional basis, it cannot be impaired by merely applying to its exercise the term "coercion"', or by alleging that the employer put pressure on employees not to join the union.[66] This reasoning is similar to that of the House of Lords in *Allen v Flood*, an English case of 'at-will' employment which concerned an industrial dispute.[67] The claimants were discharged after the defendant, representing the majority of workers, threatened to 'call out' the workers if the claimants continued to be employed. The employer therefore discharged the claimants in a bid to maintain industrial peace. The issue was whether the 'malicious' motive which prompted the defendant to procure their discharge gave the claimants a cause of action in tort. They clearly had no action for breach of contract, their employment being 'at will', and the Law Lords held that this was not affected by the allegation of 'malice'. In sum, the result of these rulings from the English and American courts is that at common law 'malice', 'coercion' and 'inequalities of fortune' do not render unlawful what is lawful particularly where the action being challenged is an essential attribute of individual liberty and the freedom of contract. The courts have long seen the right to make contracts concerning the provision of labour as an emanation of the right of personal liberty and the right of private property, and have emphasized that the right to make such contracts freely is as essential to the capitalist as to the labourer.

---

62 At 40.

63 At 9.

64 So-called 'yellow-dog' contracts by which an employee agreed not to join a union are now outlawed by the National Labor Relations Act (the Wagner Act) of 1935. See discussion in Blades. An interesting modern parallel in the UK is *Associated Newspapers Ltd v Wilson* [1995] 2 A.C. 454 (legality of financial pressure to leave union upheld on reasoning consistent with *Coppage v Kansas*) and the European Court decision in *Wilson & Palmer v United Kingdom* [2002] I.R.L.R. 568.

65 At 9.

66 At 9.

67 [1898] A.C. 1.

The idea that 'freedom of contract' is an important attribute of individual liberty still constitutes the foundation of the arguments which defend the at-will rule. For instance, in the words of Richard Epstein:

> The first way to argue for the contract at will is to insist upon the importance of freedom of contract as an end in itself. Freedom of contract is an aspect of individual liberty, every bit as much as freedom of speech, or freedom in the selection of marriage partners or in the adoption of religious beliefs or affiliations. Just as it is regarded as prima facie unjust to abridge these liberties, so too it is presumptively unjust to abridge the economic liberties of individuals.[68]

Thus the perceived equality between employer and employee remains an integral part of the courts' formulation and protection of the at-will rule, and is seen as an essential component of individual freedom. In practice the apparently equal protection of the rights of both parties affords employees less protection than their employers. Karen Orren notes that although the at-will rule developed on the basis of the freedom of both parties, the courts did not take seriously the idea that the *servant's* constitutional rights might be infringed, let alone take precedence to the rights of the master. Seeing the operations of 'business' as part of the property rights of the master, the rhetoric of liberty and private property was used to protect the master's rights against interference.[69]

The freedom of contract and substantive due process theories are no longer used to justify the at-will rule in quite the same way as in the nineteenth century. The constitutionality of employment protection statutes was subsequently firmly secured by the Supreme Court endorsement of the National Labour Relations Act in *NLRB v Jones & Laughlin Steel Corp.*[70] and both English and American law now have various forms of statutory employment protection which recognize the inequality between employer and employee. Nevertheless these early debates reveal much about how the law is understood today. Although US courts have sometimes been prepared to recognize exceptions to the at-will rule by finding that there was an implicit 'dismissal only for just cause' agreement between the parties, and some states have legislation regulating plant closures and unfair dismissal, the vast majority of US

68 Richard A. Epstein, 'In Defense of the Contract at Will' (1984) 51 *University of Chicago Law Review* 947–82 at 953.

69 Karen Orren, 'Master and Servant Law and Constitutional Rights in the United States during the Nineteenth century: A Domain-Specific Analysis' in Steinmetz (ed.). Jacoby suggests that in the US 'the strict at will doctrine was based on an ideological bias against trade unionism rather than a principled commitment to contractual equality in employment' (at 126). In this context the force of Deakin and Wilkinson's observation becomes apparent: '[h]istory shows us that the legal regulation of labour has been at its most restrictive (and on occasions repressive) in precisely those periods when free market ideas were regarded as orthodoxy by intellectuals and policy makers' (at vii).

70 301 U.S. 1 (1937). The NLRA is discussed further in Chapter 4.

firms still hire workers on at-will terms.[71] As for English law, it is often said that the presumption of reasonable notice provides a greater measure of job security than American law. But because there are no real restrictions on the giving of such notice, Feinman is correct to argue that the result is often the same in both countries where the employee may and often enough does find herself summarily dismissed with no warning. The only difference is that under English law the employee would be entitled to a sum equivalent to what she would have earned during the notice period ('payment in lieu of notice') usually not nearly enough to compensate for the impact of the job loss: for most workers being paid a month's or even three months' wages does not in any significant way alleviate the disruption and future impact of dismissal. In both countries the freedom of contract allows both parties to agree on terms that grant employment security to the worker, but despite this theoretical freedom, as Pauline Kim points out, 'fixed-term contracts are unusual and indefinite-term just-cause contracts are rarer still'.[72] Therefore it may be said that Anglo-American law still reveals the formative influences of freedom of contract and respect for private property which shaped its historical development, and these influences must be taken into account in assessing the effectiveness of regulatory provisions which shift the alignment of property rights and the managerial prerogative in the enterprise.

The Right to Work

This part of the discussion examines the 'right to work' at common law.[73] The focus of this analysis on the conceptual underpinning and underlying values of the common law requires a closer analysis of judicial opinion on rights in the employment context, therefore statutory law must continue to be put aside for now. At an analytical level the common law scepticism surrounding the idea of property rights in work relates not only to the characterization of workers' rights as *proprietary*, but more so to the existence of extra-contractual *rights* in relation to employment. The query surrounding the existence of a general right to work was enunciated by Megarry V.-C.:

---

71 Pauline T. Kim, 'Bargaining with Imperfect Information: A Study of Worker Perceptions of Legal Protection in an At-will World' (1997) 83 *Cornell Law Review* 105–60 at 107, 8; Katherine V. W. Stone, 'Knowledge at Work: Disputes Over the Ownership of Human Capital in the Changing Workplace' (2002) 34 *University of Connecticut Law Review* 721–64; William B. Gould IV, 'Job Security in the United States: Some Reflections on Unfair Dismissal and Plant Closure from a Comparative Perspective' (1988) 67 *Nebraska Law Review* 28–55. For a recent discussion see Scott A. Moss, 'Where There's At-Will, There are Many Ways: Redressing the Increasing Incoherence of Employment At-Will' (2006) 67 *Pittsburgh Law Review*.

72 Kim, at 106–7.

73 For a fuller discussion see Bob Hepple, 'The Right to Work' (1981) 10 *Industrial Law Journal* 65–83. For a discussion of the French *le droit au travail* see Freedland, 'Employment Law'.

> I pause there to say that there may well be jurisprudential questions about the true nature of such a 'right.' I have no intention of discussing the wide variety of meanings which the protean word 'right' embraces; but if a person has a right in the strict sense of the word, then some other person or persons must be subject to a duty correlative to that right. Yet who is under a duty to provide the work? Who can be sued? The 'right to work' can hardly mean that a man has a 'right' to work at whatever employment he chooses, however unsuitable he is for it; and if his 'right' is merely to have some work provided for him that is within his capabilities, then the difficulty of determining who is under the duty to provide it is increased.[74]

These perceived difficulties explain why there is no cause of action in the context of dismissal other than 'breach of contract'. The aim here is not to argue that there can be a general 'right to work' in the sense that troubled Megarry V.-C. Such an argument is not necessary in formulating a theory of property in work in the context of economic dismissals where workers in a particular firm seek to protect their investments of time, skill and labour in that firm. In this context the potential rights and liabilities arise between specific parties in a specific long-term relationship with each other, and there is no question of workers making general claims against employers at large to provide them with work. As will be seen later the idea of property in work is understood to emanate from the existing employment relationship itself and is in that sense the narrower than, and distinct from, rights-based analyses founded on fundamental human rights.[75]

The aim in this part of the discussion is to consider the potential scope for claims formulated on the basis of rights arising from the employment relationship which are *not* founded on the terms of an existing contract. This is crucial to developing the idea of property in work, as the first hurdle to overcome is the law's reluctance to depart from the contractual framework in conceptualizing the employment relationship. The discussion focuses on two cases. On the face of it, looking at the facts giving rise to these cases, the English case of *Allen v Flood* and the American case of *United Steel* appear to have nothing in common. The reason they are selected for discussion is not their facts, but the remarkable similarity in the reasoning of the Court of Appeal and an American district judge on the nature of the right to work. Although both decisions were overturned on appeal they illustrate a line of thinking which, this book argues, is well worth further attention.

The Case of Allen v Flood

It has been seen that in *Allen v Flood* the difficulty was that if there were no breach of contract, the contract being terminable at will, the 'malice' would not by itself

74 *McInnes v Onslow-Fane* [1978] 1 W.L.R. 1520 at 1528. For a helpful response to this query see Hepple, 'The Right to Work'.

75 On this perspective see Hepple, *Rights at Work*. In focusing on property rights rather than human rights this work proceeds within the general context of 'private' law rather than 'public' or 'constitutional' law'.

give rise to a cause of action in tort, and that the House of Lords held that no breach of contract had been established therefore no claim could be sustained. It was noted that the claimants were dismissed by the employer under pressure from the majority of workers, represented by the defendants, during an industrial dispute. This part of the discussion examines the Court of Appeal decision in that case, which held that the claimants *did* have a good cause of action as their right to work had been infringed by the defendant's malicious act. Although it was overruled by the Law Lords the reasoning of the Appeal Court merits closer consideration because it offers an alternative framework of analysis to 'breach of contract'. Hawkins J. preferred an analysis based on the infringement of the claimants' rights to work and to exercise their calling and trade. He relied on the principle underlying the 'restraint of trade' cases that 'The common law of England has for centuries recognized that a man has a right to work at his trade or profession without being unjustly excluded from it'.[76] Lord Denning M.R. in *Naigle v Feilden* thought that such protection did not depend on the existence of a contract; referring to previous cases in which the courts had relied on a form of implied contract to entertain claims by workers excluded from a closed shop he said:

> I think that could only be done by inventing a fictitious contract. All through the centuries courts have given themselves jurisdiction by means of fictions; but we are mature enough, I hope, to do away with them. The true ground of jurisdiction in all these cases is a man's right to work. I have said before, and I repeat it now, that a man's right to work at his trade or profession is just as important to him as, perhaps more important than, his rights of property. Just as the courts will intervene to protect his rights of property, they will also intervene to protect his right to work.[77]

Hawkins J. in *Allen v Flood* thought the same principle could be extended to a dismissal. It might be thought that for purposes of this discussion too much should not be made of *Allen v Flood* and the 'restraint of trade' cases because the courts' ready intervention in the context of industrial disputes, particularly where it appeared that an individual worker was being prevented from working simply because he did not belong to the dominant union, would be unlikely to be replicated where workers challenge an employer's decision to dismiss them for organizational or other economic reasons. It is true that Lord Denning's robust defence of the 'right to work' conveniently enabled him to 'intervene in the affairs of trade unions'.[78] However the purpose of drawing an analogy with the 'right to work' cases is not to suggest that the courts are likely to view economic dismissals as analogous to the restraint of trade or the closed shop. The aim of the analogy is simply to demonstrate that

76 *Naigle v Feilden* [1966] 2 Q.B. 633 at 644.

77 At 646. See also Lord Denning in *Lee v The Showmen's Guild Of Great Britain* [1952] 2 Q.B. 329 at 341. The 'closed shop' refers to the exclusion of non-unionists from a unionized workplace, now regulated in the UK by s. 219 and 222 of the Trade Union and Labour Relations (Consolidation) Act 1992.

78 Hepple, 'Right to Work' at 79.

the idea of rights emanating from the employment relationship, which are distinct from contract, is not without conceptual antecedents in the common law. This is a necessary first step in establishing the conceptual coherence of stakeholder theory in Anglo-American law. Therefore the significance of the reasoning of Hawkins J. outside the context of industrial disputes lies in his readiness to *extend* the notion of a right to work beyond the factual context in which it had previously arisen. Referring to the cause of action in the restraint of trade context Hawkins J. said:

> I am not debarred from using the facts applicable to such a cause of action as evidence in the case which is substantially before us, a case which rests upon a very broad and solid foundation, requiring no technical breach of contract for its support; namely, the violation by the defendant of the legal right which each of the plaintiffs, in common with every man in this country, has to pursue freely and without wrongful hindrance, interruption, or molestation that profession, trade, or calling which he has adopted for his livelihood.[79]

Hawkins J. acknowledged that this would extend the 'restraint of trade' principle to a novel situation, but he thought that the malicious infringement of the claimants' right to work was clearly unlawful, and that no authority was necessary to support such a fundamental proposition of law.[80] Citing examples from a broad reach of cases involving the exclusion of workers, traders, and even tenants, Hawkins J. summarized the nature of this right as an expectation of continuing employment:

> Involved in that right, and a component part of it, is the right to the full benefit of that valuable interest they had in what Lord Ellenborough in *Pitt v. Donovan* termed a 'probable expectation' (as distinguished from a vested legal interest), an essential element in promoting the success, and contributing to the value, of every occupation by which the means of living are obtained. The daily labourer, whose tested character for steadiness, honesty, and industry has induced his master, as a matter of course, through a long series of years, week by week to renew or continue his employment, finds in this the foundation for his 'reasonable and probable expectation' that he may rely on continual employment in the future. These 'probable expectations' are equally applicable to all trades, great and small … All rely upon 'probable expectations' attached to their trade or calling, and the law throws its protection round each and every man in his honest endeavours to earn his livelihood.[81]

This idea of 'probable expectation' in continued employment is central to stakeholder theory, and it is significant that its roots lie in the common law. Singer has argued that a 'reliance interest' arising from a long-term relationship between the parties is capable of giving rise to property rights, and it could be said that Singer's idea of a 'reliance interest' reflects the same principle as that enunciated by Hawkins J. in

79 [1898] A.C. at 14.

80 'I venture to think no authority is needed for this': at 16.

81 At 16.

this case.[82] Nor was there a lack of support for this principle from the Law Lords. Lords Halsbury L.C., Ashbourne and Morris, dissenting from the rest of the House, agreed with the 'elaborate and most able opinion' of Hawkins J. as to the nature and extent of such a right.[83] The claimants certainly had a right 'to pursue their calling unmolested.'[84] According to Lord Morris:

> At common law a workman had a *right* to work with any person who was willing to employ him. Both had a right to trade in labour as in any other commodity and as they thought fit. This was part of the personal liberty enjoyed by every man, and, like personal liberty, was the subject of peculiar safeguards, notably – it was a right which like that of personal liberty could not be bartered away …[85]

Lord Halsbury also made reference to the importance of individual liberty, saying that there was

> no right in this country under our laws so sacred as the right of personal liberty. No right of property or capital, about which there had been so much declamation, was so sacred or so carefully guarded by the law of this land as that of personal liberty … the liberty of a man's mind and will, to say how he should bestow himself and his means, his talents and his industry, was as much a subject of the law's protection as was that of his body.[86]

The fact that the action was not brought against the employer (hence Lord Morris's reference to 'any person who was willing to employ him') as a third party was alleged to have induced the dismissal, means that in this case there was no potential hurdle presented by a conflict between employer and employee. However from a conceptual perspective the main significance of *Allen v Flood* is that the judicial attempt to find an alternative basis for recognizing a cause of action by a dismissed employee, that is one that does not arise from breach of contract, went all the way to the House of Lords and in the end, as Lord Halsbury noted in his dissent, more judges supported the rights-based approach than opposed it:

> My Lords, I regret that I am compelled to differ so widely with some of your Lordships; but my difference is founded on the belief that in denying these plaintiffs a remedy we are departing from the principles which have hitherto guided our Courts in the preservation of individual liberty to all. I am encouraged, however, by the consideration that the adverse views appear to me to overrule the views of most distinguished judges, going back now for certainly 200 years, and that up to the period when this case reached your Lordships' House there was an unanimous consensus of

82 Joseph W. Singer, 'The Reliance Interest in Property' (1988) 40 *Stanford Law Review* 611–750.

83 Lord Halsbury L.C. at 68.

84 At 72.

85 At 155.

86 At 72–3.

> opinion; and that of eight judges who have given us the benefit of their opinions, six have concurred in the judgments which your Lordships are now asked to overrule.[87]

It is highly significant that the Court of Appeal and three of the Law Lords did not analyze this dispute simply in contractual terms but preferred to focus on the rights of the claimants in their work arising out of a 'probable expectation' of continued employment. Lord Halsbury was not persuaded by the argument that extending this reasoning from restraint of trade cases to the context of dismissal from work would create a new right not supported by precedent:

> It is said, indeed, that an action for the infringement of such a right is a novelty; but I do not concur that it is, or that if it were it would be a sufficient argument. The whole history of the action upon the case … affirms the principle that where cases fall under the same right and require a like remedy new precedents should be created.[88]

Lord Ashbourne considered this interpretation to be supported by 'good sense and by those considerations of justice and fair play one would expect to find in any legal system'.[89] This approach therefore sees the right to work as an attribute of individual liberty and one which is more important than any 'right of property or capital'.[90]

However, in the event, relying on the same value of individual liberty the majority of the Law Lords came to the opposite conclusion. Lords Davey, Watson, Herschell, Macnaghten, Shand and James of Hereford maintained that individual liberty implied that employment continued at the employer's will and unless the employer was in breach of contract no cause of action arose in the context of dismissal. They considered that the interpretation of the Court of Appeal was 'neither sound in principle nor supported by authority.'[91] Lord Davey declared that an employee 'has no right to any particular employment if it depends on the will of another' and therefore no right of the claimants had been infringed.[92] The majority were persuaded by counsel's argument that an employee 'has no *absolute* right to any particular employment, irrespective of circumstances. He has a right to sell his labour – but only to one who wishes to buy it'.[93] Lord Herschell observed that the employers 'were violating no contract – they were doing nothing wrongful in the eye of the law'.[94] No legal right having been

87 At 89–90.

88 At 73.

89 At 112.

90 At 39, citing *Reg. v Druitt* (10 Cox, C. C. 592) where Lord Bramwell said: 'No right of property or capital is so sacred or so carefully guarded by the law of the land as that of personal liberty. That liberty is not liberty of the body only; it is also a liberty of the mind and will, and the liberty of a man's mind and will to say how he should bestow himself and his means, his talents and his industry, is as much a subject of the law's protection as is that of his body'.

91 Lord Watson at 109.

92 At 172.

93 Counsel's argument at 4 (emphasis added).

94 At 118.

infringed, the act of dismissal was entirely lawful. The proposition then followed that a lawful act of dismissal was not rendered unlawful by the motive behind it.

The United Steel Case

Another example, this time taken from an American federal district judge who intuitively arrived at the same result as Hawkins J. and the dissenting Law Lords in *Allen v Flood*, supports this analysis of attempts to shift from a 'breach of contract' to an 'infringement of rights' analysis. Hawkins J was prompted by his certainty that a rights-based analysis was within the spirit of the law to remark that 'I venture to think no authority is needed for this',[95] although in fact his reasoning was found by the dissenting Lords to be consistent with a line of authorities 'established at least as far back as the reign of Queen Anne'.[96] A similar argument is developed by Singer in his insightful analysis of *United Steel Workers v United Steel Corp.*, an analysis which has proved to be ground-breaking in advancing stakeholder theory.[97] Singer argues that the courts' reluctance in that case to adopt a rights-based analysis for fear of crossing the line into creative law-making was unwarranted. *United Steel Workers* was an action by the union for an injunction to stop United Steel destroying the steel works which formed the basis of their community and livelihoods. At first instance Judge Thomas Lambros thought that the claimants had acquired a right arising out of their long relationship with the employer which entitled them to an injunction, but as in *Allen v Flood* there was some difficulty establishing the precise nature of this right as it clearly did not emanate from an explicit (or even implicit) contract. Lambros J. thought that the workers' 'probable expectation' of continued employment, to use the terminology of Hawkins J., might be in the nature of a property right. He speculated:

> Hasn't something come out of that relationship, something that out of which not reaching for a case on property law or a series of cases but … taking a look at the whole body of American law and then sitting back and reflecting on what it seeks to do, and that is to adjust human relationships in keeping with the whole spirit and foundation of the American system of law, to preserve property rights. It would seem to me that when we take a look at the whole body of American law and the principles we attempt to come out with and although a legislature has not pronounced any laws with respect to such a property right, that is not to suggest that there will not be a need for such a law in the future dealing with similar situations it seems to me that a property right has arisen from this lengthy, long-established relationship …[98]

Lambros J. was suggesting to counsel how the claimants' case might be defined, and reflecting on his suggestions they subsequently amended their claim to allege that they had a right of property in the steel plant arising out of their long relationship

95 At 16.

96 At 155.

97 492 F.Supp. 1. Singer, 'The Reliance Interest'.

98 631 F.2d 1264 (6th cir. 1980) at 1279; cited in Singer, 'Reliance Interest' at 618–9.

with United Steel. This claim was later described by the Court of Appeals as a 'cry for help', with the implication that it had no precise legal foundation.[99] As the claim could not be placed within the bounds of 'any formal contract law' the Court of Appeals held that it could simply not be sustained.[100] While sympathetic to the case for a new property right, the court thought it had no law-making authority to create such a right:

> This Court has spent many hours searching for a way to cut to the heart of the economic reality that obsolescence and market forces demand the close of the Mahoning Valley plants, and yet the lives of 3500 workers and their families and the supporting Youngstown community cannot be dismissed as inconsequential … Unfortunately, the mechanism to reach this ideal settlement, to recognize this new property right, is not now in existence in the code of laws of our nation.[101]

Building on his analysis of this case Singer argues that there is ample authority in the case law for the recognition of a 'reliance interest' giving rise to property rights, demonstrating that the common law recognizes 'the sharing or shifting of various property interests in situations that should be viewed as analogous to plant closings'.[102] As did the dissenting Law Lords in *Allen v Flood*, he cites ample authorities to establish such an analogy and makes a cogent case. This raises the issue of the use that may properly be made of legal principles formulated in cases arising in different contexts, a point addressed by both Singer and the Law Lords. Lord Halsbury was not persuaded that a right to work, in the context of dismissal, was 'a novelty'; he stated that 'I do not concur that it is, or that if it were it would be a sufficient argument'.[103] Singer draws attention to the importance of extending legal principles as part of the process of common law development, relying on the compelling argument of Louis Brandeis and Samuel Warren:

> That the individual shall have full protection in person and in property is a principle as old as the common law; but it has been found necessary from time to time to define anew the exact nature and extent of such protection. Political, social, and economic changes entail the recognition of new rights, and the common law, in its eternal youth, grows to meet the demands of society.[104]

In defining stakeholder rights as proprietary Singer relies explicitly on the existing legal framework understood in a broader sense, proposing that stakeholder rights can be developed and recognized by the courts in much the same way as other rights and causes of action have developed within the aegis of the common law, notably in

---

99 631 F.2d 1264 (6th cir. 1980) at 1265.

100 At 1266.

101 At 1266.

102 At 621.

103 At 73.

104 In 'The Right to Privacy' (1890) 4 *Harvard Law Review* 193 at 193; discussed in 'The Reliance Interest' at 628–29.

exercise of the courts' equitable jurisdiction. He demonstrates that courts routinely reallocate rights of property between different parties with conflicting interests in the same resource without any suggestion that they are exceeding their jurisdiction.

It is clear, then, that the supreme difficulty in developing further the idea of property in work lies not in the absence of authority for extending the principle of 'rights' to the context of dismissal, nor even in judicial reluctance to depart from the contractual framework, but rather in overcoming the apprehension that such an extension might touch upon political and economic questions which fall within the competence of parliament rather than the courts. It is true, to an important extent, that the effects of economic dismissals have inevitable political implications that make it difficult for this issue to be fully contained or comprehensively addressed within the common law framework. The case may be otherwise when rights in work are asserted within the realm of *public* law as is often the case in European law, in which context they are based on constitutional rights or general rights available to all citizens or all members of society thereby allowing an explicitly political debate about social and economic power, but that is not the avenue explored in this study. As this study is concerned with the conceptual nature of the employment relationship at common law the point to be made here is that there can certainly be no grounds for the assumption that the common law lacks suitable conceptual apparatus for constructing a theory of rights at work. Megarry V.-C. was concerned about the difficulty in establishing a correlative duty, but in voicing this concern he made no reference to the fact that the law recognizes both rights and duties arising from an existing long-term legal relationship in several contexts where the rights and duties are not of a vague or indeterminate nature but affect the parties to that particular relationship. Therefore it could be said that at the conceptual level the idea of property in work does not, as suggested by a narrow focus on the 'freedom of contract', pose difficulties for the common law. If the problem of economic dismissals in the modern corporation is viewed in historical perspective – as the most recent in a perpetual succession of diverse impediments to the continuation of the employment relationship – then by taking into account the different perspectives on the nature of the employment relationship which have emerged during the course of that history a conceptual foundation may be found for beginning to construct a theory of property in work.

The Dominance of Employment as Contract

The classical view in Anglo-American law is that the employment relationship is based on contract.[105] As this applies to both the individual employment relationship as well as the employment relationship in the firm, and because the law generally makes no conceptual distinction between these two contexts, it is worth reiterating that this book is not concerned with the individual employment relationship but only

105 Otto Kahn-Freund, 'A Note on Status and Contract in Modern Labour Law' (1967) 30 *Modern Law Review* 635–44.

with the relationship between workers as stakeholders and the firm as employer. In this context, if employment is understood as contract how much scope exists for the proprietary perspective? This book addresses this question at two levels; this part of the discussion considers the analytical level and the final chapter addresses the current legal framework.

At the analytical level, the aim in this book is not to deny the utility of the contractual model but rather to suggest how the contractual model may be complemented by alternative explanations of the role of employees within the structure of the firm. Alternative perspectives are needed because, as the conceptual foundations of the employment relationship have come under detailed scrutiny during the evolution of labour law, one recurring theme has been the inability of 'contract' to fully describe that relationship.[106] Deakin and Wilkinson point out that 'it has never been possible to give an exhaustive account of the employment relationship using the logic of contract alone'; indeed no single account can purport to be exhaustive.[107] They argue that only comparatively recently did the employment relationship at common law begin to be conceptualized as contractual – the contract of employment as understood today did not extend to all categories of workers until after 1945.[108] It has been seen that this relationship was until the end of the nineteenth century contained within the hierarchical model of the master and servant laws, and although 'higher status' workers who fell outside the ambit of the Master and Servant Acts could be said to have had their work relationships governed by contract this was not the case for the vast majority of workers. Although the terminology of 'master and servant' is no longer used there is still an important residual category of rights and duties which are determined more by status (the parties' relationship to each other, such as the employee's duty of obedience or the employer's duty to maintain mutual trust and confidence) than by agreement. Another reason why it may be helpful to move beyond contract in addressing job security is that the ideology of contract is ill-suited to the imbalance of power between employer and employee.[109] In the corporate governance context this is compounded by contractarian perspectives which exclude employees from the debate altogether, on grounds that their interests are (or can, and should be) fully protected by their contracts. Stakeholder theory attempts to take these

106 See Freedland, *The Personal Employment Contract*; Bob Hepple, 'Restructuring Employment Rights' (1986) 15 *Industrial Law Journal* 69–83.

107 Deakin and Wilkinson, at 37. They pose the question as follows: 'is the contract of employment based on agreement, or command; is it an exchange, or a relationship; is it a private law transaction or a type of status regulated by public law?'

108 At vii: 'it was not until the advent of the welfare state, in the first decades of the twentieth century, that the concept clearly recognizable to modern labour lawyers as 'the contract of employment' was definitively established as the foundation of the law governing the labour market'.

109 Furthermore the employment contract is not simply a contract like any other contract in the market, hence it is described as a 'relational' contract: Melvin Eisenberg, 'Relational Contracts' in Jack Beatson and Daniel Friedmann (eds.), *Good Faith and Fault in Contract Law* (Oxford: Clarendon Press, 1995).

factors into account, and hence seeks explanations that focus on the investments made by both parties over the course of the employment relationship. Hence some stakeholder theorists have opted to explore the potential of property rights as one possible conceptual basis for explaining employees' entitlements in the firm. By drawing attention to the proprietary nature of employee rights it becomes possible to evaluate the potential contribution of stakeholder theory to attaining a richer and more complete account of the employment relationship.

The first point to note is that the dominance of the contractual model should not *in itself* be relied upon as evidence that it is the best way of understanding the employment relationship. The dominance of particular approaches may, but does not necessarily, indicate the superiority of those approaches. Marcel Kahan and Michael Klausner suggest that over time legal rules acquire a life of their own that may have as much to do with familiarity and 'status quo bias' as with the inherent quality of those rules.[110] It is reasonable to suppose that as the reliance on the contractual framework built up over time it became increasingly more persuasive, and its attractions may well have become self-perpetuating. The benefit of relying on the 'tried and tested' rules of contract is further enhanced by a gradual process of 'social learning' involving the interpretation and adjustment of these rules. In time these rules come to be associated with greater certainty and predictability, providing them with an advantage that untested ideas lack and making it less likely that new approaches will be explored. This is particularly likely to happen in a legal system based on the doctrine of precedent. In this light, while it is possible to conclude with some confidence that the notion of contract is, for better or worse, now entrenched as the explanatory framework in regulating dismissals, it cannot be said with confidence that this proves it to be the *optimal* model.

Mark Freedland, writing in the context of the personal employment relationship, makes a similar point: 'English employment law is deeply, perhaps even irrevocably, committed to a contractual analysis of the individual employment relationship';[111] 'our system of employment law is so deeply committed to a contractual mode of analysis of employment relationships' that it may be 'more effective to [continue to] deploy a contractual concept' in understanding the nature of the employment relationship.[112] Referring to the 'notice rule' at common law Freedland observes that:

> At the moment, the unrestricted notice rule exerts a surprising hegemony in the common law concerning the termination of personal work or employment contracts. It has acquired

110 Marcel Kahan and Michael Klausner, 'Path Dependence in Corporate Contracting: Increasing Returns, Herd Behavior and Cognitive Biases' (1996) 74 *Washington University Law Quarterly* 347–66.

111 Freedland, *The Personal Employment Contract* at 6.

112 At 34. Similarly Hugh Collins remarks that 'the dead weight of tradition in the common law accounts in part for the survival of the simple contractual account of the employment relation': 'Market Power, Bureaucratic Power, and the Contract of Employment' (1986) 15 *Industrial Law Journal* 1–15 at 14.

> that hegemony, not because it has any particular moral cogency, nor because there is any special reason to believe that it accurately reflects the perceived rights and obligations of employing entities, but rather because it has become part of a web of legal rules or doctrines, which are mainly about the remedies which the common law (including the law of equity) affords for contractually wrongful dismissal. This web of rules and doctrines has become a self-reinforcing one in which each rule sustains the others. This conceals the fact that many of these rules now *lack* a clear free-standing justification.[113]

This is not to suggest that tradition alone explains the dominance of contract as a conceptual tool in understanding the employment relationship. The law of contract is a useful and valuable legal framework, and as Freedland demonstrates it is well able to adapt itself to the changing employment relationship. Freedland argues persuasively that the conceptual basis of the employment relationship is no longer based purely on the classical contractual model with its nineteenth-century assumptions of freedom of contract and equality of bargaining power, but has developed within a 'fundamentally different framework of thinking about the way in which personal work or employment contracts should be understood or interpreted';[114] away from a static towards an evolutionary conceptualization of the terms of the relationship.[115] This may explain why it is deemed prudent for the statutory employment protection framework to continue resting on notions of contract.[116] This being the case the essential task here is not to override or replace the contractual model but to acknowledge its limitations, particularly in the context of job security during corporate restructuring. The discussion earlier illustrated the difficulties which the common law courts have when trying to reconcile a judicial instinct that the workers should have a remedy with the tenets of the freedom of contract, and to a large extent this remains a problem in protecting job security in the modern firm.

Contractual Job Security

The common law action for 'wrongful dismissal' is an action for breach of contract. The classic statement of the rule is *Ridge v Baldwin* where Lord Reid said that

113 At 345.

114 At 239.

115 At 271.

116 This is particularly true of unfair dismissal law, which is defined as the termination of or failure to renew that contract: s. 95 Employment Rights Act 1996. At the level of the individual employment relationship with which Freedland is concerned, it is readily apparent that the statutory framework of unfair dismissal is based on the notion of termination of contract, although see Lord Millett in *Johnson v Unisys*: 'the right not to be unfairly dismissed is a statutory right which is not derived from contract' (i.e. the cause of action is statutory not contractual) [2003] 1 A.C. 518 at par. 75.

> the master can terminate the contract with his servant at any time and for any reason or for none. But if he does so in a manner not warranted by the contract he must pay damages for breach of contract. So the question in a pure case of master and servant ... depends on whether the facts emerging at the trial prove breach of contract.[117]

Similarly in *Malloch v Aberdeen Corp.* it was said that 'at common law a master is not bound to hear his servant before he dismisses him. He can act unreasonably or capriciously if he so chooses but the dismissal is valid. The servant has no remedy unless the dismissal is in breach of contract and then the servant's only remedy is damages for breach of contract'.[118] No attempt will be made here to analyze the wrongful dismissal action in detail, as the aim is only to make the point that there is no doubt at all that in most employment contracts the employer is well within its rights in terminating the contract for any reason or none at all, subject (in English law) to giving the requisite notice or paying a monetary sum to the employee in lieu of notice.[119] The applicable notice periods are established by reference to either a 'reasonable' period (based on the reference period for payment and the custom of the trade) or to the statutory framework.[120] In keeping with the doctrine governing breach of contract, *Addis v Gramophone* established that damages for wrongful dismissal are limited to the amount to which the employee would have been entitled had he worked through the notice period to the time when the contract could have been lawfully terminated, and do not extend to compensation for the manner of dismissal or injured feelings.[121] This principle has been justified on grounds that it 'enables the employer to identify with certainty the common law liabilities consequent on pursuing the procedures leading up to dismissal and the termination of a contract. That is desirable in itself: and it promotes the early resolution of disputes in the employment field.'[122] Of this rule Freedland writes that: 'The view that wrongful dismissal is wrongful, and remediable in damages, only because of its prematurity, its denial of a promised period of notice or fixed term of employment, has been and continues to be the dominant approach of English common law.'[123] The Supreme Court of Canada put it thus:

117 [1964] AC 40 at 65. It was argued in *Johnson v Unisys* [2003] 1 A.C. 518, albeit to no effect, that 'the law has moved on since *Ridge v Baldwin*' (at 525).

118 [1971] 1 W.L.R. 1578 at 1586.

119 For a detailed discussion see Deakin and Morris, at 396–443. Under the Employment Rights Act 1996 s. 118 there are essentially two types of awards in damages: a basic award (depending on age, length of continuous service and gross weekly pay) and a compensatory award ('just and equitable in all the circumstances' up to a £55,000 maximum). There is an 'additional' award where the employer ignores a re-employment order.

120 Governed by s. 86 et seq of the ERA 1996: see Deakin and Morris, at 398–99.

121 [1909] A.C. 488.

122 Counsel's argument in *Johnson v Unisys* [2003] 1 A.C. 518 at 525. See, however, the speech of Lord Steyn in that case. He stated (at 527): 'The supposed rule in *Addis* has been controversial for a long time'; and (at 531) 'the ratio decidendi of *Addis*' case does not preclude the recovery of special damages flowing from the manner of a wrongful dismissal'.

123 *The Personal Employment Contract* at 361.

> A 'wrongful dismissal' action is not concerned with the wrongness or rightness of the dismissal itself. Far from making dismissal a wrong, the law entitles both employer and employee to terminate the employment relationship without cause. A wrong arises only if the employer breaches the contract by failing to give the dismissed employee reasonable notice of termination.[124]

The legal requirement to give reasonable notice of dismissal is implied by law into contracts for an indefinite duration.[125] As an implied term it arises only where there are no express terms to the contrary. As the Privy Council put it in *Reda v Flag*, 'The true rule, which is not confined to contracts of employment but applies to contracts generally, is that a contract which contains no express provision for its determination is generally (though not invariably) subject to an implied term that it is determinable by reasonable notice'.[126] But where as in *Reda v Flag* a fixed term contract does provide for dismissal without cause, remaining silent as to the notice requirement, the notice requirement will not arise by implication. From this it can be seen that the notion of employment as contract is particularly problematic in the context of job security to the extent that it entails no real security of tenure unless expressly provided for in the contract. Moreover, the common law does not generally impose procedural safeguards such as the duty to give reasons or to grant the employee a warning or fair hearing before he is dismissed. This has now been partly remedied by the introduction of a statutory duty to comply with these basic procedural safeguards, failure to comply with which renders a dismissal unfair.[127] Deakin and Morris observe that one effect of this statutory procedure is that 'the employer can no longer rely on the power of the notice term to dispense with the need for procedural fairness or for adequate substantive grounds for an act of discipline or dismissal'.[128] Even so they note that these inroads are as yet 'somewhat fragile: they have not received the clear endorsement of the House of Lords and a number of doctrinal issues … remain unresolved.'[129] The position remains, as stated by Freedland, that 'under contracts of employment, the employing entity should be strongly presumed to possess a power of termination by notice which was not subject to substantive or procedural restrictions as to when and how it was to be exercised.'[130] In sum, managerial prerogative continues to take priority over job security: 'the employer retains the right to dismiss if he is sure that he wants to and is

124 *Wallace v United Grain Growers Ltd* (1997) 152 DLR (4th) 1, 39 (McLachlin J).

125 Although it is, exceptionally, possible that a contract for an indefinite duration may be deemed to be intended to continue indefinitely, so that no right to dismiss on notice will be inferred: *McClelland v Northern Ireland General Health Services Board* [1957] 1 W.L.R. 594 discussed in Deakin and Morris at 401.

126 [2002] U.K.P.C. 38 at par. 57.

127 S. 98A of the Employment Rights Act 1996.

128 At 397, referring to the Employment Act 2002.

129 At 397.

130 At 349.

prepared to face the [financial] consequences. The size of the workforce, the aptitude of the man for the job, remain in the last resort matters for management'.[131]

The Implicit Obligation of Good Faith

There have been recent indications that the common law might develop to allow breaches of contractual terms other than the notice term to give rise to a wrongful dismissal claim. In English law the implied term of 'mutual trust and confidence', under which the employer has an obligation to deal with the employee in good faith, has yielded promise as a potential way forward in developing norms preventing dismissal without just cause. In the US most states have developed limited modifications or exceptions to the at-will rule on the basis of an implied covenant of good faith and fair dealing.[132] As with the discussion of wrongful dismissal, the aim here is not to present a detailed discussion of these implied terms but to give an indication of how (if at all) notions of good faith and fair dealing have enhanced substantive job security at common law.[133]

In English law the implied term of mutual trust and confidence is defined as 'a term that the employers will not, without reasonable and proper cause, conduct themselves in a manner likely to destroy or seriously damage the relationship of confidence and trust between employer and employee'.[134] According to Lord Steyn in *Johnson v Unisys* this implied obligation 'is an overarching obligation implied by law as an incident of the contract of employment.'[135] The development of this obligation has raised the possibility that a dismissed employee might be able to bring an action for wrongful dismissal even where the requisite notice of dismissal was given, on grounds that the dismissal was in breach of the employer's implied obligation to act in good faith.[136] Although it has had a dramatic effect on the interpretation of the employer's duty in the course of a continuing employment relationship, so far this obligation has had little, if any, discernible effect on job security at common law in terms of preventing dismissals except for just cause or

---

131 Tony Honoré, *The Quest For Security: Employees, Tenants, Wives,* The Hamlyn Lectures (London: Stevens & Sons, 1982) at 8.

132 Discussed in William B. Gould IV, 'The Idea of the Job as Property in Contemporary America: The Legal and Collective Bargaining Framework' (1986) *Brigham Young University Law Review* 885–918 at 887 et seq.

133 For a detailed substantive discussion see David Cabrelli, 'The Implied Duty of Mutual Trust and Confidence: An Emerging Overarching Principle?' (2005) 34 *Industrial Law Journal* 284–307; Douglas Brodie, 'Legal Coherence and the Employment Revolution' (2001) 117 *Law Quarterly Review* 604–25.

134 Browne-Wilkinson J in *Woods v W M Car Services (Peterborough) Ltd* [1981] ICR 666 at 670, approved by the House of Lords in *Mahmud v Bank of Credit and Commerce International SA* [1998] A.C. 20.

135 At 536.

136 For a fuller discussion see Lizzie Barmes, 'The Continuing Conceptual Crisis in the Common Law of the Contract of Employment' (2004) 67 *Modern Law Review* 435–64.

on fair terms.[137] It has certainly not abolished the established common law rules by introducing a new requirement that employees can only be dismissed on fair or justifiable grounds. The main reason for this is that the scope of the implied term of mutual trust and confidence is limited, so that it applies during the continuing employment relationship but does not extend to the 'manner of dismissal.' The rationale given for this approach is that 'a common law right embracing the manner in which an employee is dismissed cannot satisfactorily coexist with the statutory right not to be unfairly dismissed'.[138] The House of Lords has expressed willingness to develop the implied notion of good faith in dismissal but is reluctant to encroach upon Parliament's intentions when it introduced a statutory framework giving workers a right not to be unfairly dismissed.

That being a matter of statutory interpretation what is more important from a common law perspective is that mutual trust and confidence as an *implied* contractual term, and not a right per se, also gives way to the express terms of the contract. In *Reda v Flag* the Privy Council reiterated that where the employer has a clear and express contractual right to dismiss the employee without cause, the implied term of mutual trust and confidence cannot qualify that right. Lord Millett said of this implied term that

> in common with other implied terms, it must yield to the express provisions of the contract … it cannot sensibly be used to extend the relationship beyond its agreed duration; and … it cannot sensibly be used to circumscribe an express power of dismissal without cause. This would run counter to the general principle that an express and unrestricted power cannot in the ordinary way be circumscribed by an implied qualification.[139]

The courts continue to draw a careful distinction between the action for damages for breach of the implied term of mutual trust and confidence as an ordinary action for breach of contract, on the one hand, and the action for wrongful dismissal on the other.[140] More recently the House of Lords has clarified that this does not mean that a claim based on breach of the implied term of mutual trust and confidence is necessarily precluded if the employee was, in the end result, dismissed.[141] The employee may bring a claim for compensation for breach of this implied term but only if he is able to do so 'without having to challenge the validity of the decision to

---

137 See Deakin and Morris, at 396–7.

138 Lord Nicholls of Birkenhead in *Johnson v Unisys* [2003] 1 A.C. 518 at 526. Ironically, in the past the employee's own liberty to quit was relied upon to justify the employer's liberty to fire him; now the existence of statutory employment protection appears to justify limitations on the scope of employee's common law rights.

139 At par. 45.

140 See judgment in *Reda v Flag* at par. 50, referring to *BG Plc v O'Brien*: 'these were not damages for wrongful dismissal (since his dismissal was not wrongful) but damages for breach of an implied term in his contract that he would not during the period of his employment and without reasonable and proper cause be treated less favourably than his fellow employees.'

141 *Eastwood v Magnox Electric Plc* [2004] I.R.L.R. 733.

dismiss him'.[142] Anderman is therefore justified in concluding that 'despite the rise of the term of mutual trust and confidence … implied terms continue to perpetuate the image of the employer as the sole owner of the business as well as to reinforce the power inherent in that property right'.[143] This is largely because the implied obligation of mutual trust and confidence, although it imposes an obligation on the employer, does not redress the imbalance between employer and employee in the context of dismissal, illustrating the difficulty in regarding implied contractual terms as a way of enhancing job security.[144] Terms implied into the contract of employment necessarily reflect the underlying assumptions of exclusive ownership rights vested in the employing entity, which means that unless the contract explicitly grants employment protection rights to workers then they remain unprotected at common law.

Therefore in the absence of express job security clauses, a satisfactory solution has so far not crystallized within the doctrine of implied contract. So far the courts have not been willing to allow implied notions of good faith to override any express contractual terms allowing dismissal at will or on notice, and there are still difficulties in the application of good faith to the dismissal itself in contrast to the conduct of the continuing employment relationship. Hence Deakin and Morris conclude that: 'The common law has stopped well short of implying into all contracts of employment an obligation upon the employer to observe natural justice, or, less specifically, to act fairly, when exercising a contractual power to discipline or dismiss'.[145] American law appears, though by a somewhat different route, to have arrived at the same result as English law. At first glance it appears to offer workers much stronger protection than the English implied term of mutual trust and confidence, mainly because the American courts do not make quite so strenuous an effort to reconcile good faith with the express terms of the parties' contract.[146] However, American courts do take into account 'the nature and purpose of the underlying contract' in interpreting this duty, and it has been suggested that acting in bad faith will not render a dismissal wrongful unless the breach of the good faith covenant amounts to a tort (and not simply a

---

142 At par. 53.

143 'Termination of Employment' at 108.

144 Anderson makes this point succinctly: '[a]lthough the implied term of mutual trust and confidence may have improved the employee's position by placing certain outer limits to the power of the employer to exercise control without restraint, it does not seem to have dislodged the sole ownership image of the employer'. This is primarily because in balancing the interests of both parties the employer's interest, unlike that of the employee, is conceptualized as proprietary': ibid, at 110.

145 At 566.

146 There are indications that unlike the English interpretation which states explicitly that implied terms of good faith must give way to any express 'dismissal without cause' terms, the implied covenant of good faith and fair dealing in the US is understood as part and parcel of a 'public policy' exception to the freedom of contract: Gould, 'The Idea of the Job as Property'. In English law the courts have declined the invitation to link 'mutual trust and confidence' to public policy in this way: *Johnstone v Bloomsbury Health Authority* [1991] ICR 269.

breach of contract).[147] The difficulties here are similar to those in English law in distinguishing the breach of the implied contractual term of trust and confidence from the well-established breach of the duty of care in tort.[148]

Statutory Rights and Conceptual Analysis

Does the answer lie in legislative intervention? It is sometimes said that contractual job security could be enhanced by further *statutory* support for implied terms of good faith or trust and confidence. This would avoid the difficulties faced by terms implied at common law which, as demonstrated above, may be avoided by express terms. Terms implied by statute into contracts of employment, as in other types of contracts, would take priority over all other terms. In the context of economic dismissals with which this discussion is concerned there is already, arguably, a vast array of employment protection statutes which achieve precisely this effect. The difficulty with this proposal is that the interpretation of employment protection statutes proceeds by reference to the conceptual structure of contract. Anderman argues that the statutory body of rights granted by protective employment legislation is an autonomous layer of employment law, distinct from the contractual framework of the employment relationship, and that by paying closer attention to this distinction the courts would be better able to interpret the protective measures of the statutes.[149] In this light the law regulating termination of employment could be viewed as emanating from two different sources, the law of contract and statutory law.

However, while most of the law relating to job security is indeed derived from statute, these statutory rights in turn derive their normative and conceptual coherence from the common law. As Freedland explains, statutory rights could be seen at one level as merely changing the 'definition or content or operation' of the employment relationship, but at another level they must also be seen as a reflection of common law norms and concepts. This means that these statutory rights cannot be fully understood without identifying the conceptual premise from which they derive their 'normative content'.[150] This at least partly explains why the courts persistently revert to contract in interpreting these statutes. Anderman has argued that statutory employment protection, especially rights conferred on workers by European law, may not be derived from contract at all, or they may go beyond contract.[151] This is markedly the case with the law governing employment protection in the context of corporate restructuring, as will be seen in the analysis of transfers of undertakings

147 See *Koehner v Superior Court* 181 Cal. App. 3d. 1155, discussed in Gould, 'The Idea of the Job as Property' at 903–4.

148 Wanjiru Njoya, 'Employment, Implicit Contracts and the Duty of Care' (2005) 121 *Law Quarterly Review* 33–8.

149 Steven Anderman, 'The Interpretation of Protective Employment Statutes and Contracts of Employment' (2000) 29 *Industrial Law Journal* 223–42.

150 *The Personal Employment Contract* at 10–11.

151 Anderman, 'The Interpretation of Protective Employment Statutes'. See also Alan Fox, *Beyond Contract: Work, Power and Trust Relations* (London: Faber, 1974).

in the final chapter. While Anderman is correct to say that this statutory framework needs to be unshackled from the restrictive bounds of contract and particularly from an 'exaggerated' view of the need for contract-based tests, nevertheless it might be helpful to offer an alternative common law framework within which to understand the nature and significance of these statutory rights.

The Proprietary Alternative

The task in this book is to consider, drawing from a long tradition of explaining the rights of the parties to the employment relationship by reference to notions of ownership and property in work, whether notions of property have anything to offer in understanding employment rights. While it is not suggested that the language of property could serve the same function in the interpretation of the Employment Rights Act as it does in, say, the Sale of Goods Act or the Land Registration Act, nevertheless it may offer a useful conceptual framework in understanding the nature of rights at work. For this purpose the proprietary framework is proposed not as a replacement for, but as a complement to, the contractual framework. The suggestion is that it constitutes an additional frame of reference in thinking about job security in the firm.

Property and contract have traditionally served as the fundamental bases for defining rights relating to social and economic participation in market activity, and both concepts are constantly evolving in their interpretation. These concepts are better understood as interlinked rather than oppositional.[152] The protection of property rights is inextricably linked to the freedom of contract as 'ownership carrie[s] with it the right to freedom of contract.'[153] It may be observed that the concepts of contract and property play a joint and interdependent role in defining and understanding the nature of the firm in economic theory. The same kind of interdependence can be identified in various aspects of legal doctrine, where property and contract often work together in creating legal relationships.[154] In this way, drawing on both disciplines, the stakeholder theory of the firm explains the employment relationship in firms with fragmented shareholding as emanating from an implicit contractual agreement between the parties and subsisting in respect of property rights in the firm.

The suggestion then is that reference may be made to both contract and property, depending on the context under investigation. Contract works better than any other

---

152 Deakin and Wilkinson observe (at 42) that the 'common law system of employment law [is] based around freedom of contract and respect for private property'.

153 Philip Selznick, *Law, Society and Industrial Justice* (New York: Russell Sage Foundation, 1969), at 137. It must be said that Selznick considers both contract and property to be equally ineffective as a basis for a 'law of associations' governing corporate enterprise: 'the received notion of property … has hindered the development of a theory adequate to deal with the internal ordering and external effects of modern economic organization' (at 63).

154 The clearest examples are the relationship between mortgagor and mortgagee, or landlord and tenant, which derive from the contract between the parties and exist in respect of property rights in the same resource: see *Bruton v London & Quadrant Housing Trust* [2000] 1 A.C. 406.

concept in many circumstances but less well in others, and by the same token there may be contexts where property works better than other conceptual tools to hand while remaining inapplicable or inappropriate in other contexts. If neither property nor contract provides a perfect 'fit' in all states of the employment relationship then the value of both lies in their analytical utility in explaining particular problems. This is not to say that the concepts of property and contract only have analytical value at an abstract level. Empirical reality may be taken into account at a policy level, allowing the selection of the conceptual framework which exhibits greatest potential in advancing particular values or explaining specific work relationships. But this book is not investigating policy choices. It is exploring the limits of the concepts which are used in explaining the employment relationship in the firm. Hence the best way of understanding property and contract in a theory of the employment relationship in the firm is to view this investigation not as a matter of deciding which is the 'winner' in a competition of concepts (contract is better than property, or property is better than contract), but of turning to different concepts that help explain the work relationship in different contexts. It is in that light that the discussion which follows, setting out the idea of property in work, should be read.

Property in Work

Property is popularly understood as 'possession-oriented and thing-centered', which would imply that it is an inappropriate way of describing an entitlement to a job.[155] However Waldron demonstrates that the essential significance of property lies in the legal relationships which it regulates, particularly in prescribing rights of access, control and use of resources amongst the parties to those relationships.[156] As mentioned in the Introduction, a common response to the notion of ownership of jobs is that employees cannot own their jobs because they cannot 'buy and sell' jobs in the same way that, say, they can buy and sell their cars. It is true that workers cannot alienate their jobs but then they do not want to – the entire purpose of this exercise is to establish a basis on which they might be able to keep their jobs or at least be consulted about losing them. Property in this context implies an element of control over the resource, and entails the right to participate in making decisions about the firm's economic structure when jobs are at risk. In the words of Davies and Freedland: 'the idea of job property is a concretization of the idea of job security. The idea of job security is in turn an abstract notion expressing the existence of social or legal mechanisms controlling and restricting the employer's freedom to terminate the employment relationship'.[157] The aim here is to explain why this notion of job security is linked to conceptions of property.

155 Selznick, at 63.

156 See Waldron's discussion at 31–7.

157 Paul Davies and Mark Freedland, *Labour Law: Texts and Materials* (2nd ed.) (London: Weidenfeld and Nicolson, 1984) at 429.

Origins of the Idea

The concept of job property or the ownership of jobs goes back to the Middle Ages. As Deakin explains, in the mediaeval guild system each trade could itself be seen as 'the collective property rights of the guild', vested in the 'collectivity of producers' who controlled entry into that trade.[158] A worker could only gain entry into a trade if he served the required apprenticeship. Only those who so qualified were allowed to work at that trade at all and it was an offence to practise the trade outside the remit of the guild.[159] Therefore, 'ownership and control of work organization rested with those within a guild'.[160] Simon Rottenburg also makes the point that those who were qualified to work in a particular trade had property in their work to the extent that they exercised control over it and determined access to engage in it, functioning in much the same way as the closed shop of the industrial era. Later property in work was linked more broadly to the idea that workers own their labour and are therefore entitled to the 'fruits' of that labour, an idea which was influential in contributing to the decline of the master and servant laws predicated as they were on the notion that the master owned the servant's labour. The preferred view by this time was that 'individuals owned themselves and were free to dispose of their energies in the marketplace'.[161] This idea was strongly associated with the philosophy of John Locke. Workers were deemed, by virtue of their labour, to acquire property in the product of their work. As Locke wrote:

> every Man has a *Property* in his own *Person*. This no Body has any Right to but himself. The *Labour* of his Body, and the *Work* of his Hands, we may say, are properly his … he hath mixed his *Labour* with, and joyned to it something that is his own, and thereby makes it his *Property*… For this *Labour* being the un-questionable Property of the Labourer, no Man but he can have a right to what that is once joyned to, at least where there is enough and as good left in common for others.[162]

Viewed independently of 'the philosophical context of his overall natural law philosophy' Locke's theory seems quaint, particularly as he spoke in context of mixing one's labour with what one 're-moves out of the State that Nature hath provided', but it has not entirely lost its appeal as a way of understanding the value of work.[163] Subsequently, the link between ownership and work passed through an era when it split into two different themes. One was associated with different

158 Deakin, 'The Contract of Employment' at 11.

159 Statute of Artificers, 1563. See Deakin, 'The Contract of Employment' at 7: 'Rules regarding competition were thereby linked to a particular conception of property rights within the enterprise.' These provisions were repealed in 1813.

160 Deakin, 'The Contract of Employment' at 8.

161 Steinfeld, at 5.

162 John Locke, *Two Treatises of Government*, II, sect. 27, cited and discussed in Waldron, chapter 6.

163 Adam Mossoff, 'Locke's Labor Lost' (2002) 9 *University of Chicago Law School Roundtable* 155–64. Selznick observes that 'The legal imagination was captured by John

forms of worker-owned firms, state-driven forms of employee ownership of firms in centrally-coordinated economies;[164] the other was linked to notions of job security and compensation for economic dismissals in free-market economies. The rest of the discussion pursues the latter theme as it is the one relevant to understanding Anglo-American law.

The impetus for 'job property' arguments in 1960s Britain and America, as technological developments caused many workers to be made redundant, was the belief that these workers were entitled to a measure of compensation which took into account more than just the loss of a few weeks' or months' wages. In the UK the Turner Report on *Labour Relations in the Motor Industry* envisaged job property as a substantive rather than merely procedural right to job security, speaking of 'more than a right of appeal against management decisions' and 'rights to a particular job at a particular place'.[165] This approach is illustrated by the early interpretation of the Redundancy Payments Act 1965, which was the first UK statute to grant general protection of employees in the context of economic dismissals, recognizing an entitlement arising from continuity of employment.[166] A number of commentators saw this statute as reflective of property rights in jobs, Michael Bennett observing that the Act 'began treating employment as a property right, by awarding compensation when positions disappeared for economic reasons.'[167] This idea was best expressed by Sir Diarmaid Conroy's ruling in the Industrial Tribunal that 'Just as a property owner has a right in his property and when he is deprived he is entitled to compensation, so a long-term employee is considered to have a right analogous to a right of property in his job, he has a right to security and his rights gain in value with the years.'[168] Lord Denning observed in the context of the unfair dismissal protection of the Industrial Relations Act 1971 that 'The Act gives the employee a right in his job which is akin to a right in property.'[169] In America, during the same period the proposal was that compensation for loss of one's job should be calculated on the basis of 'what the surrender of the [employee's] property right is worth'.[170]

Locke's model of lonely, resolute, pioneering man appropriating material objects through toil and binding his self to his possessions' (at 63).

164 See for example the discussion of employee ownership in Yugoslavia by Alchian and Demsetz.

165 Herbert A. Turner, Garfield Clack and Geoffrey Roberts, *Labour Relations in the Motor Industry: A Study of Industrial Unrest and an International Comparison* (London: Allen & Unwin, 1967) at 336; cited in White at 100.

166 Jo Carby-Hall, 'Redundancy' (2000) 42 *Managerial Law* 1–127.

167 Bennett, at 117–18.

168 *Wynes v Southrepps Hall Broiler Farm Ltd* [1968] I.T.R. 407 at 407, cited in Carby-Hall at 8; also *Marriot v Oxford and District Cooperative Society* [1970] 1 Q.B. 186; *Hindle v Percival Boats Ltd* [1969] 1 W.L.R. 174; *Lloyd v Brassey* [1969] 2 W.L.R. 310.

169 *Brindle v H.W. Smith (Cabinets) Ltd* [1973] 1 W.L.R. 1653 at 1658, cited in Carby-Hall at note 13.

170 Rottenburg, at 402. Echoing the sentiments of its British counterpart, the Industrial Tribunal, America's National Labour Relations Board held that 'The employee has a stake in

Meyers's Ownership of Jobs

In his 1964 study of the ownership of jobs which is still often cited today Frederic Meyers broke new ground in taking these ideas further, investigating the potential of 'property' and 'ownership' in analyzing and explaining employment security, and his ideas are therefore worth outlining here in some detail.[171] Meyers challenged the contractual conceptualization of the employment relationship, arguing that in focusing entirely on the terms agreed on by the parties just like any other exchange of goods and services for a fee this view 'embodies no concept of a job at all'.[172] This view implied that there was nothing to be owned and yet, Meyers argued, workers thought of their position as something which belonged to them: 'my job', rather than 'the contractual relationship between myself and my employer'. Meyers argued that '[a] job, of course, is an abstraction, but like other abstractions such as "good will" and "expectancy of profit" it may become the object of "ownership"'.[173] Meyers captured the essence of the employee's status as one that is in a sense independent of the employer-employee relationship: 'The relationship has become, basically, one of employee to job rather than employee to employer. That relationship is at least analogous to ownership'.[174] Meyers saw this as an important aspect of work relationships in the modern economy, observing that 'in major segments of the economy the employer-employee relationship is no longer a linear one, but is a complex one in which both employer and employee have an independent relationship to a job and to families of jobs'.[175] Hence Meyers spoke of 'the objectification of the job'[176] as a thing capable of being owned, 'the notion of the job as something independent of a contract of employment'.[177]

Meyers saw the notion of a 'property right in a job' as an analogy rather than a 'category' of property rights as such, and appreciated that 'the analogy between this form of property and the legally-recognized forms of property rights over tangible and intangible assets is inevitably incomplete.'[178] This is not a weakness in his argument because all concepts could be said to be, in the final analysis, imperfect analogies. The

---

the enterprise because he has spent years of his working life accumulating seniority, accruing pension rights, and developing skills that may or may not be salable to another employer. And just as the employer's interest in the protection of his capital investment is entitled to consideration in the interpretation of the Act, so too is the employee's interest in the protection of his livelihood': *Ozark Trailers Inc.*, 161 N.L.R.B. 561 (1966) at 566, cited in Gould, 'The Idea of the Job as Property' at 891.

171 *Ownership of Jobs: A Comparative Study* (Los Angeles: University of California, 1964).

172 At 2.

173 At 3.

174 At 15.

175 At 3.

176 At 99.

177 At 98.

178 At 388.

same applies to the concept of contract and notions of 'freedom of contract': they are presented as analytical constructs rather than the every-day practical reality of the employment relationship. Both property and contract fulfill the role of expressing normative values, and it would be inaccurate to interpret either of these concepts as having a literal descriptive function. In discussing the employment relationship the notion of property, just like the concept of freedom of contract, represents 'the use of words as symbols expressing a policy, an aspiration, a tradition, and not as symbols denoting a reality'.[179] Property and contract in the employment relationship both denote, not empirical reality, but a useful way of conceptualizing the rights of the parties engaging in corporate enterprise. At this level it makes no more sense to counter the property explanations of work on grounds that a job is not really a 'thing' to be owned with all the attributes of property, than it would to deny the explanatory value of contract by reference to the reality that most employees do not negotiate their terms and conditions of work but simply sign standard-form contracts. Such arguments are useful in testing the boundaries of conceptual analysis and determining where one concept works better than another, but cannot be relied upon as an exclusive test of the utility of each concept within specified boundaries.

Meyers suggested various ways in which the concept of property could enhance job security. He considered the concept useful in advancing the claim that an employee should be able to enjoy his work without fear of arbitrary dispossession by the employer; the idea of 'undisturbed possession' is a central incident of ownership. He therefore argued that employees entitled to statutory compensation for involuntary dismissal 'may be said to have property-like rights in employment'.[180] He explained the UK's unfair dismissal and redundancy legislation as examples of legal limitations on managerial prerogative, by restricting the employer's ability to unilaterally or arbitrarily separate the employee from the job. Other commentators have recently viewed the Employment Rights Act 1996 in a similar light, in so far as it contains procedural safeguards against the arbitrary termination of employment. The statutory right to bring a claim of unfair dismissal recognizes that employees have a right to continuity of employment.[181] Hence the unfair dismissal legislation was termed 'the nearest approach to a general realization of job property' that had yet been achieved when the law was first passed.[182] The clearest instance of the job conceived of as property lies in the power to order that the employee be re-engaged or reinstated, remedies allowed though infrequently used under the UK's unfair

179 Otto Kahn-Freund, *Labour and the Law* at 16.

180 At 1.

181 Freedland, *The Personal Employment Contract* at 90. As described by Deakin and Morris, 'from a doctrinal point of view, the legislation on unfair dismissal represents a major incursion into the common law, limiting the employer's otherwise open-ended power to bring the contract of employment to an end without the need for substantive justification, and imposing general standards of procedural fairness upon the process of dismissal' (at 385).

182 Davies and Freedland, *Labour Law* at 431.

dismissal legislation.[183] The reference to property in this context denoted recognition of the worker's claim founded on a form of possession, rather than simply a claim for damages, as well as the claim for a *compensation* award for losing the job rather than simply the basic award for termination of contract.[184] Meyers saw this legislation as a good frame of reference in considering the possibilities for American law.

The Modern Theory

This perspective continued to draw attention for the next two decades before it was abandoned on grounds that the analogy of jobs as property was by no means a straightforward one. Several commentators took the view which was addressed in the opening of this book, that the job does not appear in material respects to be amenable to the same 'traditional' rights of alienation and disposition as other forms of personal property, and that progress on the conceptual front therefore did not lie in the direction of property rights.[185] This decline could also be linked more generally to the growing body of opinion that the concept of property itself, irrespective of the resource in question, had outlived its usefulness and it was time to adopt new ways of thinking about social and economic resources.[186] It has been seen in the discussion of Meyers's work that the concept of job property did not purport to be based on a *complete* analogy with other 'traditional' forms of property. As noted by Kahn Freund, there was certainly a conscious awareness that it was possible to carry the analogy too far, but that nevertheless the principle underlying the analogy was one of value.[187] Even at the peak of its appeal the 'job property' claim in the UK and the US was not based on immunity from dismissal or on the assertion that workers should not be required to adapt to technological developments or downturns in the market. It was concerned instead with the computation of the compensation payable for economic dismissals. In an indirect sense the potential increase in legal safeguards or the level of compensation would be expected to make dismissal a less attractive option for managers, and therefore a strategy of last resort. However the direct focus of the job property arguments was not simply on trying to keep one's job at all costs, but on drawing attention to the true value involved when the job was lost. The job property arguments therefore focused on the 'loss of the job as a source of *future* benefits' which was argued to require an alternative reference point for calculating severance payments; the argument was that compensation should be

183 Sections 114–116 of the Employment Rights Act 1996, discussed in Deakin and Morris, at 518–22.

184 White.

185 Carby-Hall, at 8–9. Davies and Freedland suggest that 'the twenty years from 1963 to 1983 will in retrospect be regarded as the two decades which saw the rise of the idea of job property in our labour law – and also, its partial or complete fall' in *Labour Law* at 428.

186 Catherine Mitchell and William Lucy, 'Replacing Private Property: the Case for Stewardship' (1996) 55 *Cambridge Law Journal* 566–600.

187 In 'Labour Law – Old Traditions and New Developments' at 38, cited in Carby-Hall at 8.

based on the value of the workers' human capital investments in the firm rather than on the notice period.[188]

Meyers's work remains, so far, the most extensive general attempt to conceptualize the job as property. It provides a compelling framework for a proprietary analysis of job security. Nevertheless his analysis now needs to be clarified and updated in certain important respects, first by taking into account the point made by Hugh Collins that 'the law makes no attempt to establish an absolute entitlement to job security, a form of property right in a job'.[189] Collins is critical of job property as 'a right to possession of a job' or job property as 'immunity from dismissal'. The importance of Collins's analysis as contrasted with that of Meyers lies primarily in highlighting the need to clarify the meaning and definition of 'property' in the context of job security, taking a realistic view of what the law sets out to do and the limits of what law can achieve when faced with economic imperatives. Collins's critique serves the useful function of prompting advocates of the job as property precisely to map the contours of their claim.

Still, it must be reiterated that notions of property in work are not based on notions of absolute possession or immunity – it would be inaccurate to view Meyers's theory of property in work as a claim of absolute entitlement. Collins argues that there can be no absolute entitlement to job security as there is no private ownership of a specific job and a worker 'enjoys neither secure possession nor absolute control over its alienation'.[190] In arguing that the law does not recognize property rights in jobs Collins refers to 'absolute private ownership' as the 'primary meaning' of ownership.[191] But again it would be, at the very least, controversial to view absolutist perceptions of ownership and property as the 'primary meaning' of ownership. The modern idea of property is almost invariably *relative*, with important qualifications and limitations on the rights of the owner to deal with her property. As Singer explains in developing his own theory of workers' proprietary entitlement arising out of long-term work relationships, 'Property rights are more often shared than unitary, and rights to use and dispose of property are never absolute.'[192] Long gone are the days of *Bradford v Pickles*.[193]

The property owner who assumes that ownership primarily entails rights of an 'absolute private' nature soon discovers that in fact these rights are heavily

188 White, at 100 (original emphasis).

189 Collins, *Justice in Dismissal* at 9; Anne Davies makes the same point at 161–2.

190 Collins, at 10.

191 Collins, at 9.

192 Singer, 'The Reliance Interest' at 622.

193 [1895] A.C. 587 where the House of Lords upheld the absolute right of a property owner to do as he wished with his property and to prefer 'his own interests to the public good'. Mr Pickles sunk a well on his property with the sole motivation of depriving the City of Bradford of its source of water; the Lords declined to intervene. Indeed some theorists argue that it has always been the case that property has never in reality been conceived of as an absolute entitlement: see Ugo Mattei, *Comparative Law and Economics* (Ann Arbor: University of Michigan Press, 1997).

circumscribed by law and increasingly, by a duty to take the broader interests of society into account.[194] Limitations on the rights of an owner are now the dominant element in the law of property where the asset is of great social and economic significance. While rights of property in such assets cannot be infringed *at will*, it is certainly the case that they *can* be infringed. So although Collins correctly states that there can be no absolute entitlement to job security his remarks must be read alongside the fact that the stakeholder view of property in work does not rest on notions of absolute entitlement. If Meyers's insights are, therefore, to be of use in developing a proprietary stakeholder model property must be understood in a relative and not absolute sense. It has been said that property rights in work are closer in analogy to the easement than the fee simple: 'neither job rights nor access rights are held in fee simple; they cannot be sold to others'.[195] On this point Collins notes that there can be precisely defined situations in which employees have what he describes as 'conceptions of job property which have reduced legal incidents'.[196] There may be significant qualifications on the exercise of employees' property entitlements in the firm, but such qualifications do not, in themselves, deprive these rights of their proprietary status.[197]

Notions of job ownership are therefore considerably more modest than might be thought at first glance. They are not based on the kind of uncompromising stance which is often, rightly or wrongly, assumed to go hand in hand with the assertion of ownership claims or property rights. Singer has emphasized that where a firm has inevitably failed or an industry irreversibly gone into decline, the notion of job security cannot mean simply that no workers should ever be fired:

> All workers are entitled to appropriate levels of job security. This does not mean that workers can never be fired or that companies can never be restructured in ways that reduce their workforce. However, it does mean that corporations owe obligations to long-term employees that may well go beyond the scope of bargained-for contractual obligations, especially when alternative methods of preserving individual interests in access to employment are missing.[198]

There is surely a good case for at least exploring this notion of job ownership as a means of formulating an appropriate level of job security.

---

194 An interesting example of this is the 'right to roam' which renders a landowner powerless to prevent ramblers walking across his or her fields (under the Countryside and Rights of Way Act 2000). For a general discussion of the 'absolutist-relativist' tension in land law see Kevin Gray and Susan F. Gray, *Elements of Land Law* (4th ed.) (Oxford: Oxford University Press, 2005).

195 Rottenburg, at 402.

196 Collins, *Justice in Dismissal* at 9. These might include 'a right to compensation for compulsory alienation' or 'merely a right to an extended period of notice prior to dismissal'.

197 Wanjiru Njoya, 'Employee Ownership and Efficiency: An Evolutionary Perspective' (2004) *Industrial Law Journal* 211–41.

198Singer, 'Jobs and Justice' at 496.

Labour Law and Property

The relevance of property in thinking about job security in labour law has been noted by various commentators. Davies and Freedland have defined job property as 'the interest, viewed as proprietary in nature, which a worker has in the continuation of his employment as the result of legal measures or social systems which protect the expectation and security of continued employment.'[199] Deakin and Morris suggest that 'the notion of job property could be thought of … as implying a recognition not simply of the dependence of workers on their jobs for economic subsistence but, more broadly, of the need for "job satisfaction" in the sense of personal self-expression and the fulfilment of career-related and occupational goals.'[200] It could therefore be said that the current thinking about job property in labour law is not so much concerned with the simple question whether workers own their jobs, but with a more sophisticated assessment of the nature of the rights they enjoy with regard to decision-making in the firm, and the level of protection to which they are entitled when they are at risk of losing their jobs during corporate restructuring. These ideas can be linked with the stakeholder understanding of job property as an interest that arises when firm-specific human capital investments are placed at risk by a short-term focus on share value. In this sense the job ownership debate remains highly relevant to the definition and scope of job security in the modern context.

Why, given this strong tradition, has greater use not been made of job property in labour law? One answer is that the historical divide between capital and labour, in which the employer owned the place and tools of work, caused property rights to be associated more with the employer than the employee.[201] After the onset of industrialization and the factory system 'the concentration of property rights over productive assets [was] in the hands of merchant-capitalists or external equity investors'.[202] This gave impetus to the idea that the firm, which eventually took over as the employer of most workers, was the shareholders' property. There was also the idea, referred to earlier, that the master purchased the labour of his workers, their labour thereby becoming his property.[203]

Moreover it was considered conceivable that the contract of employment itself could be seen as the employer's 'property'. This was the view taken by the English Court of Appeal in *Nokes v Doncaster Amalgamated Collieries* in the context of a transfer of an undertaking, where the question arose whether contracts of employment were part of the 'property' of a company purchased by the new

199 Davies and Freedland, *Labour Law* at 428.

200 At 388.

201 Cochran and Miller.

202 Deakin, 'The Contract of Employment' at 9.

203 Steinfeld, at 81, discussing *Woodward v Washburn* where the New York Supreme Court held, citing Blackstone as authority, that the relation of master and servant is founded on 'the property that every man has in the service of those whom he has employed, acquired by the contract of hiring, and purchased by giving them wages' (3 Denio 369 (1846) at 374).

owner.[204] The Court of Appeal held that 'the right to the services of an employee is property of the transferor company',[205] as the language used to provide for the transfer of the company's 'property' and 'liabilities' was 'prima facie wide enough to include within its scope every kind of right recognized by law, including proprietary, contractual, or statutory rights of every description'.[206] This decision was overruled by the House of Lords, where the majority view was that the term 'property' takes its meaning from the context, and in the context of the transfer of a company's property on a winding up, 'property' does not include anything other than property of which the company in the course of winding up could dispose without having to obtain the consent of some third party, which clearly does not include contracts for personal services. Viscount Simon L.C. observed that 'The word "contract" does not appear in the [relevant section of the Companies Act] at all, and I do not agree with the view expressed in the Court of Appeal that a right to the service of an employee is the property of the transferor company'.[207]

As in *Allen v Flood* the position taken by the Law Lords in *Nokes* was justified as the only result compatible with individual liberty, Viscount Simon observing that any other position 'would be at complete variance with a fundamental principle of our common law – the principle, namely, that a free citizen, in the exercise of his freedom, is entitled to choose the employer whom he promises to serve, so that the right to his services cannot be transferred from one employer to another without his assent'.[208] Similarly Lord Porter held that such a right cannot be bought or sold, and the employer has no right to deal with it without obtaining the consent of the worker, so it forms no part of the employer's assets.[209] The significance of this case will be addressed in the final chapter in discussing the current legal framework governing transfers of undertakings; it is mentioned here to illustrate that the idea of the employment contract as the employer's property was not inconceivable in the common law philosophy. The employer's prerogative in making decisions to hire or fire was traditionally seen as an exercise of 'managerial authority', which in turn was conceived of as 'an incident of ownership, a matter of property right'.[210] Anderman argues that these perspectives continue to be reflected in the modern law: 'if one looks closely at a number of judicial statements there is strong evidence of the endurance of a rather absolutist assumption of the employer's "property" rights by the judiciary'; this makes it difficult or impossible to understand the modern law without taking into account '[t]he influence of sole property rights assumptions [which] help to explain a number of the historical decisions of employment law that otherwise have appeared puzzling, particularly those judicial decisions relating to

204 *Donoghue v Doncaster Amalgamated Collieries, Ltd. Nokes v Same* [1939] 2 K.B. 578; reversed by the House of Lords on appeal [1940] A.C. 1014.

205 [1939] 2 K.B. 578 at 586.

206 Sir Wilfrid Greene M.R. at 584.

207 [1940] A.C. 1014 at 1024.

208 At 1020.

209 At 1052–53.

210 Selznick, at 137.

the termination of employment.'[211] The effect of these decisions has been to associate the notion of property with *exclusion* of the employee, rather than as a shared interest between employer and employee.

Another reason which explains the current hesitance in characterizing employee rights as proprietary is the traditional preference for collective bargaining over the assertion of individual rights as a more effective means of promoting job security.[212] This preference for collective bargaining has meant that 'Until fairly recently, labour lawyers in the United Kingdom have … been generally reluctant to cast the claims of labour in the mould of rights at all.'[213] While collective bargaining involves an element of solidarity, the language of rights appears to individualize workers' entitlements. Notions of shared ownership in the firm also imply that workers should, to a degree, identify with the employers' interests as joint owners of the same resource. Hence stakeholder proposals are met with the same misgivings as notions of cooperation and partnership which imply unified interests of both employer and employee but too often end up being instrumental ways of advancing the employers' interests.[214] The traditional recognition of an inherent conflict of interests between employer and worker representatives is therefore often preferred.

This conflictual model in which the interests of workers and employers are deemed to be inherently opposed has, however, been changing in recent years. The role of collective bargaining is evolving as trade unions increasingly rely on, rather than view with scepticism, legislation protecting the rights of the individual employee. Keith Ewing has remarked that 'Trade unionists … are now using the rhetoric of rights and the rhetoric of human rights powerfully to reinforce their claims'.[215] Unions continue to play an important role even where there is an emphasis on individual rights, because such individual rights 'are more effectively upheld where there is a trade union presence'.[216] Individual non-unionized workers 'are easily intimidated, often ignorant of their rights, and reluctant to stand up to their employers for those rights' and so if rights are to be meaningfully enforced the role of unions will remain vital.[217] It will be seen in the final chapter that unions have been able to exercise a 'property-like claim on the enterprise' in the context of transfers of undertakings, relying on rights granted to individual workers to secure

211 Anderman, 'Termination of Employment' at 102.

212 Hugh Collins, *Employment Law* (Oxford: Oxford University Press, 2003).

213 Keith Ewing, 'Laws against Strikes Revisited' in *The Future of Labour Law* at 46.

214 Deakin and Morris note that direct forms of worker participation 'are predicated upon, and are generally designed to promote, a more individualistic view of the employment relationship than a representational model, together with a close identification on the part of workers with the employer's objectives' (at 823).

215 Ewing, at 46–7.

216 William Brown and Sarah Oxenbridge, 'Trade Unions and Collective bargaining' in *The Future of Labour Law* at 74.

217 Brown and Oxenbridge, at 75.

and enhance their bargaining power.[218] They have thereby rescued thousands of jobs which the individual worker, despite his or her statutory rights, would not be able to achieve.[219]

These difficulties have not altogether prevented the recognition of a measure of property in work at common law. The issue has arisen in the context of the restraint of trade, considering whether an employer can prevent a former employee from practising his trade and whether existing employees have a right to be provided with work to do by the employer.[220] The doctrine of restraint of trade is one which continues to have important implications for notions of job property in that if employees 'own' their work or have a 'right to work' then the employer should not, by contract, be able to restrict the employee from exercising that right.[221] The point has already been made that the restraint of trade cases represents the long line of authorities which the dissenting Lords in *Allen v Flood* thought could be extended by analogy to the 'malicious' infringement of a more general 'right' to work. The idea of job property also appears in public law, and where employers are public or quasi-public bodies they have been required to observe principles of natural justice such as giving employees the right to be heard and the right to be given reasons for the employer's decisions. The notion of 'security of tenure' of public officials, exemplified in *Ridge v Baldwin,* has implied that such officials could not be dismissed without just cause by making the dismissal amenable to judicial review.[222] The fact that these cases have usually arisen *outside* the context of dismissal certainly cannot be overlooked, but they nevertheless illustrate some of the ways in which the idea of property in work might be understood in labour law.

To conclude this part of the discussion it may be said that the theory of property in work has evolved from the mediaeval notion of collective ownership of the trade, with its connotations of excluding those who did not belong to it, into a much more flexible and socially desirable notion of shared interests in the firm. This conceptual transformation has been necessary to ensure the continued relevance of property, as

---

218 John Armour and Simon Deakin, 'Insolvency and Employment Protection: the Mixed Effects of the Acquired Rights Directive' (2003) 22 *International Review of Law and Economics* 443–63 at 445.

219 Armour and Deakin, discussing the 2000 case of the Rover Group, a UK car manufacturer, where the unions were able to secure the sale of Rover to a purchaser who would continue production and save up to 24,000 jobs, rather than the employer's preferred purchaser whose plan was for Rover to cease volume car production. The unions achieved this by filing compensation claims on behalf of all the workers worth more than £300 million, thereby forcing the employer to the bargaining table.

220 *Devonald v Rosser & Sons* [1906] 2 K.B. 728.

221 Freedland, at 81; 487–491. See *Naigle v Feilden* [1966] 2 Q.B. 633: a 'right not to be capriciously and unreasonably prevented from earning his living as he wills': Salmon L.J. at 653; *McInnes v Onslow-Fane* [1978] 1 W.L.R. 1520, Megarry V.-C. at 1528: 'I pause there to say that there may well be jurisprudential questions about the true nature of such a "right."'

222 [1964] A.C. 40. For further application of this idea see *Malloch v Aberdeen Corp.* [1971] 1 W.L.R. 1578 and *Stevenson v United Road Transport Union* [1977] I.C.R. 893.

exclusivist and even exploitative connotations of 'private property' have increasingly come under attack in the modern social and political environment. What has emerged is not necessarily a *new* theory of property, but certainly a distinctly modern theory of property. The next part of the discussion considers how this conceptual evolution is used to construct a stakeholder theory of the firm. The proprietary stakeholder model shifts the emphasis from managerial prerogative to a focus on the rights employees acquire in the enterprise by virtue of their status as employees. Protection of the employee's job and job prospects therefore becomes attributable not to the employer's largesse, but to the employment status itself.

The Proprietary Stakeholder Model

The modern ideas of job property which lie at the heart of the proprietary stakeholder model arose in response to the economic recession in the manufacturing industries of Britain and the US in the 1980s. Steel works and coal mines were shut down and thousands of skilled workers laid off including those working in plants that were still profitable. They were shut down not because they were loss-making but because they were technologically obsolete and it seemed cheaper to shut down than to retrain the workers and update production methods and equipment.[223] Writing in this context Singer has argued in favour of legal recognition of workers' property rights arising out of their long relationship with the firm.[224] His proposal calls for an inquiry into the organization of firms from a property rights perspective, and for a more inclusive corporate environment which would make the modern corporation better equipped to meet the challenges of rapidly changing working patterns. He examines the potential for property rights arising from long-term employment relationships to serve as a suitable normative framework within which to consider the role of workers in the corporation. These rights could be seen as a superimposition upon the contractual framework, with the workers' 'property' in their jobs emanating from and being founded upon the contractual relationship. This idea lies at the heart of the proprietary model of stakeholder theory, of which an overview is given below.

Overview of Stakeholder Theory

Stakeholder theory attempts to reconceptualize the firm as an entity which is no longer run exclusively or invariably in the interests of its shareholder-owners, asserting that corporate activity ought to maximize wealth not solely for the benefit of shareholders but also for the benefit of other participants in the firm. In general stakeholder theory conceives of the firm as a team or network involving multiple participants and interest groups who all make a contribution to corporate activity and therefore acquire a legitimate expectation to be appropriately rewarded for their

223 Singer, 'The Reliance Interest'.

224 Singer, 'The Reliance Interest'.

input.[225] In general this includes employees, creditors, suppliers, customers, the wider community or even the environment affected by its operations. But it is not just a general theory of inclusiveness. In the words of Freeman, one of the earliest stakeholder theorists, the term 'stakeholder' lends itself to more precise definition. It is 'a useful *unit of analysis* that easily depicts the social and societal effects of business' which may be focused on in order to 'show that there are broader issues at stake than just the economics of business. We can measure performance with these other groups, model good and bad performance, and revise the narrow economist's vision of business to include social issues and societal effects'.[226] It is therefore intended as a theory which may offer practical guidelines in balancing conflicting interests in the firm.

Considering that it raises fundamental questions of a social, economic and political nature, and with such a broad spectrum of interests, it is not surprising that the formulation and development of stakeholder theory still has a long way to go.[227] Part of the difficulty is that stakeholder theory has normative, descriptive and instrumental elements. This categorization is made by Donaldson and Preston, who see the greatest potential of stakeholder theory in its normative claims.[228] Accordingly the focus in this book is primarily on the normative basis of the theory, which is presented as a counter to the normative ideology of shareholder primacy.

Another difficulty is how to define the precise nature of the 'stakes'. Various possibilities have been explored, and undoubtedly the most promising strategy is to situate stakeholder theory within a theoretical and conceptual framework which already has well-established foundations. Again, Donaldson and Preston did most to prompt the realization that 'The normative basis for stakeholder theory involves its connection with more fundamental and better-accepted philosophical concepts'.[229] They present the challenge as one of defining 'stakes' and 'stakeholders' using terms which already have a solid doctrinal basis and hence well-defined conceptual parameters, and suggest that a good way of doing this is by grounding the stakeholder

---

225 Margaret M. Blair and Lynn Stout, 'A Team Production Theory of Corporate Law' (1999) 85 *Virginia Law Review* 247–328.

226 At 171.

227 Margaret Blair and Thomas Kochan, 'Introduction' in Margaret M. Blair and Thomas Kochan (eds.), *The New Relationship: Human Capital in the American Corporation* (Washington D.C.: Brookings Institution Press, 2000) 1–27 at 25: 'considerable use of the term "stakcholders" and "stakeholder firms" can be found in different social science literatures … yet these terms often lack analytical precision. Moreover, they are only beginning to be translated into testable theories or propositions that would support empirical examination'. They add that there is a need to formulate 'more precise stakeholder models of the firm'.

228 Although Freeman suggests (at 174) that 'in the messy world of management it is simply impossible and not very useful to be precise about what claims are normative and what claims are empirical etc., though there will surely be times when such careful delineation has a purpose'.

229 At 81.

interest within a property rights framework.[230] Writing from the perspective of management science they do not rely on 'formal' conceptions of property rights. They suggest that

> One need not make the more radical assertion that such stakes constitute formal or legal property rights … All that is necessary is to show that such characteristics, which are the same as those giving rise to fundamental concepts of property rights, give various groups a moral interest, commonly referred to as a 'stake,' in the affairs of the corporation.[231]

They have, however, struck a chord within the legal discourse on property rights. One of the ways in which pluralist ideas of property have made an appearance in English and American courts is through the argument that the identification of 'formal' legal rights capable of founding a cause of action is derived from a compelling 'moral interest' such as that described by Donaldson and Preston. As stakeholder theory continues to evolve it would benefit from further investigation of the extent to which support for 'stakes' as 'legal property rights' may be derived from ideas of property in work in the common law tradition. This book takes a step in that direction. The starting point is to delineate the boundaries of the stakeholder model as conceptualized in this discussion.

Theories of the Firm

There are various stakeholder models, which rest on different theories of the firm. This study is concerned with the stakeholder model which selects the 'property rights theory of the firm' as the context for investigating the relationship of employees to the employer organization.[232] There is an ongoing debate as to which theory of the firm is most cogent in terms of accuracy and explanatory force, but rather than engaging with that debate this study investigates the proprietary model. This model is certainly no less appealing than other approaches to stakeholder theory in terms of its analytical value and insights into the nature of the firm. It also benefits from the level of interest invariably associated with all theories of property. This part of the discussion therefore brings together different perspectives on property rights in the firm in order to assess, in its entirety, the picture that emerges from these different perspectives. The aims of the proprietary stakeholder model may be better appreciated if it is recalled that this discussion seeks to demonstrate how job security can be

230 For recent discussions see Cheryl C. Asher, Joseph M. Mahoney and James T. Mahoney, 'Towards a Property Rights Foundation for a Stakeholder Theory of the Firm' (2005) 9 *Journal of Management and Governance* 5–32; Margaret M. Blair, 'Closing the Theory Gap: How the Economic Theory of Property Rights Can Help Bring "Stakeholders" Back into Theories of the Firm' (2005) 9 *Journal of Management and Governance* 33–9.

231 At 85.

232 For an accessible review of the property rights theories of the firm see Oliver Hart, 'An Economist's Perspective on the Theory of the Firm' (1989) 89 *Columbia Law Review* 1757–74.

understood *within* that theory. Therefore it is not claimed that job security can only, or will automatically, be enhanced within this proprietary framework. Here, as in the context of understanding the conceptual nature of the employment relationship, the idea is to offer a more nuanced analysis by adding to, not replacing, other theories of the firm. Again, if the corporate governance debates were allowed only one theory of the firm, or limited to a single reference point in explaining the different attributes of the employment relationship, then it would be necessary to assert the superiority of the proprietary stakeholder model. However on the assumption that there is room for more than one explanatory theory of an institution of such legal, social and economic importance as the modern firm and the role of employees within it such an assertion is not made.

Large Publicly-Traded Firms

The stakeholder model is concerned with ownership and control of large publicly-held corporations. As an interdisciplinary exercise this discussion uses the terms enterprise, firm, corporation and company interchangeably to refer to the large entities that dominate the Anglo-American economy, attaching no significance to technical or legal distinctions between those terms within different disciplines. In this context the 'personal' aspect that characterizes the relationship between an individual employer and her employees is lacking, and employees' security of tenure may be considered without being overly hindered by the difficulties of establishing mutuality of obligation and the appropriateness of specific performance. It is not as problematic to enjoin a large firm from dismissing its workers without prior consultation as it would be to impose the same requirement on an individual employer. In referring to employer corporations as 'employing entities' rather than simply 'employers' Freedland draws attention to the fact that in this context the employment relationship is not individual and bilateral but a complex and multilateral one. He observes that in the modern economy, only in relatively few cases is the employer 'an individual human person in a simple bilateral relation with the worker'.[233] Davies and Freedland have pointed to the need for a re-examination of the relationship between workers and employing entities, and it is suggested here that this need becomes particularly acute when the employer is a large publicly held corporation governed in accordance with an emphasis on maximizing share value.

The focus of stakeholder theory, concerned as it is with the firm's proprietary structure, is therefore not on the 'personal' relationship between employer and employee, but on the respective roles which both parties play within publicly held corporations. In concentrating on employment security in the context of corporate restructuring stakeholder theory is not directly concerned with the security of tenure of the individual worker but with the employment security of workers at risk of being laid off in their hundreds or even thousands. Mass redundancies not only involve the sacking of individuals but also have more profound social implications.

233 Freedland, *The Personal Employment Contract* at 37.

They may affect entire neighbourhoods, towns or regions, with knock-on effects for other industries and institutions. The problem of plant closures is perhaps the best illustration of this phenomenon. It is a familiar scenario today, as outsourcing becomes widespread. Concerns about job security in this context are heightened by the fact that there is no suggestion of 'fault' on the part of the workers – blame is laid instead on impersonal market forces, which may intensify the sense of social displacement felt by those affected particularly where the job cuts are not perceived to be inevitable.

Finally, the differences between firms of different sizes are crucial. The employer-employee relationship in the large professionally managed firm is quite different from that in the small owner-managed firm. It is one thing to require the managers of a large firm with thousands of employees to consult employee representatives before making important decisions, and quite another to impose the same obligation on a family-run business with a handful of employees. In this regard private owner-managed firms are better classified with individual employers than with large publicly-traded employing entities. This distinction is reflected in the law regulating workers' rights in the firm. For instance in Germany the Codetermination Act of 1976 requires firms to have two-tier boards of directors with employee representatives constituting half of the supervisory board, but this only applies to enterprises with over 2000 employees. Private companies must have employee representatives constituting a third of the supervisory board, if they have more than 500 employees.[234] Likewise this discussion takes the importance of the firm's size into account and limits its claims to large firms whose shares are traded publicly on the stock market.

The Classification of Employees

The stakeholder model, in this discussion, generally assumes that 'managers' represent the employing entity, despite the fact that managers are often amongst the very employees whose firm-specific human capital investments in the firm are placed at risk by restructuring. This approach requires some justification. After all, in law the corporation is a separate and independent legal person which means that the firm *itself* is the employer.[235] The corporate entity as the 'employer' is distinct from the actual people who exercise the managerial prerogative to hire and fire workers but are themselves 'employees' of the firm who in reality may not always have absolute

234 In Italian law, reinstatement of a wrongfully dismissed employee 'is the natural remedy for all firms of more than 15 employees': Anderman, 'Termination of Employment' at 123, discussing the Italian *Statuto di Lavoratori*, Article 18. In the UK 'from 6 April 2005 employees in organisations with 150 or more employees have a right to be informed and consulted on a regular basis about issues in the organisation they work for. Organisations with 100 or more employees will come within the scope of the legislation in April 2007, and those with 50 or more employees in April 2008' (<www.dti.gov>).

235 See Simon Deakin, 'Workers, Finance and Democracy' in *The Future of Labour Law* at 80–82; Teubner, 'Company Interest'; Max Radin, 'The Endless Problem of Corporate Personality' (1932) 32 *Columbia Law Review* 643–67.

discretion in job creation and loss and may well themselves be controlled, or even be at risk of being dispensed with altogether, by the firm's directors. Managers also have an interest in job security. This issue is compounded by the modern tendency to describe as 'managers' many workers who in fact have no more real decision-making authority than other workers. Nevertheless the stakeholder model as developed in this discussion relies on various assumptions about managerial prerogative and the role of managers as 'employer'. It makes no reference to these distinctions for the following reasons. The main interest is in the allocation of ownership and control in the firm. The classical theory of the firm terms as managers those with decision-making power at the highest level, an approach which is necessary to enable a useful discussion of control and decision-making in the firm. In discussing the allocation of control between the various parties and its impact on job security it is usually convenient to refer to 'the employer' although in reality the employer is an artificial entity and decisions are taken by managers. As Davies and Freedland have observed: 'The purpose of the term "employer", certainly in individual employment law and more broadly in labour law, is to capture all the relevant bearers of management powers, so as to bring them within the fold of regulation'.[236] This aids clarity of exposition, allowing a fuller appreciation of the role and influence of managerial prerogative as the right of the employer to hire and fire.[237]

For similar reasons the discussion refers to non-managerial employees interchangeably as 'employees' or 'workers', despite the legal distinctions between the two terms and the diverse types of employees in the modern firm. There are obvious difficulties with this approach. In so far as it exists, job security generally extends only to those workers defined in law as 'employees', and there are usually qualifying conditions such as length of continuous service. No matter how far job security advances, it seems that as long as the need to categorize workers exists there will always be too many workers unable to take full advantage of these protections. Deakin and Wilkinson have noted that 'it is no exaggeration to think of the classification of work relationships as the central, defining operation of any labour law system.'[238] Many of those falling outside the definition of an employee are atypical workers in short-term, fixed-term, temporary or part-time jobs; many who are classified as 'independent contractors' rather than 'employees' are in reality working for the firm in exactly the same way as they would if they were employees.[239] In order to devote attention to the subject at hand it is not possible within the confines of this discussion

236 Paul Davies and Mark Freedland, 'The Employment Relationship in British Labour Law' in *The Future of Labour Law* at 135.

237 For a study which takes account of managers as employees see Teresa Ghilarducci, James Hawley and Andrew Williams, 'Labour's Paradoxical Interests and the Evolution of Corporate Governance' (1997) 24 *Journal of Law and Society* 26–43.

238 At 4.

239 On the definition of the worker see Sandra Fredman, 'Labour Law in Flux: The Changing Composition of the Workforce' (1997) 26 *Industrial Law Journal* 337–52; Hugh Collins, 'Independent Contractors and the Challenge of Vertical Disintegration to Employment Protection Laws' (1990) 10 *Oxford Journal of Legal Studies* 353–80. On the definition of

to address the important matter of how a property-based classification of workers would compare with the contract-based classification, in terms of the comparative *proportion* of workers who would fall within the remit of employment security laws. This is a matter requiring empirical investigation. For present purposes tentative conclusions may be drawn about the value of a property-based classification by relying on what is known about the social costs of corporate restructuring.

The Social Cost of Corporate Restructuring

The effect of corporate restructuring on job security depends largely on pressures external to the firm such as the regulatory and institutional environment, the markets within which the firm operates, and the overall social, political or economic conditions. It goes without saying that if firms are not profitable then in the long run there will be no firms to provide jobs. At this general level more profits for shareholders means more jobs for workers. Here the strength of Walter Cabot's argument cannot be ignored:

> We should not put on blinders and focus only on the micro level of concern for a given employee who at age fifty-seven is forced out of a company. I think we all can and should have compassion for that individual. But we will all end up with the same fate unless we address the greater questions … If we continue to protect inefficient, uncompetitive companies, we're all going to be out of work … As to the individual employees displaced by a plant closure, the free market will operate to produce more jobs, because the industry and corporate America will be functioning more competitively.[240]

According to an empirical study conducted by the Cambridge Centre for Business Research (the Cambridge Study) similar sentiments are echoed by managers in the UK: 'Our business is about profits and shareholder value. If it's jobs before shareholder interests, the answer is no … it simply prolongs the agony'.[241] The reasoning here is that pursuing profits is in everyone's best interests: 'maximizing profits for equity investors assists the other "constituencies" automatically'.[242] The argument is that if corporations are efficiently run, which requires allowing managers to make tough decisions from time to time, all workers will ultimately be better off as the economy will sustain 'more and better' jobs.

---

the employer see Simon Deakin, 'The Changing Concept of the Employer in Labour Law' (2001a) 30 *Industrial Law Journal* 72–84.

240 Walter M. Cabot, 'The Free Market Promotes Long-Term Efficiency that Benefits All Stakeholders' (1991) 21 *Stetson Law Review* 245–52 at 248.

241 Simon Deakin, Richard Hobbs, Sue Konzelmann and Frank Wilkinson, 'Anglo-American Corporate Governance and the Employment Relationship: A Case to Answer?' ESRC Centre for Business Research, University of Cambridge Working Paper No. 308 June 2005 at 10.

242 Frank H. Easterbrook and Daniel R. Fischel, *The Economic Structure of Corporate Law* (Cambridge, Massachusetts: Harvard University Press, 1991) at 38.

However the social cost of job losses cannot always be assumed to be necessary in the interests of efficiency or overall wealth benefits to society. During corporate restructuring substantial gains for shareholders are often made at the expense of employment and wage losses. Andrei Shleifer and Lawrence Summers point out that this is often the case in the context of hostile takeovers which generate wealth benefits for shareholders by reneging on earlier promises made to the workers, usually promises that were given to induce those workers to put more effort into their work at their own cost, in the expectation of future rewards such as promotions.[243] The workers' effort based on these implicit promises is a lost investment if they are fired by new managers after the takeover. This fact is often overlooked, if attention is paid solely to the firm's rising share value. The Cambridge Study found evidence of share values rising as a direct result of job losses. The study cites the example of managers faced with the threat of hostile takeover who responded by making their own offer of short-term gain to their shareholders 'to retain their loyalty', an offer which was financed by firing workers. The offer

> took the form of a promise to return cash to the shareholders which would be generated in large part by a redundancy exercise aimed at cutting costs. Thus halfway through the bid process, the target announced that it would be cutting 17% of its workforce … in the event it went even further, dismissing nearly 1,000 workers while the bid was in progress, including 500 in one day.[244]

This illustrates the concern which lies at the heart of the stakeholder debate, which is that profit maximization should not come at the expense of workers' jobs when this is not necessary for productive purposes. Shleifer and Summers observe that this form of activity results in wealth redistribution from employees to shareholders, and not wealth creation. This suggests that gains in share value should be measured against the real cost of job loss in deciding whether it is justifiable.

Cost of Job Loss, Downsizing and the Stock Market

Once a job is lost it may prove difficult or impossible to find an alternative of comparable worth, an effect sometimes felt for the remainder of the worker's career. One empirical study 'find[s] substantial and long-lasting effects of job loss on annual

---

243 Andrei Shleifer and Lawrence Summers, 'Breach of Trust in Hostile Takeovers' *National Bureau of Economic Research Working Paper No. W2342* (May 1989). Published in Alan J. Auerbach (ed.), *Corporate Takeovers: Causes and Consequences* (Chicago: University of Chicago Press, 1988).

244 Deakin et al, 'Anglo-American Corporate Governance and the Employment Relationship' at 13. Despite the sacrifice of all these jobs the strategy was unsuccessful in preventing the takeover.

earnings and wages' over the long term, from which many workers never recover.[245] The cost of job loss has been defined as

> the difference between the utility value of being in the current job and that of the next best alternative. The utility gained from the current job is primarily determined by the wage received, while the alternative level of utility is affected by the wages on offer, the chances of securing another job, and whatever utility is derived, in terms of both replacement income and leisure time, from unemployment.[246]

The next best alternative is often worth far less than the job lost, which means that the cost of job loss has lifelong effects for most workers.[247] This is clearly problematic where the dismissal involved no element of 'fault'. Margaret Blair points to the fact that in the US 'long-tenured employees laid off through no fault of their own (as a result of plant closings, for example) typically earn 15 to 25 percent less on their next jobs'.[248] Derek Simpson makes a similar case in relation to the British manufacturing industry, where 'those people who lose their jobs in manufacturing and who find work in another sector, suffer an average 40 per cent pay cut. Only 13 per cent find another job in manufacturing' and 'these workers' reduced spending power impacts hugely on the local economy'.[249] Simpson is right to express concern not just for the workers who lose their jobs but also for the local economy, as corporate restructuring which results in thousands of job losses allows corporations to accumulate wealth for their shareholders by externalizing the costs of economic progress onto the local community. In this way the corporation is 'effectively transferring to the public sector the costs of maintaining these displaced workers'.[250] This suggests the need for a more socially-desirable balance between profits and jobs.

---

245 Robert Topel, 'Specific Capital and Unemployment: Measuring the Costs and Consequences of Job Loss' (1990) 33 *Carnegie--Rochester Conference Series on Public Policy* (Allan Meltzer and Charles Plosser (eds.), *Studies in Labor Economics in Honor of Walter Oi*) 181–214 at 181.

246 Francis Green and Steve McIntosh, 'Union Power, Cost of Job Loss and Workers' Effort' (1998) 51 *Industrial & Labor Relations Review* 363–83 at 365–6.

247 Topel, at 183.

248 Margaret M. Blair, 'Firm-Specific Human Capital and Theories of the Firm' in Margaret M. Blair and Mark Roe (eds.), *Employees and Corporate Governance* (Washington D.C.: Brookings Institution Press, 1999) at 61. She observes that in fact 'these are conservative estimates' (at note 5).

249 Derek Simpson, 'Manufacturing: What We Want From Warwick' (2005) 55 *Federation News* 28–9 at 28.

250 Joseph W. Singer, 'Jobs and Justice: Rethinking the Stakeholder Debate' (1993) 43 *University of Toronto Law Journal* 475–731 at 496, explaining that 'Mass lay-offs create substantial negative externalities, imposing costs on the workers' families, public services, and other businesses in the community. Because the costs of economic transition are partly borne by taxpayers, allowing employers to fire workers en masse without minimum levels of benefits subsidizes those employers'.

The problem is compounded when workers are fired without warning. In the UK workers' entitlement to notice before dismissal has not prevented employers sacking thousands of workers without warning. One newspaper reported how a company sacked 'almost all 2,500 of them without so much as a minute's notice before their phones started ringing. A text message on their mobiles told them an expected pay day had been cancelled and to ring a phone number that played another message, this time from liquidators PricewaterhouseCoopers, saying they had lost their job'.[251] Another factor compounding the problem is the impression that job cuts were not inevitable or unavoidable. Firms often boost their profits by firing workers especially when advantage can be taken of cheap labour in other parts of the world, made possible by the increasing use of modern information technology which reduces the need for workers to be physically present at the workplace. According to the Organization for Economic Co-operation and Development (OECD) the industries most affected are accounting, consulting and financial services, industries which play a significant role in both the UK and US economies.[252] News reports abound of jobs lost as firms move their operations offshore.[253] Firms certainly need to be flexible and respond quickly to changes in the global market. Workers generally accept that sometimes the firm has no other realistic option than to shut down. Nevertheless there is sometimes a real choice to be made between shareholder and employee

251 Phillip Inman, 'When You Get the Sack by Text' *The Guardian*, 7th June 2003 at 23; and see Wedderburn of Charlton, *The Future of Company Law: Fat Cats, Corporate Governance and Workers* (London: Institute of Employment Rights, 2004). The picture is much the same as that in the US where 'An employer may give any or all of its employees the 'weekend farewell,' notifying them on Friday that they are terminated as of the end of the day. One department store simply posted a notice on its locked doors on Monday that the store was being sold to another company and all employees were terminated. The management of a college called members of its staff to a meeting in an auditorium, told them they were immediately dismissed, and prohibited them from going back to their workplaces. Another more ingenious employer that had decided to close its plant sounded a fire alarm and, when all of its employees were out, locked the gates and announced that all employees were terminated': Clyde W. Summers, 'Worker Dislocation: Who Bears the Burden? A Comparative Study of Social Values in Five Countries' (1995) 70 *Notre Dame Law Review* 1030–78 at 1036.

252 Organization for Economic Co-operation and Development (OECD) Directorate for Science, Technology and Industry *Report of the Working Party on the Information Economy: The Share of Employment Potentially Affected by Offshoring – An Empirical Investigation*, DSTI/ICCP/IE (2005) 8/Final.

253 'Norwich Union Britain's biggest insurer yesterday said that it would move 950 jobs from Britain to India and Sri Lanka during 2005, with a further 2,350 to be moved offshore during the following two years … In October 2003 HSBC, Britain's largest bank, said that it would send 4,000 jobs offshore, while Lloyds TSB plans to transfer 1,500 jobs to India by the end of this year. Troika, the consultancy, estimates that 100,000 British financial services jobs will be moved offshore by 2010': Christine Seib, 'NU Plans to Send 7,000 Jobs to Asia by 2007' *The Times* (September 23, 2004). See, more recently, Phillip Inman, 'Royal & SunAlliance to Cut Tenth of Workforce' ('as part of an efficiency drive to reduce annual running costs by £130m') *The Guardian* (June 20, 2006).

interests. An example may be taken from the British manufacturing industry which according to *Amicus*, the union representing workers in this industry, was losing 10,000 to 12,000 jobs a month in 2005. *Amicus* argued that:

> we believe that manufacturing decline is not inevitable. At the centre of our strategy for recovery is the need for stronger employment rights which will not only help protect UK workers but will also be good for business, boosting productivity, providing greater export opportunities, and generating more inward investment.[254]

This reasoned reaction from the trade unions indicates that they protest against job losses not out of a misguided sense of absolute entitlement to hold their existing jobs 'for life' but precisely because they perceive that there is a genuine alternative to be explored, such as the idea of temporary wage reductions to allow the firm to weather an economic downturn in the market.

In the Cambridge Study worker representatives expressed the view that 'when share prices fell, management was prone to making 'knee jerk reactions' and attacking costs simply to demonstrate to financial analysts that some action was being taken'.[255] This undue focus on short-term share value is another major source of contention. In the UK it is said that 'It has become accepted wisdom in parts of the City [of London] that companies in difficulty can restore share prices by instituting large-scale redundancies'.[256] The Cambridge Study cites the instance of a company which 'announced a major restructuring programme with the loss of 6,000 jobs. There was no prior consultation with employee representatives. On the day of the restructuring announcement, the company's share price increased by 11%'.[257] The situation is the same in the US, where 'downsizing' of staff is sometimes done not with the aim of enhancing productivity but simply to enhance the firm's value on the stock market.[258]

It might seem logical that firms would not unnecessarily fire their workers because they cannot exist without workers. However the crucial issue is the time-frame taken into account in decision-making, and whether managers allow a short-term gain in stock-market value to take priority over the long-term interests of the firm. Here Adam Smith's observation is pertinent: 'In the long run the workman may be as necessary to his master as his master is to him; but the necessity is not

254 Simpson, at 28.

255 Deakin et al, 'Anglo-American Corporate Governance' at 13.

256 Simon Deakin and Giles Slinger, 'Company Law as an Instrument for Inclusion: Regulating Stakeholder Relations in the Context of Takeovers' ESRC Centre for Business Research, University of Cambridge Working Paper No. 145 September 1999 at 13.

257 Deakin et al, 'Anglo-American Corporate Governance' at 10.

258 Marleen A. O'Connor, 'Organized Labor' as Shareholder Avtivist: Building Coalitions to Promote Worker Capitalism' (1997) 31 *University of Richmond Law Review* 1345-98 at 1375, citing a study in which 'fewer than half of [downsizing] firms subsequently increased profits; only a third reported higher productivity'.

so immediate'.[259] If the firm means to continue in business then downsizing may be only a very short-term strategy, but short-term decisions of this kind may boost the firm's stock market value considerably which is no insignificant consideration when the daily performance of its shares is being watched closely by investors and competitors.[260] This tendency is mostly associated with the large publicly-held firms that dominate the Anglo-American economies, but it appears to be increasingly common around the world as globalization impels corporations to converge in their managerial philosophy and practices.

Wages are not the only significant cost which may be cut to maximize profits, nor are workers the only constituency in the firm whose interests may be in conflict with shareholders' interest in profit maximization. The same conflict extends to other parties dealing with the firm such as suppliers or customers who may be adversely affected by cost-cutting measures. Advocates of corporate social responsibility therefore focus on the balance to be struck between maximizing profits on the one hand, and the corporation's duty to society on the other. All contributors to corporate activity are important. It is evident that firms rely on all their participants, including their shareholders.[261] The focus of this study on workers' interests in the firm is not based on the view that workers are invariably or automatically more important than other stakeholders, but rather on the view that they are sufficiently important to merit a more careful assessment of their role in the firm. This focus is necessary because in the predominant theories of the firm unwarranted emphasis on the importance of shareholders obscures or overlooks the role played by workers. Some balance may be restored by giving prominence here to the crucial role played by workers in the modern firm.

Justifying Economic Dismissals

The difficulty with enhancing job security lies in reconciling this with the fact that corporate restructuring may *genuinely* be intended to enhance flexibility, efficiency and productivity, and job losses may sometimes be a necessary cost in achieving this

---

259 Smith, T*he Wealth of Nations* Book 1, Chapter VIII: 'In all such disputes the masters can hold out much longer. A landlord, a farmer, a master manufacturer, a merchant, though they did not employ a single workman, could generally live a year or two upon the stocks which they have already acquired. Many workmen could not subsist a week, few could subsist a month, and scarce any a year without employment.'

260 Meyers, at 39. Meyers remarks on occasions when employers would afterwards rehire staff laid off for economic reasons, sometimes with the same benefits and perks that they were entitled to before they were dismissed, raising the question whether the dismissals had been necessary in the first place.

261 See, however, Majorie Kelly, 'The Incredibly Unproductive Shareholder' (2000) 80 *Harvard Business Review* 18–19. Henry Hansmann in *The Ownership of Enterprise* (London: Belknap Press, 1996) explores other potential sources of finance other than shareholders. Meeting the firm's capital needs may not be as difficult as might be expected if the firm can borrow the capital on reasonable terms.

end. This tension is certainly acknowledged by the stakeholder theory of the firm. It does not assume that *all* corporate restructuring is a deliberate attempt to maximize profits by expropriating workers' human capital investments. Not all reorganizations are a pretext for firing workers. As Freeman puts it

> Stakeholder capitalism is no panacea. It simply allows the possibility that business becomes a fully human institution. There will always be businesspeople who try to take advantage of others, just as there are corrupt government officials, clergy and professors. Stakeholder capitalism bases our understanding and expectations of business, not on the worst that we can do, but on the best. It sets a high standard, recognizes the common-sense practical world of global business today, and asks managers to get on with the task of creating value for all stakeholders.[262]

On this issue this study aims as far as possible to remain cognizant of the need to balance job security with other economic imperatives. As noted earlier the law recognizes that in genuine situations of 'economic dismissals' it would not be appropriate to apply the same kind of employment protection measures that apply to other unfair or wrongful dismissal cases. Nevertheless, in drawing the boundaries of its regulatory provisions the law recognizes that not all dismissals which take place during restructuring can be justified. First and foremost, in considering the effect of corporate restructuring on employees it is important to appreciate the value of rights at work. Sir Bob Hepple argues that 'When we assert [such] rights we are claiming that we want work not only to survive, but also to achieve personal and social fulfilment'.[263] He therefore criticizes regulatory approaches which prioritize competitiveness at the expense of 'the welfare of the human being at work'.[264] Corporate restructuring which boosts the stock market value of firms, and therefore increases overall shareholder wealth, may ultimately come at too high a social cost when masses of workers are laid off. The social costs of job losses may well be unquantifiable:

> The loss of a job … may be far more hurtful than a term in jail. When these deprivations are inflicted arbitrarily, and there is no recourse, a gap in the legal order exists. We become more sensitive to that gap when the decisions are made by organizations that seem large, powerful and impersonal ...[265]

This has been recognized in the context of unfair dismissal litigation in the UK, Lord Millett observing that 'many people build their lives round their jobs and plan their future in the expectation that they will continue. For many workers dismissal is a

262 Freeman, at 178.

263 Hepple, *Rights At Work* at 2.

264 Bob Hepple and Gillian Morris, 'The Employment Act 2002 and the Crisis of Individual Employment Rights' (2002) 31 *Industrial Law Journal* 245–69 at 246.

265 Selznick, at 38.

disaster'.[266] For this reason the book draws attention to perspectives which question the shareholder primacy norm and point to the need to enhance job security in the context of corporate restructuring. As Singer expressed it, the aim 'should be to encourage desirable economic change without unnecessary social misery'.[267]

Conclusion

This chapter considered the links between work, property and liberty from the early days of master and servant to the modern stakeholder economy. It showed that throughout this period the idea of rights in work has represented a significant theme in the common law, formulated by a number of judges, philosophers and academic commentators as rights of property. Liberty and property were seen to go hand in hand as fundamental values, invoked to support *both* the rights of workers and the rights of employers. The chapter argued that this fact has been obscured by the overwhelming tendency to associate these values *exclusively* with employers' rights. The result is that stakeholder theory and ideas of property in work are presumed to be inherently opposed to these fundamental values and thereby to go against the grain of the common law tradition. The reality, as this chapter has shown, is that ideas of property in work are rooted in an intellectual heritage that can be traced back to the mediaeval guilds. The chapter argued that this line of thinking, as manifested in the law, should not be overlooked simply because it lies buried in dissenting opinions and decisions reversed on appeal. It was seen that in *Allen v Flood* and *United Steel Workers* various judges recognized the existence of extra-contractual or property rights in the context of the employment relationship. It was not argued that these opinions represent 'good law' in a doctrinal sense, but they were relied upon to illustrate that prevailing notions such as employment at will and employment as contract are far more controversial in the common law tradition than is commonly supposed, and that the idea of property in work is by the same token far less controversial than appears at first sight. In this way the chapter has illustrated that the common law tradition is rich enough to encompass different conceptual analyses of the employment relationship.

The focus was on three main aspects of the common law. First on some of the historical influences that shaped the conceptual nature of the employment relationship, focusing on notions of liberty and property and the eventual establishment of employment at will. It was suggested that the English requirement of reasonable notice has not made significant inroads into the overriding idea of termination 'at

266 In *Johnson v Unisys* [2003] 1 A.C. 518 at par. 72.

267 'The Reliance Interest' at 623. Similarly Margaret Blair and Lynn Stout argue that 'the proper purpose of the public corporation is not maximizing shareholder wealth, but promoting long-term, value-creating economic production … in a fashion that provides surplus benefits not only to shareholders but to other groups that make specific investments in corporations as well': 'Specific Investment and Corporate Law' (2006) 7 *European Business Organization Law Review*. <www.ssrn.com> at 1.

will', but has manifested itself as a right to monetary compensation for wages that would have been earned during the notice period. The second aspect explained how this is interrelated with the contractual basis of the employment relationship. The suggestion was made that in the context of job security in the firm the proprietary model is able to capture aspects of the employment relationship in the firm which are not fully addressed within the contractual framework with its emphasis on damages. Third, the chapter considered different perspectives on property in work. Over time the idea has enjoyed varying fortunes, but it has never quite disappeared. The proprietary model of stakeholder theory was distinguished from these historical approaches, as the aim of this book is not to advocate a return to past ideas but to evaluate the potential of a modern and evolving theory of property rights to explain the allocation of ownership and control in the modern firm, and to offer a means of recognizing the participation of employees in the governance of these firms. This chapter has illustrated that the idea of 'ownership' in explaining the role of employees in the firm is not alien to or incompatible with the common law tradition. The fact that it has not acquired predominance is not in itself a reason to abandon it. Instead its valuable attributes may be extracted and used as analytical tools in clarifying the nature of ownership and control in the modern enterprise. This idea is explored in the next chapter which considers the question: 'who owns the firm?'

Chapter 2

Ownership of the Firm

> When several parties share legal rights in property, any identification of a single person as the 'owner' is likely to be arbitrary and misleading. It is arbitrary because we could just as easily identify someone else as the owner. It is misleading because it denies the existence of joint interests and the need to determine the legal relations among all the persons with legally protected interests in the property.[1]

Introduction

Waldron depicts the idea of ownership as an 'organizing idea'. It is 'an essential point of reference by which the operation of … very detailed and complicated rules is to be understood'.[2] Notions of ownership and property rights have long been used to explain the interrelationship and co-existence of conflicting interests in the same resource. In the context of corporate restructuring the main conflicting interests in the firm are the workers' interest in the continuity of their jobs, the managerial prerogative exercised on behalf of shareholders, and the economic imperatives of efficiency and competitiveness.

If the firm is owned *exclusively* by its shareholders then there can be no room for employee claims of ownership. This proposition is compelling in a free society founded on the respect for private property. This chapter argues that while shareholders have good grounds to claim a form of ownership in the firm it is not necessary to understand that claim as an absolute entitlement to maximize profits by cutting jobs regardless of the impact on employees' firm-specific human capital investments. In some circumstances these human capital investments give employees a valid ownership claim. Stakeholder theory accommodates *both* shareholder and employee claims within a pluralist model of co-ownership. To assess the feasibility of this argument the chapter analyzes the degree of support given in English and American law to the idea that shareholders own the firm. Finding that shareholder ownership is not an explicit legal construct but operates instead as an underlying assumption, the chapter argues that this assumption should give way to a theory of shared and contingent ownership which allows the reconciliation of conflicting interests in the firm.

1 Singer, 'The Reliance Interest' at 638.

2 Waldron, at 42. Similarly Harris refers to property as a 'complex organizing idea'.

Ownership of the Firm

The first way of discussing ownership in the firm is by reference to the ownership of physical assets, explaining why a firm might choose to own its assets instead of hiring or leasing them. Ownership of these assets has the advantage of bringing within the boundaries of the firm the resolution of any potential conflicts of interest over maintenance and use, hence keeping transaction costs down.[3] Sanford Grossman and Oliver Hart focus on asset ownership to explain the decision by one firm to acquire another.[4] The mechanism of vertical integration places the physical assets at different stages of production under the unified ownership of the acquiring firm, granting the acquirer decision-making rights in the new firm. Ownership therefore explains the decision by one firm to merge with or take over another. In similar vein, highlighting the importance of asset ownership, the proprietary structure of the firm has also been explained in terms of 'asset partitioning'. This has most significance in the context of insolvency, where property rules 'partition corporate assets from the assets of individuals associated with the company'.[5]

But ownership in the firm need not be understood solely in terms of specific 'assets'. The concept of property is more concerned with the mutual rights and obligations amongst individuals with conflicting interests in the same resource than with the ownership of physical 'things'.[6] Ownership signifies a 'bundle of rights', a 'complex bundle of relations', which includes the right to the firm's revenues and to determine the firm's operations and strategy.[7] It is in this sense that the concept of ownership has greatest relevance for decision-making in the firm, and for employee-participation claims. In this context ownership is often used in a normative sense, to designate a right of which the owner ought not to be deprived without his or her consent.[8] Ownership in the firm is also best understood as a qualified rather than absolute notion. Here the importance of the normative, as opposed to descriptive, notion of ownership is highlighted by the fact that in the large publicly-held firm the definition of shareholders as owners is hardly descriptive of actual practice, in that the rights exercisable by the shareholders do not include the entire range of rights exercisable by any owner of property. Most shareholders understand that they

---

3 Benjamin Klein, Robert G. Crawford and Armen A. Alchian, 'Vertical Integration, Appropriate Rents and the Competitive Contracting Process' (1981) 89 *Journal of Political Economy* 615–41.

4 Sanford Grossman and Oliver Hart, 'The Costs and Benefits of Ownership: A Theory of Vertical and Lateral Integration' (1986) 94 *Journal of Political Economy* 691–719.

5 Armour, at 3.

6 Kevin J. Gray, 'Property in Thin Air' (1991) 50 *Cambridge Law Journal* 252–307.

7 Waldron, at 28–9.

8 Calabresi and Melamed. Employees' rights of information and consultation prior to corporate restructuring may be understood as ownership claims in this sense, *if* they are coupled with sanctions which ensure that depriving them of these rights will invalidate the managers' unilateral decision. As will be seen in Chapter 4 this is the case in some European member states, though not in the UK.

do not have the same rights of access to the premises of companies in which they own shares as they do in their own homes.[9] As Waldron remarks in referring to the description of shareholders as owners of the company, 'of course, they do not have all the rights of ownership on, say, Honoré's list, but then neither does a landlord or a mortgagor'.[10] This point may also be illustrated by the description of shareholders in law and economics. Emphasis is on the formal control exercised by shareholders as providers of equity capital, despite the fact that a shareholder has no right to control directors in their day-to-day management of the corporation.

Ownership as Control

In the different disciplines which contribute to the study of corporate governance the 'owner' is identified as the party who is entitled to control the firm and to make important decisions when its future is at stake. Rights of ownership therefore determine the allocation of control between all the contributors to the firm's activities. In this way, to use Waldron's language, ownership serves as a central organizing mechanism in the allocation of control within the enterprise, providing a framework for a system of rules governing access to and control of the firm's resources. Much therefore depends on identifying the party in whom ownership rights are vested.

In discussions of ownership in the firm the concern is often not with the actual authority wielded by corporate participants in practice but much more with the formal allocation of control. Henry Hansmann describes as the firm's owners 'those persons who share two formal rights: the right to control the firm and the right to appropriate the firm's profits, or residual earnings', and formal control as 'the right to elect the firm's board of directors and to vote directly on a small set of fundamental issues, such as merger or dissolution of the firm'.[11] If control is defined in a formal sense as the ultimate right to make decisions or to delegate decision-making authority then it follows that a firm is shareholder-owned if formal control, through voting rights, is vested in shareholders. Thus a firm in which employees also own shares, and exercise formal control in their capacity as shareholders, cannot be said to be employee-owned in this sense even if employees might be said to have a claim to the firm's residual earnings.[12] This focus on formal control allows the shareholder ownership assumptions of corporate law to remain unaltered by the separation of ownership and control and the fact that actual control is often exercised by managerial employees.[13]

---

9 On the corporation's right to exclude see *Porter v Metropolitan Police Comr* [1999] All E.R. 1129.

10 At 58.

11 At 11.

12 Gregory Dow and Louis Putterman 'Why Capital (Usually) Hires Labor: An Assessment of Proposed Explanations' in Blair and Roe.

13 There is no inconsistency here – there are other examples in law of split ownership where the legal title is devoid of practical or actual control over the thing owned: see Njoya, 'Employee Ownership and Efficiency'.

The idea of ownership is useful not only in identifying *who* owns rights of control, but also in prescribing *how* these rights are exercised. In a real sense, as Luigi Zingales points out, the exercise of control rights determines the bargaining position or power of the firm's participants and affects the processes of collective decision-making within the firm, by determining the effectiveness with which the parties in control are able to protect their interests. This has significant practical implications extending not only to bargaining power within the firm but also to the bargaining power wielded by corporations in the economic and political debates in society generally.[14] To the extent that the firm's ownership structure enhances or detracts from the bargaining power of the firm's participants it has a crucial effect on the ability of employees to bargain for job security. Ownership as control therefore offers a way of understanding the interplay of conflicting interests of various participants in the corporate enterprise.

In explaining the link between ownership and control of the firm Hansmann also highlights the importance of investment incentives. He argues that ownership, defined as a claim to the firm's residual earnings, provides the owner with the incentive to use control to maximize those earnings. A misallocation of the residual rights of control would lead to the distortion of the parties' incentives to invest in the firm – unless owners have control they will not invest in the firm, resulting in a net loss of wealth in society and making everybody worse off.[15] Ownership is therefore a vital consideration in both the determination of who has the right to exercise control of the firm as well as in the conferment of incentives to maximize production.[16] Within this framework it is crucial to determine the most efficient allocation of ownership rights in the firm, as that will in turn point to the optimal allocation of control rights in the firm. The central idea is that control rights should be allocated so as to maximize investment incentives.

Control rights should be allocated so as to minimize transaction costs. The basic idea is that the structure and size of the firm are ultimately determined largely by the need to avoid external contracting processes, in the market outside the firm, which are not cost-free. The Coase theorem suggests that if contracting in the market were costless the initial allocation of property rights within the firm would not matter as the parties would simply redistribute these rights amongst themselves through contract, and ownership would therefore be irrelevant. The invisible hand of the market would simply reallocate property rights to the party who valued those rights most.[17] In a world devoid of transaction costs the role of the law is limited to defining

---

14 On this basis the notion of shareholder ownership has been used to explain the power wielded by the large public company in the modern economy: John Parkinson, *Corporate Power and Responsibility: Issues in the Theory of Company Law* (Oxford: Clarendon Press, 1993).

15 Oliver Hart, 'Incomplete Contracts and the Theory of the Firm' in Oliver E. Williamson and Sidney G. Winter (eds.), *The Nature of the Firm: Origins, Evolution and Development* (Oxford: Oxford University Press, 1993).

16 Zingales.

17 Derived from Smith, *Wealth of Nations*.

property rights with precision and allowing all parties the freedom to contract for those rights which they value.[18] Ownership becomes relevant and necessary because it may be prohibitively costly for such contractual reallocations to be viable. The initial allocation of residual rights of control in the firm must be considered carefully because it may not in the event be possible for the parties to redistribute these rights through negotiation or agreement. Therefore the question who the owner is becomes highly significant, as the optimal or efficient allocation of ownership rights in the firm cannot reliably be expected to emerge spontaneously through market contracting. [19]

Shareholder and Stakeholder Owners

Because shareholders are often referred to as 'owners' of the firm the framework of corporate governance is premised on the idea that managers act on behalf of and are accountable to the shareholders.[20] At a general level the argument that the corporation belongs to its shareholders may be readily appreciated. The Companies Act 1985 defines the members of the company as its shareholders.[21] It appears logical that the shareholders' purchase of shares in the company gives them an ownership stake within it. Shares are a valuable, indeed arguably the most valuable, form of property in the modern economy, having long surpassed the importance of land ownership.[22] The property rights theory of the firm defines ownership as 'possession of "residual" control rights, the rights to make all decisions (at least those that have not been delegated to others by contract) and receive whatever is left over after all payments specified by contract have been paid'.[23] Drawing from this definition it seems reasonable to describe shareholders as the firm's owners, as all control rights vest in them other than those they delegate to managers to exercise on their behalf. In contrast to claims of shareholder ownership, it is more difficult to discern the basis

---

18 Coase.

19 Therefore it could be said that in economic theory property refers to 'those attributes left over after all maximizing contracts that are possible within transaction-cost constraints have been exploited'; Property is 'a stand-in for the assignment of use rights that is employed only when the possibilities for contracting run out': Merrill and Smith, at 377 and 378.

20 For instance the Cadbury Committee *Report on the Financial Aspects of Corporate Governance* stated that 'the shareholders as owners of the company elect the directors to run the business on their behalf and hold them accountable for its progress' (1992) at par. 6.1. 'Contemporary discussions of corporate governance have come to be dominated by the view that public corporations are little more than bundles of assets collectively owned by shareholders (principals) who hire directors and officers (agents) to manage those assets on their behalf': Blair and Stout, 'A Team Production Theory' at 248.

21 S. 22 Companies Act 1985.

22 'The large enterprise … has brought with it new modes of belonging and dependency. It has undercut the worth of contractual freedom and has lessened the significance, even for the middle-class man, of traditional forms of property, notably the ownership of chattels and land': Selznick, at 36.

23 Blair, 'Firm-Specific Human Capital' in Blair and Roe, at 77–8.

of the employees' claim to ownership. After all it could be said that the workers are simply hired by the company to do a specific job for which they are paid, and that their interest in the firm stops there. Employees are deemed to be outsiders with whom the firm deals at arms' length through the mechanism of contract: 'a firm is a fairly well-defined entity whose interests are simply the interests of its owners. By this assumption, employees are contracting with the firm but are not, themselves, part of it'.[24]

The result is that shareholder-owners are deemed to have the exclusive right to make strategic decisions in the firm, which in practice means that they have the right to appoint the firm's managers and to have those managers act as their agents in pursuing their best interests. This perspective is justified on different grounds but the argument of particular interest in this chapter is that based on the prerogatives of ownership. The basis of this argument is that the owner of property has the right to make all decisions affecting that property – 'I own it, so I can do what I want with it'.[25] This idea draws support from the neoclassical economic theory of the firm, which is concerned with the 'agency' relationship between shareholder owners (the principals) and managers (the agents).[26] The focus of this theory is on ensuring that managers, who are inclined to shirk and to divert the firm's income to themselves, are constrained to pursue profits on behalf of shareholders. This conflict of interests attracts most attention in agency theory, a theory associated with the defining characteristic of the Anglo-American public corporation: the separation of ownership and control. The firm is defined as a bundle of assets managed on behalf of absent shareholder-owners by hired managers, the primary concern of corporate law being to align the incentives of the managers with those of the shareholder-owners.[27] As this model does not address the conflicts of interest arising in relation to other stakeholders, giving the impression that such interests are of no significance to a theory of the firm, the model has long been criticized:

> A concept of the corporation which draws the boundary of 'membership' thus narrowly is seriously inadequate … the line between those who are 'inside' and those who are 'outside' the corporation is the line between those who are recognized as entitled to a regularized share in its processes of decision and those who are not. A more spacious conception of 'membership,' and one closer to the facts of corporate life, would include all those having a relation of sufficient intimacy with the corporation or subject to its power in a sufficiently specialized way.[28]

---

24 Blair, 'Firm-Specific Human Capital' in Blair and Roe, at 65–6.

25 Williams, at 302.

26 Hart, 'An Economist's Perspective'.

27 Corporate governance is thought to be essentially about 'reducing "agency costs" by keeping directors and managers faithful to shareholders' interests': Blair and Stout, 'A Team Production Theory' at 248–9.

28 Abram Chayes, 'The Modern Corporation and the Rule of Law' in Edward S. Mason (ed.), *The Corporation in Modern Society* (Harvard: Harvard University Press, 1959) cited in Selznick, at 51.

Stakeholder theory proposes one method by which this 'more spacious conception' can be achieved, by arguing that ownership understood as residual control and the right to make decisions in situations not governed by explicit contracts does not inevitably point to shareholders as the firm's exclusive owners. The stakeholder model conceptualizes the firm as a network of multiple participants each of whom is entitled to a return on their contribution to corporate productivity. The question how this return should be defined and quantified, particularly when the interests of different stakeholders are in conflict, is answered by defining these 'stakes' within the proprietary framework of the firm. The idea that employees' interest in the firm is limited to their wages is countered by defining employees as investors whose interests are not fully captured by the terms of their employment contracts. This allows job security to be understood as an interest founded on employees' property rights in the firm.

This argument draws inspiration from the suggestion of Blair that employees often have just as much claim to be considered the owners of the firm as do the shareholders.[29] Blair argues that ownership in the modern firm is shared or split between myriad shareholders who contribute finance capital and employees who contribute the skill, innovativeness and ideas on which the firm's productivity and profitability is based. It is increasingly evident in the modern economy that in a particular firm the people who work for it may be even more vital to its success than its shareholders. Over the centuries the nature of work has changed quite dramatically, from an era when the employer exercised almost total discretion over the way tasks were performed, to the modern age in which many workers have almost autonomous discretion over the performance of their work. In an earlier age workers were expected to 'do what they are told promptly and without asking questions or making suggestions … it [was] absolutely necessary for every man to become one of a train of gear wheels.'[30] By contrast in the modern firm workers are priced for the ability to 'manage themselves', as it is often put. Creativity and the capacity to work independently are often an explicit and indispensable requirement in recruitment. These new values alter the allocation of ownership and control of the firm. Blair argues that in this 'new employment relationship' central to the modern firm, the contribution of employees' skills and knowledge has become much more central to productivity, in many ways replacing the role previously played by finance capital: 'human capital is often as important as physical capital in creating value'.[31] Ideas and intellectual input have become an increasingly vital part of corporate enterprise in what has been termed the 'new economy'.[32]

29 Blair, *Ownership and Control.*

30 Frederick Taylor, quoted in Fox, *Beyond Contract* at 193.

31 Blair and Roe, 'Introduction' in Blair and Roe, at 2.

32 O'Connor, 'Organized Labor.

Who Owns the Firm?

If shareholders own the firm then they are entitled to the same legal protection accorded to property owners in a free market society. This leads some commentators to consider it unacceptable for the interests of employees to be taken into account alongside those of shareholders, or for employee welfare to be deemed as important as maximizing profits in defining the goals of corporate enterprise. As noted earlier the view that profit maximization on behalf of shareholders is the sole standard to which managerial decision-making should aspire places reliance on the role of property 'in providing a source of security against a range of interfering forces in society at large.'[33] The corporation is an institution of private property. The notion of property implies non-interference in the owner's dealings with respect to the thing owned, and especially freedom to buy and sell or otherwise dispose of the property – 'an unfettered sphere of action, an island of privacy'.[34] If property owners have a legal right 'to exclude an indefinite and anonymous class of marauders, pilferers, and thieves',[35] similarly they have a right to exclude all alleged stakeholders making what are thought to be unsubstantiated claims on the firm. In this light proposals that corporations should be run in the interests of all who have a stake in it are depicted as an unacceptable attack on the property rights of the firm's owners.[36]

Commandeering Corporate Property

In the UK context Elaine Sternberg depicts stakeholder theory as an attempt by stakeholders to 'commandeer corporate property'.[37] She argues that

> Stakeholder theory undermines private property, because it denies owners the right to determine how their property will be used. In so far as assets are held or utilised by organisations, stakeholder theory stipulates that those assets should be used for the benefit of all stakeholders. The owners of those assets are thereby prevented from devoting their property unequivocally to the ends of their choice … Since most property is manufactured, financed, distributed or otherwise processed through organisations, it would leave almost no property subject to owner control.[38]

---

33 Merrill and Smith, at 363.

34 Selznick, at 63.

35 Merrill and Smith, at 362.

36 Elaine Sternberg, 'The Defects of Stakeholder Theory' (1997) 5 *Corporate Governance* 3–10; Confederation of British Industries, *Boards Without Tiers: A CBI Contribution to the Debate* (London: CBI, 1996). For a US perspective see Mark E. Van der Weide, 'Against Fiduciary Duties to Corporate Stakeholders' (1996) 21 *Delaware Journal of Corporate Law* 27–86.

37 At 8.

38 Ibid.

Similarly in the US, William Cabot has argued against stakeholder-oriented laws on grounds that 'the sanctity of shareholder property rights should be preserved'.[39] He advances the view that 'individual stock ownership rights are fundamental rights, grounded in the U.S. Constitution' and that 'the traditional marketplace respects these ownership rights by making it clear that directors have a duty to act in the interests of shareholders':

> It's difficult for me to emphasize how sacred I feel the concept of private property is to our nation. Here is an example to which many will relate: many Americans own their homes today. If a legislature were to say they did not 'own' them anymore by taking away one or more of their property rights, for whatever reason, they would suffer a loss in value … Ownership rights are sacred, but employees are not owners … If shareholders must face the prospect of losing their inherent ownership rights … this would lead to the demise of corporate America.[40]

These critiques raise two important issues: first, whether shareholders' property should be held subject to stakeholder claims on the ground that there are inherent limitations on private property; that is, whether shareholders should be *divested* of some of the rights ordinarily inherent in property. The second issue is the more fundamental question whether shareholders own the firm in the first place, and, if so, the *extent* of shareholder property rights in the firm. After all shareholders cannot be divested of what they do not own. The distinction between these two issues is significant because it reflects the two main ways in which stakeholder theory makes use of the notion of property. The first is the recognition that ownership carries with it a measure of liability. The second asks whether employees and other stakeholders might well have independent property claims in the firm which do not depend on notions of shareholder liability but arise from their own investment in the firm. It is important to separate these two ideas from each other, and part of the weakness in the Sternberg and Cabot critiques is that while they address the first idea, they do not address the second. They see the stakeholder claim as simply one based on the inherent limits of property. They appear to presume that the status of shareholders as exclusive owners of the firm is self-evident (shareholders own the entire 'bundle of sticks' representing ownership of the firm), and that the stakeholder claim is purely one concerning the appropriate limits (if any) to be implied within the framework of an 'exclusive property' theory of the firm (shareholders should be compelled to give some of their sticks to the employees). They do not consider the implications of employee investments (employees create their own sticks; the firm's 'bundle of sticks' is an amalgam of both shareholder and employee investments). These two distinct ideas are considered further below.

39 At 250.

40 At 250–51.

Inherent Limitations on Property

Sternberg argues that there are no good grounds for curtailing shareholder property rights: 'Stakeholder theorists sometimes attempt to justify curtailing property rights by indicating that property rights are seldom absolute. But the fact that some limitations apply is not an argument for imposing others …'[41] In this way her critique responds to the element of the stakeholder argument which relies on the existence of exceptions to the exercise of all rights, including the rights of liberty and property, particularly where such exceptions are necessary in the public interest. This element of stakeholder theory will be referred to in this part of the discussion as the 'limitations' approach.

The 'limitations' approach is relied upon in support of corporate social responsibility arguments, which assert that shareholder owners are responsible for the effects of corporate activity on the rest of society. In this sense the 'limitations' approach imposes an important qualification on the idea that shareholder ownership requires exclusive attention to shareholder interests, but it has the disadvantage that it still allows a defence of shareholder dominance, if it can be shown that corporations *do* take into account the effect of their operations on other constituencies. It is also susceptible to the claim that the shareholder primacy norm does not prevent other constituencies from protecting their own interests through specific contracts or the regulatory role of the state in the manner, for example, of the Employment Rights Act or any other regulatory law geared towards protecting the weaker party in market transactions. This, it is often argued, is nothing to do with corporate law.[42] The 'limitations' argument is therefore vulnerable to the Sternberg critique that the existence of limitations on property rights does not *in itself* call for employees or other stakeholders to have a decision-making role in the firm. In the end corporate social responsibility must rest on additional premises and not solely on a 'limitations' argument. John Parkinson's argument for corporate social responsibility relies, for instance, on various grounds including the fundamental need for corporate power in modern society to be justified.[43]

The 'limitations' argument also leaves itself open to the response that these limitations are adequately taken into account by the common law in its modern formulation of the 'enlightened shareholder theory'.[44] The discussion of directors'

41 At 8.

42 See for example Easterbrook and Fischel; Hansmann and Kraakman.

43 Similarly Blades argues that 'It is a widely accepted proposition that large corporations now pose a threat to individual freedom comparable to that which would be posed if governmental power were unchecked … Foremost among the relationships of which this generality is true is that of employer and employee' (at 1404). See also Mary Stokes, 'Company Law and Legal Theory' in Sally Wheeler (ed.), *A Reader on the Law of the Business Enterprise* (Oxford: Oxford University Press, 1994).

44 For a discussion of 'enlightened shareholder value' in historical context see Wedderburn of Charlton, 'Employees, Partnership and Company Law' (2002) 31 *Industrial Law Journal* 99–111.

duties in Chapter 4 will illustrate that both English and American law have settled on the proposition that it is in shareholders' own best interests to look out for the interests of other constituencies who contribute to corporate wealth, and good managers will take this into account in making decisions. The law encourages, and sometimes compels, them to at least think about stakeholders, although what they decide to do after that 'taking into account' process is entirely up to them. The test is entirely procedural. In this way the law seeks to balance the interests of stakeholders with managerial prerogative and the shareholder primacy norm, an approach consistent with the 'limitations' arguments. The 'limitations' approach therefore appears to be open to the response that corporations do recognize sensible limits on shareholder entitlement – managers know that it pays to protect employee interests because in the long run this pleases the workers and satisfied workers will work harder to make more profits for the shareholders.

The danger with this kind of approach is that employees will be well aware that their welfare is only deemed important as a means of increasing the productivity of the firm and its share value, with potential adverse consequences for building trust and cooperation within the firm. This danger is pointed out by Giles Slinger, when he argues that employees and other stakeholders are able to distinguish instrumental behaviour from similar actions motivated by genuine concern on the part of management.[45] Slinger argues that a calculative approach by management in its advancement of employee welfare is communicated to employees through 'micro-signals' inherent in the managerial approach, thereby destroying the vital spirit of cooperation in the firm. A 'calculative' approach by management, with employee welfare calculated simply to boost profits, may have the effect of devaluing employees' contribution in the perception of those employees. Shleifer and Summers also point to the value of trust as one of the most valuable assets in the firm, and the importance of trustworthiness in inducing employees to give their best to the firm. William Brown and Sarah Oxenbridge make the same point in the context of collective bargaining – employee participation should be seen as a means of according dignity and respect to employees and an expression of mutual trust, not just as a 'handy management technique'.[46] For these reasons stakeholder theory steers clear of the instrumental approach. Instead it emphasizes that 'The interests of all stakeholders are of intrinsic value. That is, each group of stakeholders merits consideration for its own sake and not merely because of its ability to further the

---

45 Giles Slinger, 'Spanning the Gap: The Theoretical Principles That Connect Stakeholder Policies to Business Performance' (1998) University of Cambridge: ESRC Centre for Business Research Working Paper Series (WP 11).

46 'There is a large econometric literature concerned with whether or not employers obtain tangible "efficiency gains" from collective bargaining. … But that is beside the main point, which is that, whether or not greater profits may flow through collective bargaining than through autocratic management, employers may prefer collective bargaining because they feel it to be more respectful of their employees … The support for collective bargaining is not presented as a handy management technique, but as a right and duty of employers and employees' (at 65).

interests of some other group, such as the shareowners'.[47] The importance given by directors to the interests of employees should not necessarily depend on showing that this will somehow advance the interests of shareholders, although in practice this will often be the case. Instead the validity of employees' claim to a stake in the ownership of the firm should rest on an independent claim.

The Independent Rights Claim

A better approach might be to ask whether employees have independent property claims which do not depend on the enlightenment of shareholders or largesse of corporate managers. The theory of property rights is highly suitable for grounding such an independent justification because 'the concept of property is a way of distinguishing what is settled and substantial from what is ephemeral, elusive or dependent on the will of another'.[48] Stakeholder theory does not merely suggest that shareholders should hold their property subject to community or stakeholder interests and uses. To the extent that they have a proprietary interest in the firm, shareholders are entitled to the legal protection of this entitlement and this element of the Sternberg–Cabot critique is persuasive. A free-market society does not lightly devalue or readily impose restrictions on the right to private property simply because all rights are subject to legitimate exceptions and limitations. However the second issue raised by the stakeholder debate is a more fundamental one. It asserts that other stakeholders may well have interests in the firm similar to those enjoyed by shareholders, not derived from rights taken from shareholders or from compelling shareholders to share what is rightfully theirs, but arising from the independent contribution made by stakeholders to the firm. If ownership of a resource could indeed only be exclusive to one party then there would necessarily be a tension between shareholders and one or other stakeholder constituency. However understanding ownership in the firm as shared by the different participants makes this theoretical battle unnecessary.

Stakeholder theory has been developing over several decades. Modern formulations of the theory suggest that in some contexts it is inaccurate to see the firm as shareholders' exclusive property in the first place, most compellingly in firms characterized by the separation of ownership and control. The important idea which Berle and Means advanced was that the separation of ownership and control constitutes a challenge to the 'traditional logic of property'. They contended that it was no longer realistic to view the corporation as being subject to the traditional understanding of private property in the firm, or shareholders as its exclusive owners in the traditional sense. The fact that shareholders are generally defined as the firm's owners in an exclusive sense is more accurately attributed not to its basis in empirical fact but to a particular historical approach to notions of property in the firm. In the modern era, with labour playing an altogether different role in the firm, it is possible

47 Donaldson and Preston, at 67.

48 Selznick, at 63.

to take into account a more realistic, fair and accurate view of their contribution and revise the definition of ownership of the firm accordingly.

Property Rights and Stakeholder Theory

There are two main implications of basing stakeholder theory on property rights. On the one hand stakeholder theory is opposed to the idea of shareholder ownership and questions whether it is useful to think about the corporation in terms of property rights at all. On the other hand it recognizes the potential benefits to be gained from proceeding within a proprietary framework. This paradox is remarked upon by Donaldson and Preston: 'There is a subtle irony in proposing that the stakeholder model can be justified on the basis of the theory of property, because the traditional view has been that a focus on property rights justifies the dominance of shareowners' interests'.[49] The main advantage of proceeding within a proprietary framework is that this engages with, rather than ignoring or attempting to dismiss entirely, the property rights theory of the firm. It also allows stakeholder theory to benefit from broader and more inclusive notions of ownership. Central to the proprietary basis of stakeholder theory is the understanding of property as an 'evolving theory', one which is constantly adapting itself to suit transformations in the nature of social and economic institutions.[50] It is important that a theory of property must not impose rigid categories of entitlement that unduly hamper efficient production, therefore neither shareholder nor employee interests should automatically take priority. Singer argues that 'the definition and allocation of property rights … must be both dynamic and contextual' in the sense that:

> (a) Property rights will differ depending on the context within which they are exercised and the effects they have on other market actors; and (b) they must be redefined over time to prevent the illegitimate concentration or use of power in ways that prevent individuals from participating in the market system on equal terms.[51]

A context-specific reassessment and reinterpretation allows the interests of the different parties to be defined in different ways at different stages. As Singer suggests, it allows the law to take into account both the economic context in which these rights are asserted and the effect the exercise of such rights would have on other affected parties. Thus it is possible to make an open-ended claim concerning rights of property in work, without being attached to particular fixed or pre-determined outcomes but allowing this to depend on the context. The notion of property has often been flexible in this way, the courts having a broad discretion to take into account the merits and

49 Donaldson and Preston, at 83.

50 Munzer.

51 Singer, 'Jobs and Justice' at 487.

circumstances of each situation in defining rights and allocating remedies.[52] This open-ended approach meets the need for both protection of employee interests as well as flexibility in decision-making. Donaldson and Preston also endorse the potential benefits of adopting this approach as the normative basis for stakeholder theory. They argue that the trend in thinking about property rights is towards theories such as Munzer's that are pluralistic, with more than one fundamental principle playing a role in determining the rights and responsibilities that give rise to property. They suggest that 'if a pluralistic theory of property rights is accepted, then the connection between the theory of property and the stakeholder theory becomes explicit'; it becomes clear that protecting the rights of property not only allows, but actually requires, the protection of the interests of all stakeholders.[53] As stated at the outset this rests entirely on a concept of ownership in a shared resource which is possible only on a relativist, and not absolutist, understanding of property rights.

Defining Stakeholders

This broad pluralist and dynamic concept of property in the firm does not mean that any constituency which is in any way affected by corporate activity can stake a claim to the firm's output. Clearly that would be impractical, and stakeholder theorists such as Freeman have often pointed to the need for more precise definitions and terminology capable of lending guidance to managers involved in day to day decision-making. Deakin and Slinger, emphasizing that stakeholder theory does not suggest that members of society generally should invariably or automatically have rights to participate in corporate governance, clarify that not all 'affected parties' on whom the corporation has an impact are stakeholders.[54] John Coffee also cautions that stakeholder protection should not grant those who have only a marginal interest in the processes of corporate governance any absolute 'veto' power in decision-making, suggesting that the board of directors should play the role of mediator between different stakeholder groups.[55] Sceptics of stakeholder theory therefore have no reason to fear that anybody who felt affected in any way by corporate activity would henceforth have rights to participate in decision-making.[56] Even within the limited context of employees as stakeholders managers would not henceforth be obliged to consult all the workers about every aspect of corporate strategy prior to making decisions. As Donaldson and Preston put it, 'The theory does not imply that all stakeholders (however they may be identified) should be

52 There is no suggestion, for instance, that if employee rights are proprietary they will always get an injunction to prevent dismissal. Claims based on property are often met with a remedy in damages or indeed a mere declaration that rights have been infringed: *Jaggard v Sawyer* [1995]1 W.L.R. 269.

53 Donaldson and Preston, at 84.

54 Deakin and Slinger, 'Company Law'.

55 John C. Coffee, 'Unstable Coalitions: Corporate Governance as a Multi-Player Game' (1990) 78 *Georgetown Law Journal* 1495–1549.

56 Deakin and Slinger, 'Company Law' at 5.

equally involved in all processes and decisions'.[57] A number of suggestions have been made as to the best definition of stakeholders. Deakin and Slinger propose that: 'A company's stakeholders are those whose relations to the enterprise cannot be completely contracted for but upon whose cooperation and creativity it depends for its survival and prosperity'.[58] Care is therefore taken to distinguish the use of the term 'stakeholder' in the corporate governance context from the general sense in which it is used in other arenas such as politics where frequent reference is made to the need to involve all stakeholders through democratic processes.

In the context of workers as stakeholders this implies that not all workers would necessarily be entitled to participate in the ownership and control of the firm – indeed not all workers would desire such a role. For instance those whose knowledge and skills are general rather than specialized to a particular firm would not necessarily be interested in making a claim on the firm beyond that to which they are contractually entitled. For unionized workers different unions may well take the view that extra-contractual claims would not be in their members' best interests.[59] Here it must be remembered that the reason for asserting property rights in the context of job security is not in order to *assert power* on behalf of workers, but rather *to protect them* when they are at risk of losing their jobs in certain contexts. As Selznick describes it, job property

> is more self-protective than assertive. The job is not a capital resource for the employee who 'owns' it, neither is it a personal possession to be changed or disposed of at will. In the usual case, the right to a job embraces two defensive claims: (1) seniority and (2) freedom from arbitrary dismissal, discipline and discrimination in hiring.[60]

This emphasis is important. It explains why the nature of this interest has been depicted as a form of estoppel, a shield and not a sword. It arises to prevent the firm's managers reneging on implicit promises made to employees that they will not be arbitrarily dismissed after devoting a lifetime's work to the firm.

Defining the Stakes

Formulating a definition of who is a stakeholder is only half the task. It still remains to determine the content of the stakeholder's rights. Moreover, the circumstances which trigger these rights must be capable of clear definition. The question then is how to determine when employees would be entitled to make a proprietary claim on the firm. The starting point is to overcome the assumption that employees' rights are fully defined by their employment contracts. When unforeseen contingencies arise that require some form of organizational restructuring, to fall back onto the terms

57 At 67.

58 Deakin and Slinger, at 7.

59 John C. Coffee, 'The Uncertain Case for Takeover Reform: An Essay on Stockholders, Stakeholders and Bust-ups' (1988) *Wisconsin Law Review* 435–65.

60 At 68.

of those contracts may well have the effect of leaving unprotected their interests which have subsequently arisen over time during their long-term relationship with the firm.[61]

A similar context in which this problem arises is in relation to the interests of creditors. Corporate lawyers concede that creditors are an important non-shareholder constituency group which quite appropriately expects its interests to be protected within the boundaries of corporate law. When the firm goes into insolvency the interests of creditors would be defeated if they had to rely exclusively on the precise contractual terms specified long in advance of the insolvency. Moreover the transaction costs of securing credit would rise exponentially if creditors had to specify in advance all the terms that would secure their interests in any unforeseen eventuality that affects the financial fortunes of the firm. Instead, corporate law recognizes that as soon as the firm becomes insolvent the creditors' interest crystallizes into a legitimate claim on the assets of the firm. In *West Mercia Safetywear Ltd v Dodd* it was held that in a solvent company the proprietary interests of the shareholders entitle them as a general body to be regarded as 'the company' but once a company is insolvent the interests of creditors override those of shareholders since the company's assets now belong in a practical sense to the creditors.[62] The legal process by which the claims of creditors are determined during insolvency has been extended by analogy to ascertaining the claims of employee interests during corporate restructuring.[63] The persuasive force of this analogy between creditors and employees as potential 'members' of the firm in addition to shareholders has also been noted by Lord Wedderburn of Charlton, making the point that the creditor contributes finance to the company while the employees contribute labour, and many of the same considerations that require creditor protection also require protection of employees' interests.[64]

Contingent Claims

Employees' proprietary claims depend on the risk of losing their human capital investments in the firm. Human capital refers to workers' skills and knowledge, acquired in the course of long service, which adds value to the firm. This human capital may be generic, allowing the workers to transfer readily to alternative employment with no consequent expropriation. However where human capital investments are highly specialized to the particular firm and therefore of value only to that firm then the workers' years of invested effort is lost when they are dismissed.[65] The nature of firm specific human capital will be considered further

---

61 Singer, 'The Reliance Interest'.

62 [1988] B.C.L.C. 833.

63 Deakin and Armour; Wedderburn, 'Employees, Partnership and Company Law' at 108.

64 Wedderburn of Charlton, *Company Law Reform*, Fabian Tract 363 (London: Fabian Society, 1965).

65 Blair, 'Firm-Specific Human Capital' in Blair and Roe.

in the next chapter, but at this stage it is crucial to note that it provides one good reference point in ascertaining when employees' proprietary claims arise. Armour and Deakin suggest that these firm-specific human capital investments may give rise to 'contingent claims' which are triggered when placed under threat by corporate restructuring. Restrictions on managerial prerogative in the context of economic dismissals could then be interpreted as 'aiming to protect the firm-specific human capital of the employees. In essence, they provide employees with a property-like claim on the enterprise'.[66] This is a contingent property right just like that enjoyed by creditors who assume, in effect, the status of owners when a firm is insolvent in so far as their interests take priority to those of shareholders:

> Just as the institutions of insolvency law allow for creditors' property rights to be triggered in this way when their interests are placed directly in peril by the impending failure of the enterprise, the employees' rights are triggered when there is a major restructuring (most often a transfer or insolvency situation) which puts at risk the employees' firm-specific human capital.[67]

In this sense the employees' rights would only be activated on the occurrence of certain contingencies, that is firm-specific investments placed at risk by restructuring, and would not have the kind of constant operation which might obstruct managerial decision-making and cause internal governance costs to become an impediment to efficiency. More will be said in the next chapter about the problem of distinguishing between different types of human capital investment, but the idea is offered here as one way in which the law could recognize that property in the firm is a shared, not exclusive, notion, yielding to different constituencies in different circumstances.

The Armour–Deakin proposal suggests a precise means of defining employees' claims on the firm, thereby protecting employee interests while at the same time imposing necessary limits and safeguards upon the exercise of their claims. In this way the stakeholder model does not content itself with asserting a vague entitlement, but proposes a claim which is activated only in particular pre-defined circumstances. This theory of a contingent rights form of protection is consistent with the partial constituency theory of the firm formulated by Sheldon Leader.[68] In a full constituency principle parties other than shareholders would have to be placed in positions of control over fundamental matters such as alteration of the company's articles of association and the appointment of directors. This would be unacceptable to shareholders. However under a partial principle the rights of different constituency groups vary with and depend on the particular set of circumstances. In this way stakeholder theory is able to place employees firmly within the firm's proprietary structure by viewing their ownership interest as one which may, on the

66 At 445.

67 At 460.

68 Sheldon Leader, 'Private Property and Corporate Governance Part I: Defining the Interests' in Fiona Patfield (ed.), *Perspectives on Company Law: I* (London: Kluwer Law International, 1995).

occurrence of certain contingencies, allow their interests to take priority over those of shareholders.

Shareholder Ownership in English Law

The discussion now turns to consider in more detail the influence of ownership assumptions on the doctrinal rules of company law. Within the common law the company is understood as a 'private' association owned by its shareholders.[69] Shareholders are not the *legal* owners of the company's assets but they are often understood, in theory if not in doctrine, as the substantial or *beneficial* owners by virtue of contributing the company's capital.[70] This interpretation is a logical extension of the fact that the Companies statutes define shares as personal property.[71] The conceptualization of shareholders' rights as property in the American cases has usually involved derivative actions against directors for breach of the fiduciary duty owed to the company. This cause of action is thought to vest in shareholders because of their proprietary interest, and other stakeholders who lack such an interest therefore have no legal standing to litigate the best interests of the company. In Australia the proprietary character of shares becomes most relevant in regulating the capacity of the majority shareholders to acquire the minority's shares. Although today the legal nature of the share as property is no longer of direct concern in litigation, this interpretation continues to influence the underlying norms and assumptions of company law. Historically litigation turning on the legal nature of the share in the English cases was limited to the context, in the early nineteenth century, of distinguishing between shares as real property and shares as personal property. Before the twentieth century shares could constitute either realty or personalty depending on the nature of the assets owned by the company.[72] The definition of shares in the modern Companies Acts as 'personal estate' or 'moveable property' was not intended to clarify the essential legal nature of shares (there was no doubt that they were property) but to clarify that all shares, even in a land-owning company,

---

69 Grantham; Kay and Silberston.

70 In early company law 'the theory seems to have been that a corporation held its assets on trust for the members': Paul Davies, *Gower's Principles of Modern Company Law* (6th ed.) (London: Sweet and Maxwell, 1997) at 21 note 11. The law now is that the directors do not ordinarily act as trustees for the shareholders: *Percival v Wright* [1902] 2 Ch. 421; their fiduciary duty is owed to the company. For an American view that 'shareholders are the legal owners of the company' see Van Der Weide; and Wright, 'Ownership and Accountability in Corporate Governance' in Saleem Sheikh and William Rees (eds.), *Corporate Governance and Control* (London: Cavendish, 1995).

71 The Companies Act 1985 s. 182 provides that 'the shares or other interest of any member in a company (a) are personal estate or, in Scotland, moveable property and are not in the nature of real estate or heritage.

72 *Townsend v Ash* (1745) 3 Atk. 336 discussed in Davies, *Gower's Principles of Modern Company Law* at 21.

were personalty.[73] This approach carries through to the way the company itself is conceptualized. The interpretation of early company law treatises is well illustrated by Gower's *Principles of Modern Company Law:*

> the contract constituted by the articles of association defines the nature of the rights, which however, are not purely personal rights but instead confer some sort of proprietary interest in the company though not in its property. The company itself is treated not merely as a person, the subject of rights and duties, but also as a *res*, the object of rights and duties.[74]

The early treatises did not trouble to define shares, as it seemed self-evident that 'a share is a certain amount of interest in a particular company'.[75] Paddy Ireland notes that there was initially no distinction between the shareholder's ownership of his 'shares' in the company and his ownership of the assets of the company, and indeed no distinction between the shareholders and the company. As Ireland notes, the company's subscribers 'formed themselves' by statute into a company, and hence 'the shareholders *were* the company'.[76] The term 'share' was originally used to denote the shareholder's 'interest in the assets of the company', so that owning a share in a company implied ownership of a part of the company's assets.[77] This becomes easier to understand if it is recalled that modern company law is derived from the law of partnership, under which the partners in a firm may be deemed collective owners of the firm's assets.[78] Just after the turn of the century, the law was that 'every shareholder in a joint stock company is, from the practical, financial standpoint, a partner in the enterprise and, indeed, in the case of certain chartered Companies and Companies formed by Act of Parliament, is actually known as a *proprietor*'.[79]

---

73 It had been suggested that shares in a company whose assets entirely comprised land could themselves be real property: *Bligh v Brent* (1837) 2 Y & C Ex. 268; *Watson v Spratley* (1854) 10 Ex. 222. There was not thought, at the time of the early cases, to be any difficulty regarding the legal nature of shares as property, the only question being what kind of property. For a fuller discussion see Robert R. Pennington, 'Can Shares in Companies be defined?' (1989) 10 *Company Lawyer* 140–44.

74 4th edition (1979) at 399.

75 Pennington, at 140, citing Charles Wordsworth, *The Law of General and Other Joint Stock Companies* (6th ed., 1854) at 99.

76 Ireland, 'The Myth of Shareholder Ownership' at 39.

77 Ireland, 'the Myth of Shareholder Ownership' at 40. Ireland observes (at 39) that 'Like ordinary partnerships, all joint stock companies tended, therefore, to be conceptualised as aggregates of individuals'. See also Ireland, 'Capitalism Without the Capitalist: The Joint Stock Company Share and the Emergence of the Modern Doctrine of Separate Corporate Personality' (1996a) 17 *Legal History* 40–72.

78 Davies, *Gower's Principles of Modern Company Law*; Wedderburn of Charlton, 'The Legal Development of Corporate Responsibility: For Whom Will Corporate Managers Be Trustees?' in Gunther Teubner and Klaus J. Hopt (eds.), *Corporate Governance and Directors' Liabilities* (Berlin: Walter de Gruyter, 1985).

79 Horace B. Samuel, *Shareholders Money: An Analysis of Certain Defects in Company Legislation with Proposals for their Reform* (London: Sir Isaac Pitman & Sons Ltd, 1933) at

This idea prompted the argument in *Percival v Wright* that 'the undertaking' of the company is merely the sum of the shares: 'no doubt at law it belongs to the company, but in equity it belongs to the shareholders.'[80] The argument did not succeed, the court being unwilling to define the company as property held on trust by directors for the benefit of individual shareholders as this would be difficult to reconcile with the company's statutory independent legal personality. The rule in *Salomon v Salomon & Co. Ltd* clarified that the incorporated company is a legal entity distinct from the shareholders, meaning that in law directors are trustees for the company (owing this duty directly to the company) and not for the shareholders.[81] This legal proposition did not entirely, as illustrated by *Percival v Wright*, eradicate the widespread perception at the turn of the century that in some respects the shareholders inter se were in the same position as partners or shareholders in an unincorporated company.

Subsequently, Lord Evershed in *Short v Treasury Commissioners* emphasized that shareholders do not have any proprietary rights in the assets of the business: 'shareholders are not, in the eye of the law, part owners of the undertaking. The undertaking is something different from the totality of the shareholdings'.[82] This prompts some commentators to highlight the distinction between ownership of shares and ownership of the company. Leader suggests that the courts have implicitly moved away from protecting the shareholders' property right in the company, to a focus on protecting their property right in their own shares. Ross Grantham goes further, attaching significance to the fact that shareholders are no longer able to directly control the management of the company, and that there is an increasing recognition that the business is not run exclusively for their benefit. He concludes that the law no longer conceives of shareholder rights as a consequence of their status as owners. These observations are pertinent because English law refers to shareholders as 'members' of the company rather than 'owners', but in so far as the dominant view is that the shareholders are entitled to have the company operated exclusively for their benefit it would be going too far to conclude that English company law has completely severed its historical links with the idea of the company as co-extensive with its shareholders as owners. The idea that the ownership rights which shareholders enjoy over their capital are 'carried through' into the enterprise is thought to mean that when shareholders invest they become 'part owners of the company, or at least of its business'.[83] The modern definition of shares in English law is stated as:

> A fraction of the capital, denoting the holder's proportionate *financial stake* in the company and defining his liability to contribute to its funding. Secondly, it is a measure of the holder's interest in the company as *an association* and the basis of his right to become

---

231.

80 [1902] 2 Ch. 421 at 424.

81 [1897] A.C. 22.

82 [1948] 1 K.B. 116 at 122.

83 Gavin Kelly and John Parkinson, 'The Conceptual Foundations of the Company: A Pluralist Approach' (1988) 2 *Company Financial and Insolvency Law Review* 174–97.

> a member ... thirdly it is a *species of property*, in its own right, a rather complex form of chose in action, which the holder can buy, sell, charge, etc, and in which there can be both legal and beneficial interests.[84]

In the modern context the understanding of shares as property has practical implications for the rights of shareholders inter se, allowing disputes between minority and majority shareholders to be interpreted as disputes about property rights. This is best illustrated by *Gambotto v WCP Ltd*, a decision of the Australian High Court.[85] The majority shareholders passed a resolution which had the effect of compulsorily acquiring Mr Gambotto's shares and 'freezing him out' of the company. One of the grounds on which the resolution of the majority was declared invalid was that it did not 'attach sufficient weight to the proprietary nature of a share'.[86] The court held that 'a share is liable to modification or destruction in appropriate circumstances, but is more than a "capitalized dividend stream": it is a form of investment that confers proprietary rights on the investor'.[87] An earlier decision of the same court held that 'a share in a company is property consisting of proprietary rights as defined by the articles of association'. The shareholder's right to vote is itself 'an incident of property'.[88] Commenting on this case Deborah DeMott observes that 'how we think about the nature of shareholding has major practical consequences'.[89] It would therefore be inaccurate to state that shareholders have no proprietary interest in the company. Significant property rights are attached to share ownership, 'such as rights to dividends based on profits and the rights to any surplus left on a winding up, and rights to call management to account'.[90] Hence the idea remains influential that 'the shareholders are the "*real* owners" of the company's assets'.[91]

Shareholder Ownership in American Law

In the American context the proprietary character of shares became an important basis of distinguishing those who were entitled to represent the interests of the

---

84 Leonard S. Sealy, *Cases and Materials in Company Law* (7th ed.) (London: Butterworths, 2001) at 442.

85 (1995) 182 C.L.R. 432.

86 At par. 28.

87 At par. 31.

88 *Peters' American Delicacy Co. Ltd V Heath* (21 (1939) 61 C.L.R. 457).

89 'Proprietary Norms in Corporate Law: An Essay on Reading Gambotto in the United States' in Ian Ramsay (ed.), *Gambotto v WCP Limited: Its Implications for Corporate Regulation* (Melbourne: Centre for Corporate Law & Securities Regulation, 1996) at 97.

90 Simon Deakin and Giles Slinger, 'Hostile Takeovers, Corporate Law and the Theory of the Firm' University of Cambridge: ESRC Centre for Business Research Working Paper Series (WP 56, 1997) at 4. Published in (1997) 24 *Journal of Legal Studies* 124–51.

91 Waldron, at 58 (original emphasis). See also Ireland, 'Corporate Governance, Stakeholding, and the Company: Towards a Less Degenerate Capitalism?' (1996b) 23 *Journal of Law and Society* 287–320.

corporation as an artificial entity. The underlying principle was that those entitled to bring a derivative action alleging that the directors were in breach of their duties to the company, were the owners of the company. Shareholders, by virtue of their ownership of shares, were deemed to be such owners; while creditors lacking a shareholding interest were held not to be such owners. The matter would of course be different if the corporation were insolvent, in which case the courts would recognize that 'ownership' had shifted to the creditors. However the purpose of this discussion is not to investigate the shifting ownership interests of shareholders and creditors, but to draw attention to the proprietary nature of shares and the way this was thought to extend to ownership of the firm.[92] In *Brooks v Weiser* the proposition was held to be beyond dispute that shareholders' right to sue derivatively, that is, on behalf of the company for breach of a duty owed to the company, is 'an attribute of ownership':

> The fact that among the plethora of derivative suits brought over the generations none even discuss the issue reflects the obviousness of the proposition that the right to sue derivatively is an attribute of ownership, justified on the theory that the plaintiff in such a suit seeks to recover what belongs to the corporation, because as a co-owner, it also belongs to him.[93]

Similarly *Kusner v First Pennsylvania Corp.* established three important principles; first that the shareholder's right to bring a derivative action is based on the proprietary nature of his interest, second that only a proprietary interest in a business entity vests a party with the requisite legal standing to prosecute a secondary or derivative action, and third that only a shareholder has such a proprietary interest.[94] It is interesting that here the decision was not based on the rights of shareholders as 'members', subscribers to the company's memorandum and articles of association, but instead emphasis was placed on the proprietary nature of the shareholders' interest. The claimant in *Kusner* was a creditor who had an option to purchase shares. He argued that this made his interest 'sufficiently akin to shares that the law should accord him the status of a shareholder' for the purposes of seeking to protect the interests of the company.[95] The claim was denied on the ground that in determining whether a claimant had sufficient standing to maintain a derivative action the court would not look beyond his 'complete lack of share ownership' and engage in a comparative analysis of his actual interest and the interest he would hold if he owned shares.[96]

92 On the argument that 'creditors of a solvent corporation should have a statutory right to bring suit in the name of the corporation against its directors for conduct breaching the trust of their office' see Yale Law Journal, Note, 'Creditors' Derivative Suits on Behalf of Solvent Corporations' (1979) 88 *Yale Law Journal* 1299–318.

93 57 F.R.D. 491 (S.D.N.Y. 1972) at 494.

94 395 F.Supp. 276 (1975).

95 At 281.

96 'despite the appropriateness of this method of legal analysis when rights accompanying the ownership of different classes of stock are at issue, the concept of proprietary interest is distorted beyond analytical usefulness when the holder of a mere option to purchase shares who has not yet exercised his option or legally committed

Translated into the discourse of the stakeholder debate this means that non-shareholder stakeholders have no standing to represent the interests of the company, irrespective of the facts making their interest the same, or as important, as that of the shareholders in economic terms. Higginbotham J relied on the ruling in *Kauffman v Dreyfus Fund, Inc.* that

> only by virtue of the shareholder's interest, which has been described as 'a proprietary interest in the corporate enterprise which is subject to injury through breaches of trust or duty on the part of the directors', does equity permit him to step into the corporation's shoes … Standing is justified only by this proprietary interest created by the stockholder relationship.[97]

Nor, once the shareholding requirement is satisfied, does its practical ineffectiveness matter. Suffice it that an 'ownership' interest exists; no significance will be attached to limitations on the exercise of that interest. This is illustrated in *Ashwander v Tennessee Valley Authority* where it was argued that the shareholders were *in effect* merely creditors because of restrictions placed on their class of shares, and that they therefore had no standing to bring a derivative action. It was decided that:

> We find no distinctions which would justify us in refusing to entertain the present controversy … plaintiffs are not creditors but shareholders, and thus they have a proprietary interest in the corporate enterprise which is subject to injury through breaches of trust or duty on the part of the directors who are not less the representatives of the plaintiffs because their shares have certain preferences.[98]

The reasoning appears to be that if a genuine economic interest does not give a creditor the requisite proprietary interest, conversely the lack of a genuine economic interest does not deprive a shareholder of his proprietary status. In a recent case this reasoning has been applied by a Delaware court in deciding that a shareholder may bring a derivative action by virtue of his proprietary interest even if he has suffered no financial disadvantage as a result of the directors' breach of duty.[99] This perspective has direct implications for stakeholder theory, which relies heavily on demonstrating that stakeholders' economic interest in the firm is qualitatively identical or comparable to that of shareholders. The courts insist that only a proprietary interest can give rise to a claim to represent the best interests of the company, yet no clear explanation is given as to why this proprietary interest should be attached exclusively and invariably to *shares*. Indeed there has long been an argument that linking the proprietary interest in the firm to the ownership of shares is

---

himself to the exercise of his option is held a shareholder … In this instance plaintiff does not hold Trust shares and the interest which he does hold is non-proprietary' (at 282).

97 434 F.2d 727, (1970) at 735–36 (notes omitted). Higginbotham J was partly reversed on appeal (531 F.2d 1234) but his reasoning on the proprietary nature of the shareholders' interest was not in issue on appeal.

98 297 U.S. 288 (1936) at 321 (brackets omitted).

99 *Cede & Co. v Technicolor, Inc.* 634 A 2d 345 (Del 1993).

an unacceptably narrow way of understanding ownership in the firm. The cases cited above have not been universally followed by the American courts and they remain controversial.[100] The argument has been advanced, primarily on behalf of creditors, that 'the law recognizes a broader scope of interests in the corporation' which is not limited to the ownership of shares.[101] As will be seen later, the development of this argument in the context of creditors' interests has served as a good analytical starting point in thinking about the interests of other non-shareholder interests in the firm, primarily the interests of employees.

Conclusion

This discussion shows that the fundamental underlying assumptions of shareholder ownership are influential in both English and American law. Indeed it is doubtful whether there is any effective means of severing the conceptual link between the ownership of shares and an ownership interest in the company, despite the straightforward distinction which can be made as a matter of law. The expectations associated with the status of ownership help to sustain the reluctance to accept stakeholder arguments in corporate law. A number of commentators see stakeholder theory as an attack on shareholders' property rights even though stakeholder proposals do not interfere with the ownership of shares as such, which suggests that as long as the 'share' itself constitutes a valuable item of property, the status of shareholders cannot be entirely dissociated from the normative ideology of 'ownership' and property rights in the company. At the same time there is no reason why shareholders' proprietary interest in the firm should be deemed to be an *exclusive* interest. The proprietary basis of stakeholder theory is not that property rights are to be taken away from shareholders to be given to other constituencies, but that other constituencies may themselves independently acquire property rights in the firm. Thus the analytical starting point is not that exclusive property belonging to shareholders must be given up, but that the nature of ownership in firms characterized by the separation of ownership and control in which human capital investments are a crucial asset is not exclusive. Although one element of the proprietary stakeholder model shares common values with theories of corporate social responsibility, this model is distinct from and does not itself rest on the 'social responsibility' of corporations. As a rights-based model it does not depend for its validity on managerial goodwill.

In going beyond instrumental approaches that attempt to balance shareholder and non-shareholder interests the stakeholder approach is not normatively neutral, but seeks actively to enhance the position of employees. On this issue the point made in the Introduction about striking a balance between employees' interest in job security and shareholders' interest in profit maximization should be revisited. The general approach preferred in this book is that of Davies and Freedland, whose

100 Larry E. Ribstein and Kelli Alces, 'Directors' Duties in Failing Firms' (2006) Illinois Law and Economics Working Papers Series, Working Paper No. LE06–004 (January 2006).

101 Note, 'Creditors' Derivative Suits' at 1305.

'normative stance is one which seeks to reconcile the worker's claims to autonomy, dignity and security with the needs of the employing enterprise for efficiency in the performance of its institutional tasks and maintaining its viability or profitability'.[102] Job security is not to be advanced at all costs. Efficiency and profits matter. However this should not be taken to mean that utilitarian approaches of the 'happy workers produce more profits' variety are a sufficient basis for advocating job security. There is a limit to the scope for achieving a reconciliation between jobs and profits by reference to an objective or uncontroversial standard agreed upon by all parties which advances all their interests. Donaldson and Preston observe that 'Although those who use the stakeholder concept often cite its consistency with the pursuit of conventional corporate performance objectives (and there is no notable evidence of its inconsistency), few of them would abandon the concept if it turned out to be only as equally efficacious as other conceptions'.[103] Beyond a certain point it becomes necessary for stakeholder theory to resort to a normative ideology that favours job security over profit maximization. The key task is to identify where that point lies. One starting point is to consider how much weight should be attached to the 'efficiency' arguments, an issue to which the next chapter turns. The lesson to be carried forward from this chapter is that while evidence that firms protective of employee interests enjoy enhanced profitability would be a welcome illustration of the positive outcomes of employee participation, that would not in itself constitute the sole justification for allowing such participation. That justification rests on a claim of property in work.

102 Davies and Freedland, 'The Employment Relationship' at 130.

103 Donaldson and Preston, at 81. They carry this argument even further, noting (at 87–8) that 'the ultimate justification for the stakeholder theory is to be found in its normative base. The plain truth is that the most prominent alternative to the stakeholder theory (i.e., the 'management serving the shareowners' theory) is morally untenable. The theory of property rights, which is commonly supposed to support the conventional view, in fact – in its modern and pluralistic form – supports the stakeholder theory instead'.

Chapter 3

Efficiency and Shareholder Primacy

Introduction

A necessary link is presumed to exist between shareholder primacy and economic success, implying that employee participation in ownership and control is incompatible with efficiency and competitiveness. A useful context for considering this argument is corporate restructuring such as takeovers. The response to takeovers reveals the principles and norms according to which the corporation is governed, and these are in turn reflected in the law. If efficiency (understood as aggregate social welfare) dictates that the overriding goal should be to maximize profits for shareholders, and if the law should adopt rules that allow efficient outcomes, then this would be expected to necessitate rules allowing or inducing firms to respond to takeover offers in ways that maximize shareholder value. Current UK takeover regulation is consistent with this expectation but this has not always been the case, and significantly in the US legal rules allow directors considerable scope to resist takeover attempts even when this would be in the best interests of shareholders. It would be difficult to explain this from a simple efficiency-based perspective which sees the emergence of the market for corporate control as an inevitable consequence of the separation of ownership and control and as the most efficient way of making managers accountable to shareholders.

This chapter argues that the link between shareholder primacy and efficiency is therefore not as clear as is commonly supposed. This implication is corroborated by reference to empirical studies showing that the efficiency outcomes of takeovers are uncertain. To shed further light on this conundrum the discussion considers the process of market evolution, with a critical analysis of the theory that rules which proliferate in the market are the outcome of a kind of 'natural selection' which guarantees the efficiency of those rules. Finding that the process of evolution is open-ended with regard to its efficiency outcomes the chapter then examines the efficiency implications of employee ownership. The argument on this issue is that the efficiency-based arguments against employee participation in ownership and control are not conclusive. The chapter concludes that in view of employees' firm-specific human capital investments in the firm which are placed at risk by an exclusive focus on shareholder value there is a need to reevaluate the dominance of shareholder primacy. The argument developed in this chapter is not, in itself, new. The central aim of this chapter is not to present new ideas but to bring together different perspectives on efficiency which have emerged in a variety of studies, in order to consider the implications of these perspectives for notions of property in work. This task is a necessary element of the overall argument in this book, as it would clearly be inadequate to formulate a theory of property in work which took no account of what is already known about the likely efficiency outcomes of reallocating rights of ownership and control in the firm.

Shareholder Primacy and Takeovers

In making a choice between enhancing profits and retaining jobs an extremely influential role is played by the 'shareholder primacy norm'.[1] Corporate law lends its support by providing that the directors' duty to make decisions in good faith in the best interests of the company is 'a duty owed to the company and not to its employees'.[2] In the classical doctrine the interests of 'the company' are the interests of the shareholders, 'both present and future'.[3] Hence Lord Wedderburn's observation that the model of modern company law is that of a 'shareholders' democracy' in which directors' primary duty is to maximize profits in the interests of shareholders.[4] Recent legislative responses to corporate scandals in both Britain and America have focused attention even more strongly on managers' accountability to shareholders, and it is widely thought that this shareholder primacy norm is now accepted globally as the most efficient and successful way to assign rights to ownership and control of the firm.

This has prompted Henry Hansmann and Reinier Kraakman to conclude that corporate ideology around the globe is converging on the Anglo-American shareholder primacy norm. They argue that there is

> a broad normative consensus that shareholders alone are the parties to whom corporate managers should be accountable … as a consequence of both logic and experience, there is convergence on a consensus that the best means to … the pursuit of aggregate social welfare is to make corporate managers strongly accountable to shareholder interests and, at least in direct terms, only to those interests.[5]

They contend that corporate law has reached the pinnacle of its evolution: 'The triumph of the shareholder-oriented model over its principal competitors is now assured'.[6] This represents the 'end of history' for corporate law, and the stakeholder debate really has no new ideas to offer. This chapter challenges the view, reflected

1 D. Gordon Smith, 'The Shareholder Primacy Norm' (1998) 23 *Journal of Corporation Law* 277–323.

2 *Reda v Flag Ltd* [2002] U.K.P.C. 38 at par. 43.

3 *Gaiman v National Association for Mental Health* [1971] Ch. 317 at 330, Megarry J.

4 Southey Memorial Lecture, 1984: 'The Social Responsibility of Companies' (1985) 15 *Melbourne University Law Review* 4–30.

5 At 441.

6 At 468.

in the 'end of history' thesis, that the shareholder primacy norm has triumphed in a competition of different models all of which proved either to be failures or to be less successful than the Anglo-American shareholder primacy model.

This chapter questions the view that shareholder primacy is the inevitable outcome of change and development of corporate enterprise over time. It begins by tracing the roots of the shareholder primacy norm, investigating its origins in the takeover era. The history of takeover regulation reveals important influences on the rise of shareholder value, and therefore on the prospects for recognition of employee and other stakeholder interests in the firm.[7] There are important differences between British and American takeover regulation. American law permits a broad range of takeover defences which allow managers to enjoy almost unfettered discretion in decision-making. UK law generally leaves little room for managers to resist a takeover which would favour shareholder interests. This divergence of approach suggests that the link between efficiency and the shareholder primacy norm is not as strong as is commonly supposed in the Anglo-American context – such a strong link would be expected to prompt much greater congruence of takeover regulation to ensure the primacy of shareholder interests, which has not in fact happened.

Shareholder primacy in the UK

This overview of takeover regulation is drawn largely from Leslie Hannah's and Alexander Johnston's studies of the history of takeover activity in the UK.[8] A summary of their main findings is necessary to enable a meaningful comparison with the emergence of shareholder primacy in American law. The main insight that emerges from Hannah's study is that shareholders did not always enjoy the degree of power and dominance in the firm which is now widely assumed to be an inherent attribute of the separation of ownership and control. This suggests that shareholder primacy was not a spontaneous effect of the separation of ownership and control. Although this separation was complete before 1932 when Berle and Means published their study of ownership and control, Hannah shows that hostile takeovers were virtually unknown before 1950. The takeover bid did not become established in Britain until well after an active market for the sale of publicly quoted shares emerged.[9]

---

7 Simon Deakin, 'The Coming Transformation of Shareholder Value' (2005a) 13 *Corporate Governance* 11–18.

8 Leslie Hannah, *The Rise of the Corporate Economy* (London: Methuen, 1983); Hannah, 'Takeover Bids in Britain Before 1950: An Exercise in Business "Pre-History"' (1974) 16 *Business History* 65–77. Alexander Johnston, *The City Takeover Code* (Oxford: Oxford University Press, 1980).

9 Less than 5 percent of the firms quoted on the London Stock Exchange in 1924 were acquired by other firms in the following 15 years, a much lower percentage than since the development of takeover bidding. Between 1948 and 1961, 25 percent of the companies quoted on the London Stock Exchange were taken over by other quoted companies: Hannah, 'Takeover Bids' at 67.

Hannah explains this by reference to two main factors. First there was the fact that during the interwar years (1918 to 1939) founding families often retained control of decision-making in publicly traded firms and takeovers could happen only with their consent. Second, even if it was conceivable that an offer could be made over their heads directly to the shareholders this possibility was impeded by what Hannah terms 'informational constraints': there was little information available to shareholders and potential bidders during this period. This made it difficult to anticipate the terms which would be most attractive to shareholders, and more importantly made it quite impossible for shareholders to ascertain whether or not the offer was attractive. The shareholders therefore simply accepted their directors' recommendation to refuse a bid. Hannah observes that directors could and did refuse offers which the shareholders would have welcomed had the question been put directly to them. During these years shareholders' interests were clearly subordinate and there was no legal intervention to ensure their primacy. The contemporary view was that during takeovers 'the negotiations must obviously be conducted by the directors. In order to preserve proper secrecy, it is not possible for the directors to acquaint the shareholders of the matter'.[10] Hannah notes that during takeover negotiations the shareholders were therefore passive agents whose interests were not paramount in the decision-making process, remarking that the 'the history of their attempts to thwart the decisions of directors and achieve a better bid price is largely a study in failure'.[11] Because contested takeover bidding was considered a complex and risky business the preferred merger and acquisition strategy was to forge an agreement between the boards of the companies involved, rather than mount a hostile bid, and the board usually did not consult the shareholders directly in deciding how to respond to an offer.[12] This was especially so during the wartime years leading up to 1945 when the loyalty of shareholders to directors was strong and not easily challenged by the directors of another company.

Both factors highlighted by Hannah began to change dramatically in the years after 1945. The proportion of family-dominated firms declined and takeover bids became easier to mount. They also became potentially more lucrative as share values had been depressed by a combination of factors: 'rising asset values, conservative accounting practices and dividend restraint'.[13] It was now well worth the cost and effort of venturing to take over a desirable target. More importantly the lack of adequate information which had impeded the effective participation of shareholders was largely resolved by new accounting standards introduced by the Companies Act of 1948 which 'forced companies to disclose more about their true assets and

10 Arthur E. Cutforth, *Methods of Amalgamation and the Valuation of Businesses for Amalgamation and Other Purposes* (1982 edition) (New York: Garland Publishers, 1926) at 37.

11 Hannah, 'Takeover Bids' at 68.

12 Johnston.

13 Hannah, *The Rise of the Corporate Economy* at 149.

profits'.[14] The situation was further ameliorated by the 1959 *Notes on Amalgamation of British Businesses*, a code of conduct commissioned by the Bank of England which gave further support to the idea that shareholders were entitled to receive all necessary information about the bid. The *Notes on Amalgamation* provided that 'it is for the shareholder to decide for himself whether to sell or retain his shares' and that 'to enable him to come to a considered decision, the shareholder should have in suitable form and at the right time, all relevant information, and it is the duty of the Board of his company to make every effort to ensure that such information is provided and to give him their advice'. This advice was to include 'the fullest information about the future prospects of the combined company'.[15] This was a remarkable development and it played a significant role in establishing the view that the proper exercise of managerial prerogative was to be assessed by reference to the interests of shareholders. Johnston's review supports Hannah's assessment; he observes that by the 1960s the financial press was brimming with news about the 'Take-over Bonanza' with emphasis on the shareholders' prospects of reaping substantial rewards.[16] Directors who stood in the way of potentially lucrative offers were viewed with suspicion, as the view became accepted that their duty was to act for the benefit of shareholders. Questions were raised about the best interests of the company in the context of a takeover and 'the financial press disliked directors who seemed to regard their own retention as inseparable from the interests of the company'.[17] Johnston argues that this point marked the beginning of the association of takeovers with the interests of *shareholders*, as a way of emphasizing that directors should not seek to serve their own interests in their response to a takeover bid.

The current approach in the UK continues to emphasize that the primary decision-maker during takeover bids should be the shareholders of the target company and not the management or even the courts. Therefore the main aim of the *City Code on Takeovers and Mergers*, the modern successor to the *Notes on Amalgamation*, is to safeguard the interests of shareholders. The Code prohibits the directors from taking any action that would frustrate a bid, such as initiating litigation after an offer is imminent.[18] To avoid tactical delays intended as a form of defensive strategy the Takeover Panel makes decisions swiftly and without undue formality.[19] The UK has in this way managed to avoid the highly dramatic litigation that characterizes takeovers in the US.[20] The Code ensures that shareholders are given all the information they need to make their decision, by requiring shareholder approval for any action proposed by the directors which could have the result of preventing the shareholders

14 Hannah, at 149.

15 Johnston, at 20.

16 Johnston, at 42.

17 Johnston, at 12.

18 Panel Statement 1989/7, *Consolidated Gold Fields* and Panel Statement 1989/20, *BAT Industries*.

19 Davies, *Gower's Principles of Modern Company Law* at 774–5.

20 Ibid; Bernard Black and John Coffee, 'Hail Britannia?: Institutional Investor Behavior Under Limited Regulation' (1994) 92 *Michigan Law Review* 1997–2087.

from deciding on the merits of the bid.[21] General Principle 9 of the Code states that 'it is the shareholders' interests, taken as a whole, together with those of employees and creditors, which should be considered when the directors are giving advice to shareholders'. This is supported by Rule 24.1 which requires the bidder to state 'its intentions with regard to the continued employment of the employees of the offeree company and its subsidiaries'. The ability of the management of the target company to block hostile takeover bids or prevent the bid from being presented to the shareholders is constrained by General Principle 7 which provides that, after a bona fide offer has been made, or is imminent, the board must not take action which could frustrate the offer or deny shareholders an opportunity to consider it.[22] It can be seen that in this Code the interests of target shareholders take priority.[23]

Takeover Regulation in the US

In contrast to the earlier rise of takeovers in the UK the modern form of the takeover did not become established in the US until the 1980s.[24] Martin Lipton and Morris Panner observe that as late as the 1970s, long after hostile takeovers were well established in the UK, this form of acquisition was not well regarded by American managers and influential investment bankers. They attribute the shift in opinion to the involvement in 1974 of the reputable *Morgan Stanley* in a highly publicized and successful hostile takeover, followed before too long by the 'takeover entrepreneur' whose sole function was to target vulnerable companies and acquire them for short-term gain, often 'busting up' the company for cash.[25] The question is how the law responded to the rise of takeover activity in the US, and whether, as in the UK, it attached priority to shareholder interests. The regulatory approach to takeovers in America differed radically from that in England, as remarked on by Bernard Black and John Coffee. US takeover regulation places far less emphasis than the UK Code on ensuring that directors act in the best interests of shareholders. Instead US directors enjoy considerable scope to take defensive action in resisting takeover bids.[26] Regulation began with the federal Williams Act, a 1968 amendment to the Securities and Exchange Act 1934. The Williams Act regulates the content and dissemination of information during tender offers but unlike the UK Code does

---

21 Davies, *Gower's Principles of Modern Company Law.*

22 Ibid, at 783.

23 Deakin and Slinger, 'Hostile Takeovers'.

24 Mark J. Roe, 'Takeover Politics' in Margaret M. Blair (ed.), *The Deal Decade: What Takeovers and Leveraged Buyouts Mean for Corporate Governance* (Washington D.C.: The Brookings Institution, 1993), discussing also the prior practice of proxy contests and tender offers. See also Henry Manne, 'Mergers and the Market for Corporate Control' (1965) 73 *Journal of Political Economy* 110–21.

25 Martin Lipton and Morris Panner, 'Takeover Bids and United States Corporate Governance' in Dan D. Prentice and Peter R.J. Holland (eds.), *Contemporary Issues in Corporate Governance* (Oxford: Clarendon Press, 1993) at 117.

26 Black and Coffee.

not require directors to provide independent financial information to shareholders. Moreover, directors usually have the discretion to 'just say no' to a takeover bid even where the bid would enhance the short-term interests of shareholders.[27]

One of the factors explaining the less dominant role of shareholders in US takeovers, as compared to directors, is that institutional shareholders are not as powerful as they are in the UK. Paul Davies observes that the greater emphasis in the Takeover Code on the decision-making role of shareholders, as contrasted with US law, is partly a result of the strong influence of institutional shareholders in London's financial markets.[28] In the UK institutional shareholders hold about two thirds of publicly held shares, while US institutions hold about half of the publicly held shares and play a less proactive role in the equity markets than their UK counterparts.[29] Another point of divergence is that the US is uniquely influenced by the inter-state competition for corporate charters.[30] The US federal system allows managers to select as a corporate base whichever state in their view provides the most conducive regulatory environment, particularly by lacking undue restrictions on managerial decision-making. This effect is absent in the UK although there are now suggestions that this effect may be replicated by competition for incorporation within the European Union.[31] During the takeover wave of the 1980s, the already broad power of American directors to resist takeovers was broadened further as anti-takeover statutes were passed and various defensive mechanisms endorsed. Many of these statutes also allow managers to take into account non-shareholder constituencies in considering a takeover offer, and to reject offers on the ostensible grounds that they have adverse effects on these constituencies.[32] This is unlike the regulatory framework of the UK which does not concern itself with the implications of a takeover bid for non-shareholder groups but is exclusively geared towards ensuring that 'the decision on the acceptability of the offer is made by the shareholders of the target company and not, say, by its management'.[33] From this brief comparison it may be said that the particular response of each jurisdiction to the incidence of takeovers has been determined by factors peculiar to its own corporate climate. If efficiency were they key explanatory factor for the selection of rules of corporate law then much more similarity between the US and UK takeover regulation would be expected, and the fact that they have developed quite different regulatory responses to the same

27 Michael Kahan and Edward B. Rock, 'How I Learned to Stop Worrying and Love the Pill: Adaptive Responses to Takeover Law' (2002) 69 *University of Chicago Law Review* 871–916; *Paramount Communications, Inc. v Time, Inc.* 571 A.2d 1140 (Del. 1989).

28 Davies, *Gower's Principles of Modern Company Law.*

29 Black and Coffee.

30 Roberta Romano, 'Corporate Governance as Ideology' (1993b) 102 *Yale Law Journal* 2021–37.

31 See Lucian A. Bebchuk, and Allen Ferrell, 'Federalism and Takeover Law: The Race to Protect Managers from Takeovers' (1999) 99 *Columbia Law Review* 1168–99.

32 Roe, 'Takeover Politics'.

33 Davies, *Gower's Principles of Modern Company Law* at 779 (brackets ommited).

problem raises at least an element of doubt as to whether shareholder primacy is the result of, or indeed necessarily linked to, a quest for efficient markets.

Questioning Efficiency[34]

It is often said that takeovers are an efficient way of replacing under-performing corporate managers with a team better able to ensure that the corporation meets its full potential.[35] The conclusion is then drawn that shareholder primacy is a necessary part of this process, allowing the takeover market to function effectively, and any resultant adverse effect on employees is a necessary price to pay in the interests of efficient reorganization. The foregoing discussion shows that the regulation of takeovers is in fact an 'adaptive response' to various institutional, political conditions and not a response deliberately designed to yield efficient results. In turn, shareholder primacy is an adaptive response dictated to a great extent by regulatory responses to the hostile takeover.[36] There is further support for this argument outside the context of takeovers. David Millon depicts shareholder primacy as a reaction to 'managerialism'. He argues that the creation of 'a class of professional managers' meant that the question of whose interests the corporation existed to serve became important, and shareholder interests came to be seen as a way of keeping managerial power in check.[37] Berle and Means argued that far from shareholders being a powerful constituency, changes in the nature of the corporation brought about by the separation of ownership and control had made shareholders powerless to influence decision-making in the large corporation. As shareholdings in large corporations became widely scattered power devolved into the hands of management, giving legitimacy to the argument that power should be restored to the shareholders who, as owners, were entitled to have the corporation run in their interests. What began as a means of dealing with the dangers of managerial excess, a solution which seemed the most appropriate or best available at a particular stage in the evolution of the firm, was later associated with assumptions about efficiency and the optimal structure of corporations.

It emerges from these facts concerning the emergence and ascendance of the shareholder primacy norm that there is no straightforward or necessary association between the choice of regulatory rules and the imperatives of efficiency, giving cause to be skeptical about the link between efficiency and the evolution of market institutions. The 'presumptive efficiency' perspective is contrasted with explanations

34 A study by Shleifer and Summers 'questions the common view that share price increases of firms involved in hostile takeovers measure efficiency gains from acquisitions. Even if such gains exist, most of the increase in the combined value of the target and the acquirer is likely to come from stakeholder wealth losses, such as declines in value of subcontractors' firm-specific capital or employees' human capital' (abstract).

35 See discussion below on the market for corporate control.

36 Deakin, 'The Coming Transformation of Shareholder Value'.

37 At 229.

which emphasize the limitations of economic considerations in explaining governance choices, and the crucial role played by historical, cultural and institutional factors.

Market Selection and Efficiency

The apparent association between efficiency and the prevailing structures of market institutions raises the apprehension that sharing ownership and control with employees as proposed by a stakeholder model would have unacceptable efficiency costs. It is argued that the predominance of shareholder-primacy is itself persuasive evidence that it 'offers greater efficiencies than the principal alternatives'.[38] This perspective becomes more difficult to sustain when the rise of shareholder primacy is viewed in historical context. A more comprehensive evolutionary perspective focusing on the processes of change, viewing corporate law as dynamic rather than static, allows an appreciation of the complex reality which determines the choice of governance structures. This approach reveals that the efficiency explanations are only one part of the picture. This complexity is demonstrated by Mark Roe, who explains variations in corporate governance systems around the world by reference to the influence of political and social conflict settlement ('social peace') in determining the choice of governance structures. Roe argues that 'prevailing explanations' of variations in corporate governance which focus on economic factors are incomplete in so far as they leave out the political element.[39] It is not easy to assess whether such political factors have been more influential than economic factors, but at the very least it is clear that non-economic influences are sufficiently important to merit acknowledgment. This means that too much reliance should not be placed on the predominance of shareholder primacy, and it should not be too readily concluded that sharing ownership and control with employees is somehow presumptively inefficient.

Natural Selection

One way in which the influence of historical development has been understood is by a process of natural selection in the market: over time, efficient rules and institutions survive while inefficient alternatives are weeded out.[40] From this it is thought to

38 Hansmann and Kraakman, at 449.

39 *Political Determinants of Corporate Governance* (Oxford: Oxford University Press, 2003).

40 That is rules and institutions which are 'Pareto efficient'. 'Pareto efficiency' refers to a situation where no party could be made better off without another party being made worse off – its application to corporate law assumes that trying to enhance employee welfare any further would adversely affect shareholder interests. A non-efficient distribution of property rights would be expected to continue to produce incentives for repeated litigation until a state of efficiency is reached: Robert Cooter and Lewis Kornhauser, 'Can Litigation Improve the Law Without the Help of Judges?' (1980) 9 *Journal of Legal Studies* 139–63.

follow that the existing corporate structure with ownership and control vested in shareholders may be presumed to be efficient. It has survived a long process of evolution in competitive markets. In a free market where the parties choose their own rules of corporate organization, they would be expected to choose employee controlled firms if this were the more efficient arrangement. Countries whose legal systems facilitate shareholder primacy appear to perform better, economically, than those with stakeholder-oriented systems. This perspective is associated with Frank Easterbrook and Daniel Fischel, who state that 'self-interested entrepreneurs and managers, just like other investors, are driven to find the devices most likely to maximize net profits'.[41] The 'invisible hand' which orders and directs the market will tend to punish those firms that choose inefficient choice mechanisms and reward those that choose efficient ones:

> Over tens of years and thousands of firms … tendencies emerge. The firms and managers that make the choices investors prefer prosper relative to others. Because the choices do not impose costs on strangers to the contracts, what is optimal for the firms and investors is optimal for society. We can learn a great deal just by observing which devices are widely used and which are not.[42]

The orthodox evolutionary theory of the firm in economics relies on a variant of Darwin's 'survival of the fittest' theory, on the premise that 'competitive selection forces will drive from an industry all but the efficient profit maximizers'.[43] Milton Friedman postulates that whenever the behaviour of firms is 'consistent with rational and informed maximization of returns, the business will prosper' and firms which do not adopt such behaviour will not survive.[44] For several decades this has been accepted as the best explanation of the separation of ownership and control: it is seen as 'efficient specialization', with shareholders specializing in residual risk bearing

---

41 At 6. For a fuller treatment of the debate see Robert Clark, 'The Interdisciplinary Study of Legal Evolution' (1981) 90 *Yale Law Journal* 1238–74; James G. March, *Decisions and Organizations* (New York: Basil Blackwell, 1998).

42 At 6. In other words, 'absent fiat, the form of organization that survives in an activity is the one that delivers the product demanded by customers at the lowest price while covering costs': Eugene F. Fama and Michael C. Jensen, 'Separation of Ownership and Control' (1983) 26 *Journal of Law and Economics* 301–25 at 301. More directly on the question of efficient ownership is Hansmann's 'survivorship test'. He anticipates that 'over the long run, cost-minimizing forms of organization will come to dominate most industries. Two mechanisms press in this direction. The first is conscious design and imitation on the part of the entrepreneurs who organize firms … The second is market selection: higher-cost forms of organization tend to be driven out of business by their lower-cost competitors. If we observe that a particular form of ownership is dominant in a given industry, this is a strong indication that the form is less costly than other forms of ownership would be in that industry' (at 22).

43 Richard R. Nelson and Sidney G. Winter, *An Evolutionary Theory of Economic Change* (Cambridge: Belknap Press, 1982) at 139–41.

44 'The Methodology of Positive Economics' In *Essays in Positive Economics* (Chicago: University of Chicago Press, 1953) at 22.

(by diversifying their portfolios) and professional managers specializing in running the firm.[45] As for employee interests, the argument is that if it were desirable for them to have any residual control or decision-making power in the firm then this could be specified in the explicit or implicit terms of their employment contracts. This approach is supported by the view that the common law, as distinct from statutory law, is itself the efficient result of a selection process of efficient rules over time and should therefore be relied on as a framework for corporate law with little or no statutory intervention.

Selection and Adaptation

The foregoing approach relies on an explanation of market evolution which is somewhat flawed to the extent that it overlooks the complexity of that process. Deakin makes the point that survival in the market is not a straightforward matter of being 'the fittest' overall, but rather of being 'best fitted for adaptation in a given environment'.[46] The institution best adapted to survive and indeed excel in its own institutional and cultural environment at a particular time is not necessarily the most efficient institution possible in *all* environments. It would therefore be a mistake to assume that a spontaneous process of natural selection within the market leads to the survival of *optimal* institutions. This is an important qualification of the evolution-to-efficiency perspectives. As Deakin points out the process by which firms struggle to survive is an attempt to adapt as well as possible to existing conditions in which they happen to find themselves. The question of adaptation to a specific environment is a key factor: adapting to existing conditions occurs without any quest (or any need) for optimality. Market institutions 'are adaptive without being optimal: they reflect an internal dynamic of change which is shaped by historical conditions, rather than predestined convergence on a single, uniquely efficient form or "evolutionary peak".'[47] This suggests that the 'end of history' convergence claims are only one part of the story, and one which should not be read in isolation.

Richard Nelson and Sidney Winter also criticize 'sweeping claims that economic selection forces drive individual firms and whole systems to optimal behavior' pointing out that there is an important distinction between selection from institutions which are in existence in the market, and selection from a full range of feasible possibilities.[48] Armen Alchian draws attention to the fact that as this selection process is made ex post; it is more in the nature of acknowledging firms which have proved successful than of choosing firms which have the prerequisites for success.[49] In

45 Frank Knight, *Risk, Uncertainty and Profit* (New York: Houghton Mifflin Co., 1921), reprinted in Louis Putterman and Randall Krozner (eds.), *The Economic Nature of the Firm: A Reader* (Cambridge: Cambridge University Press, 1996).

46 Deakin, 'Evolution for our Time' at 5.

47 Deakin, at 2.

48 Nelson and Winter, at 142.

49 Armen A. Alchian, 'Uncertainty, Evolution and Economic Theory' (1950) 58 *Journal of Political Economy* 211–21.

particular there can be no assumption that the reason why a firm has been successful, surviving competition in the market, is explained by *efficiency*. Nor should it be assumed that selection by market forces inevitably produces the best result from a set of possible alternatives. Alchian insists that 'what really counts [in market selection] is the various actions actually tried, for it is from these that "success" is selected, not from some set of perfect actions'.[50] Therefore result of selection in the market will not necessarily coincide with the optimal choice. Market selection is limited to choosing not only from existing institutional structures, but also within the existing economic conditions. This means that the market is not able to 'select' firms which might be 'optimal' for current conditions but which are not available for selection because they were 'weeded out' when introduced at an inopportune time when economic conditions were not right. Nelson and Winter therefore caution that while a given set-up may be the best possible out of *existing* alternatives in a given context, this does not prove conclusively that it would be the best alternative in all given states. Current structures should not, by their mere existence and survival in the market, be assigned too much weight when faced with alternative proposals.

Therefore the process of market evolution should not be understood as a process that is deliberately designed to produce the result which it in fact does produce.[51] It is instead very much influenced by historical accidents.[52] Teubner is therefore correct to depict the 'evolution to efficiency' approach as anachronistic.[53] He criticizes theories 'in which a particular direction is attributed to processes of change, such as progress, logic of development, and perfection', approaches which imply 'natural causation, necessity, universality, irreversibility, unilinearity'.[54] Such approaches imply that any attempt to deviate from existing patterns would be misguided because the market left to run its course would unerringly proceed in the best possible direction. Teubner's point is that it would be mistaken to presume that institutions which survive over time are necessarily 'better' than their predecessors: 'survival of the fittest' is not necessarily the mechanism of selection in the market. Instead, the market supports 'the co-existence of a variety of viable socio-cultural phenomena'.[55] Deakin goes further, arguing that market survival does not necessarily imply 'that these institutions are the best available; if anything, it strongly implies the opposite, namely that, through the amplifying effects of feedback between institutions and their environment, certain other paths, some of them beneficial, have been closed off'.[56] These studies suggest that no assumptions about efficiency should be made

50 At 220.

51 Daniel C. Dennett, *Darwin's Dangerous Idea: Evolution and the Meanings of Life* (London: Simon & Schuster, 1995) at 56.

52 'The institutions observed in a given nation or at any particular point in time may be partly an accident of history, rather than an optimal solution to a current economic problem': Blair and Roe, 'Introduction' in Blair and Roe, at 12–13.

53 *Law as An Autopoietic System* at 48.

54 Ibid.

55 At 52.

56 Deakin, 'Evolution for our Time' at 25.

purely from observing the structures that predominate in the market. Shareholder primacy only appears to be triumphant if quite narrow and static definitions of efficiency, as well as overall wealth and social welfare, are adopted. An alternative explanation must be sought for the entrenchment of shareholder primacy. This is the lesson that emerges from Roe's work, that a more critical assessment of the process of evolution within the market indicates that the choice of rules and structures within the firm is determined as much by political and institutional factors as by a quest for efficiency.[57]

Political and Institutional Context

Industrialization and the increasing sophistication of production methods have brought about a shift in the organization of work around the globe, with workers assuming increasing discretion over the performance of their work. Yet not all jurisdictions have responded with the same or similar rules governing the balance between managerial prerogative and workers' rights. The divergence of national laws governing labour relations reflects differences in the overall political and institutional context in each jurisdiction. This in turn prompts different responses to the employment relationship in the firm. Labour relations and labour laws continue to diverge sharply in different jurisdictions and there is no reason to expect this trend to change.[58] European workers are more likely than their Anglo-American counterparts to expect long-term, sometimes lifelong, employment in the same firm.[59] In contrast, employees in the Anglo-American context generally expect to move across several firms during the course of their careers.[60] Differences in labour law and labour relations inevitably affect the norms which govern the corporation. Indeed one of the main insights emerging from studies such as Roe's is the significant degree to which corporate governance depends on the rules and norms of the labour market.

57 Mark Roe, 'Chaos and Evolution in Law and Economics' (1996) 109 *Harvard Law Review* 641–68.

58 Susan Christopherson, 'Why Do National Labor Market Practices Continue to Diverge in the Global Economy? The "Missing Link" of Investment Rules' (2002) 78 *Economic Geography* 1–20; John Pencavel, 'Unionism Viewed Internationally' (2005) 26 *Journal of Labor Research* 65–97.

59 For instance Sigurt Vitols and Lutz Englehardt note that in the German labour market 'employees are oriented towards long-term careers with the same company ... training and socialization takes place after entry into this company' (at 19). They contrast this with the US which has a strong mid-career labour market, noting that the mid-career 'mobility rate in the UK is almost twice as high as the rate in Germany' (at 21): 'National Institutions and High Tech Industries: A Varieties of Capitalism Perspective on the Failure of Germany's "Neuer Markt"' Social Science Research Center Berlin February 2005, available at <www.ssrn.com>.

60 Christopherson.

Social Democracies

In a study which offers valuable lessons for comparative corporate governance, Roe argues that 'strong social democracies' influence the structure of the corporation and the norms according to which it is governed in favour of worker participation and employment protection. Roe's observations are particularly pertinent in the European context. It is useful at this stage to consider in more detail the governing norms of European corporate governance in order to appreciate the significance of Roe's argument, that there is a much richer array of factors affecting the choice of corporate governance norms than a narrow focus on 'natural selection' might suggest. Roe defines social democracies as 'nations committed to private property but whose governments … favour employees over capital-owners when the two conflict'.[61] This creates a strong political expectation that managers will take their 'social responsibility' into account. In France, for example, there is a 'strong state voice in the corporation, a voice that typically has taken labor's side when there was conflict'.[62] In Italy 'corporate governance structures have had to adapt to the power of labor in the political arena'.[63] There is much greater politicization of the justice of the employer-employee relationship with regard to the firm's management and direction especially in the context of termination of employment and greater appreciation of the role of 'social partnerships' in determining various aspects of economic policy. Strong political pressure to side with employees still enhances the importance and impact of the employee participation in decision-making.[64]

German codetermination is a good example of Roe's theory about the important influence of politics and political history on corporate governance. In Germany works councils (*Betriebstrat*) and employee representatives on the management board of large corporations (*Mitbestimmung*) emerged from an influential tradition of industrial democracy. Codetermination is traced back to the early nineteenth century, arising as a means of achieving 'social peace' by allowing employees to

61 *Political Determinants* at 24.

62 At 11. Since 1986 the French state has withdrawn considerably from direct control over corporations (Rebérioux) but continues to exercise significant political influence (see Roe, *Political Determinants*, at 45).

63 At 14–15.

64 Irene Lynch Fannon cites the 1997 example of the Renault automakers who closed a plant in Belgium without prior consultation with its workers. This action was criticised by a resolution of the European Parliament stating that the Parliament 'strongly condemns the actions of Renault management which demonstrates arrogance and disdain for the most fundamental rules of social consultation which is an essential element of the European social model'. The European Commission 'passed a resolution urging the French government not to provide additional funding to Renault, a state-owned company': *Working Within Two Kinds of Capitalism: Corporate Governance and Employee Stakeholding US and EC Perspectives* (Oxford: Hart Publishing, 2003) at 43.

participate in decision-making and profit-sharing in the firm.[65] The modern legal framework is rooted in legislation introduced after the First World War and enhanced after the Second World War.[66] It provides a stark contrast to American corporate governance where labour plays a very limited role in decision-making and control of the firm, and explains why commentators within the US often consider worker-participation to be a function of labour law which is irrelevant in understanding the underlying ideology of corporate governance norms. As contrasted with Europe it may well be possible to understand American corporate governance without taking labour politics into account. Roe observes that

> labor unions and labor-oriented political parties are not as powerful in the United States as they have been in continental nations. Many American politicians ignore them and survive, and American corporate law is made in contexts (such as Delaware's legislature and courts) where labor's influence is indirect and weak … Because the underlying American social reality does not continually press managers to side with employees, the long-run effects of constituency statutes have been limited.[67]

Roe's analysis suggests that strong differences persist between the labour markets and labour politics of Europe and the US. These differences make it hazardous to draw linear conclusions about efficiency based on a US experience which applies less well to the wider context of global norms. This wider context requires a fuller appreciation of the European worker participation model.

---

65 Rheinhard Richardi, 'Worker Participation in Decisions Within Undertakings in the Federal Republic of Germany' (1982) 5 *Comparative Labor Law* 23–50. For a modern context see Theodore Baums, 'Company Law Reform in Germany' (2003) 3 *Journal of Corporate Law Studies* 181–89; Dieter Sadowski, Joachim Junkes and Sabine Lindenthal, 'The German Model of Corporate and Labor Governance' (2000) 22 *Comparative Labor Law and Policy Journal* 33–66.

66 Roland Köstler, 'Germany' in Rolf Simons and Norbert Kluge (eds.), *Workers' Participation at Board Level in the EU-15 Countries: Reports on the National Systems and Practices* (Brussels: Hans Böckler Foundation and European Trade Union Institute, 2004) <www.seeurope-network.org>; the Coal and Industry Co-Determination Law of 1951, the Works Constitution Act of 1952 and the Co-Determination Law of 1976. Kathleen Thelen, *Union of Parts: Labor Politics in Postwar Germany* (Ithaca: Cornell University Press, 1991); Thelen, 'Varieties of Labor Politics in Developed Democracies' in Peter A. Hall and David Soskice (eds.), *Varieties of Capitalism: The Institutional Foundations of Comparative Advantage* (Oxford: Oxford University Press, 2001).

67 *Political Determinants* at 45, referring to constituency statutes which will be discussed below. Roe observes that 'Even during the American era closest to a social democratic one – the New Deal – American political institutions did not attack the public firm' (at 105). Similarly Pencavel remarks that 'Continental Europeans appear more concerned with wide disparities of consumption and income, much less enamored of long work hours, and much more troubled if workers lack mechanisms for representation at their workplaces compared with, say, Americans' (at 74), factors which indirectly influence the rules and norms of labour and corporate law.

European Worker-Participation Norms

This chapter began by noting the claim that as a result of globalization the Anglo-American shareholder primacy norm is now universally accepted as the normative basis of corporate law, Hansmann and Kraakman arguing that 'there is no longer any serious competitor to the view that corporate law should principally strive to increase long-term shareholder value'.[68] They suggest that alternative models such as the stakeholder model have no significant appeal in any jurisdiction and 'worker participation has steadily lost power as a normative ideal.'[69] This claim has been strongly contested.[70] Although as noted in the Introduction to this book there is growing reference in the European policy debates to competitiveness and flexibility, it would be an exaggeration to assert that worker participation is no longer viewed as an attractive or desirable ideal.[71] The European 'social model' continues to place significant reliance on employee participation in corporate governance. Moreover, recent legal developments run counter to the expectation of a rapid decline in the appeal of employee-participation.

In accounting for the continuing persistence of the European worker-participation model Hansmann and Kraakman rely on two main propositions. The first is that the framework of worker-participation rules and practices does not necessarily discount their prediction about the likely course of future developments because their convergence claim concerns the *normative ideology* of corporate governance; hence their claim is not necessarily disproved by continuing evidence of divergent law and practice. A long-term view is to be taken of the convergence process. If Hansmann and Kraakman are correct then the current framework of employee participation should be seen as a residual form of divergence which may persist in the short-term but which even if efficient will 'continue to decrease relatively quickly'.[72] Their second proposition is that employee-participation mechanisms are external to the firm and therefore outside the scope of corporate governance. Their discussion of the normative ideology of shareholder value is based on the view that while employees are important the protection of their interests is to be sought outside the scope of corporate law. This would imply that the continuing political, institutional and legal support for employee participation in Europe is of no significance to debates about the convergence of corporate governance. These two propositions will be considered in turn. First the future prospects for European worker-participation norms will be

---

68 At 439.

69 At 445.

70 See for example David Kershaw, 'No End in Sight for the History of Corporate Law: The Case of Employee Participation in Corporate Governance' (2002) 2 *Journal of Corporate Law Studies* 34–81; Jonathan Michie and Christine Oughton, 'Employee Participation and Ownership Rights' (2002) 2 *Journal of Corporate Law Studies* 143–59.

71 For the US context see Adam Winkler, 'Corporate Law or the Law of Business? Stakeholders and Corporate Governance at the End of History' (2004) 67 *Journal of Law and Contemporary Problems* 109–33.

72 At 464.

considered. Secondly it will be argued that the Hansmann and Kraakman thesis relies on an artificial corporate-labour divide, and that in considering the normative appeal of the European 'labour' model the worker participation Directives should be taken into account.

Convergence Prospects

The crucial question here is whether European worker-participation norms are politically-derived sub-optimal forms of divergence which will disappear in due course. Since the end of the 1990s when the 'convergence' thesis began to gain credence European employee participation has shown no sign of diminishing in appeal. The European Commission continues to support and extend the Directives giving legal protection to workers within the framework of its Social Policy Agenda. Referring to the 2001 Worker Involvement Directive accompanying the European Company Statute[73] and the Information and Consultation Directive of 2002[74] it has been said that 'it is hard to exaggerate the importance of these [new Directives] in corporate governance matters: they mark the explicit recognition of a European model, as opposed to the Anglo-Saxon one'.[75] The Worker Involvement Directive has been hailed as 'a historic compromise whereby workers' participation on management or supervisory boards becomes standard practice'.[76] This model is gaining increasing influence in the UK where it has led to a substantial revision of the law, and in the context of globalization there is no reason in principle why European traditions should not influence US law in a similar if less direct way.[77] The normative appeal of European worker-participation norms should therefore not be underestimated.

Two further examples will suffice to illustrate this point. The Forum to promote convergence of corporate governance within Europe, launched by the European Commission in October 2004, focuses on strengthening shareholders' rights *as well as* advancing stakeholder interests. In promoting the convergence of Europe-wide takeover regulation they refer to prospective benefits for non-shareholder constituencies:

73 Council Directive 2001/86/EC.

74 Council Directive 2002/14/EC, establishing a general framework for consultation of workers at a national level.

75 Antoine Rebérioux, 'European Style of Corporate Governance at the Crossroads: The Role of Worker Involvement' (2002) 40 *Journal of Common Market Studies* 111–34 at 126.

76 Simons and Kluge, at 4.

77 In developing their convergence thesis further Hansmann and Kraakman do recognize that forces of convergence may well be pulling in both directions (at 458); see also Marley S. Weiss, 'The Impact of the European Economic Community on Labor Law: A Comparative American Commentary' (1993) 68 *Chicago-Kent Law Review* 1427–68.

> convergence not only strengthens shareholders' rights and the protection of third parties such as creditors and employees, it makes it easier for investors to compare investment opportunities. That leads to a more efficient allocation of capital, which matters to everyone because it is the basis for creating growth and jobs.[78]

In another example a recent report on the social aspects of corporate restructuring commissioned by the European Commission places emphasis on 'avoiding the social risks linked with restructuring operations'.[79] The report makes explicit reference to both the corporate governance debate and the debate on corporate social responsibility – the two are seen as interlinked.[80] This report identifies various corporate aims including employee involvement in corporate governance, secured through information and consultation followed by a role in decision-making. The report envisages a role for corporations in promoting the 'employability' of their workers, which is described as reducing the risk of unemployment by ensuring that employees acquire and develop skills which will secure new jobs if they are laid off. This report is a recent example of a general trend to which attention has been drawn by Irene Lynch Fannon: 'when officials within the European Union attempt to describe business and economic policy for the coming decade and beyond, it is clear from policy documents, that improving overall living and working conditions is a social aspiration for which all major institutions, including corporations, take responsibility'.[81] Although policy reports issued by the European Commission are couched in aspirational terms, these reports are understood by regulators as 'soft law' instruments. They are not legally binding but are taken into account in determining legal liability under binding measures of 'hard law'. They outline social policy goals which are institutionalized through various Directives which are legally binding on all member states.[82] By contrast in Britain and America social policy is not generally seen as an intrinsic part of the responsibility of large corporations as reflected in corporate law and governance.

---

78 Press Release, Brussels, 18th October 2004 (SPEECH/04/460 and see SPEECH/05/392 of 28th June 2005). The Action Plan (adopted 21st May 2003) states that 'The Commission will not apologise for aiming for more shareholder democracy. It's what most investors want and many existing corporate governance codes refer to it as an aim'.

79 *Anticipating and Managing Change: A Dynamic Approach to the Social Aspects of Corporate Restructuring*, adopted by the European Commission on 15th January 2002, at 6.

80 The same is true of the Green Paper on *Corporate Social Responsibility* COM (2001) 366.

81 Fannon, at 9. And see <europa.eu.int/comm./dg05/esf>: goals of social policy to be implemented by 'social partners, i.e. trade unioins and works councils, industries and professional associations *and individual companies*', cited in Fannon, at 32 (emphasis added).

82 Paul Craig and Carol Harlow (eds.), *Lawmaking in the European Union* (Dordrecht: Kluwer, 1998).

The Corporate-Labour Divide

The normative claim that legal mechanisms to protect stakeholder interests *should* lie outside corporate law must not be translated uncritically into a descriptive claim that the legal framework affording employees a central role in the decision-making and control of European firms is a matter unrelated to corporate law and governance. That Hansmann and Kraakman do not attach much significance to this legal framework in identifying the normative goals of European corporate governance may be attributable to an assumption that these laws operate entirely outside the scope of corporate law, thus having no bearing on their convergence thesis. Part of the error lies in their narrow definition of corporate governance, a definition which applies to the American context but for reasons highlighted by Roe would not be meaningful in the European context.[83] The value of Roe's work is in constructing an avenue for incorporating key elements into corporate governance which if left out result in an all too simple, hence inaccurate, assessment. Quite clearly if European worker-participation rules and norms are left out of the analytical frame then the governance of European corporations looks very similar to the Anglo-American rules and norms, and the end of history appears to have arrived, or at least to be imminent. What makes it unsafe to disregard worker-participation laws in understanding European corporate governance is that they are not restricted to the scope of employment or labour law.

The centrality of labour in European corporate governance is eloquently demonstrated by Fannon in her comparative study of US and European law which draws attention to the tendency of American commentators to overlook the scope and continuing support for European worker participation.[84] For instance Hansmann and Kraakman see collective bargaining as 'an approach that lies outside corporate law, since it is not dependent on the organizational structure of the firms with which the employees bargain'.[85] This is true in the Anglo-American context. However collective bargaining in the European context cannot be separated in this way from the firm's organizational structure. Indeed this is one of the difficulties faced by the UK in implementing European collective bargaining rights. The continental countries already have sophisticated support mechanisms *within* the firm to support the role of collective bargaining, while in the UK as in the US the single-channel model of collective representation takes place almost entirely through unions which are not in

83 Roc, *Political Determinants of Corporate Governance*.

84 'From a comparative perspective, American academic literature on corporate governance, does not fully appreciate the extent of the influence of the Social Policy, nor the extent to which the laws of all the member states of the EU are affected by legislative policy formulated in Brussels' (at 27).

85 At 445. Within the American debate even those critical of the Hansmann–Kraakman perspective often view the potential impact of employee-participation rules and stakeholder-oriented regulatory measures as lying outside the scope of corporate law; see for example Winkler.

any way (and generally have no desire to be[86]) linked to the institutional framework of the firm. The European model of collective bargaining is complemented both by rights of information and consultation and the firm's works councils.[87] In Germany, for instance, it is difficult to separate collective bargaining entirely from the firm's institutional structure as trade unions representing the firm's workers have the right to nominate employee members to the firm's supervisory board of directors, and it is possible for union officials to sit on the board in this capacity even though they are not themselves employees of the firm.[88] In practice codetermination works closely with works councils and employee board representatives, with significant overlap in the personnel of the three institutions, and in any event 'the law proceeds from the assumption that the works councils are in close contact with the trade unions'.[89] Trade unions constitute a 'legal basis for electing works councils' and works councils in turn are legally entitled to delegate one or two members to sit on the supervisory board of directors.[90] These works councils are often 'made up exclusively of employees' representatives' but 'act as counterparts to the employer'.[91] Similarly in France there is an institutionalized role for trade union representatives within and alongside the firm's works council (*comité d'entreprise*).[92]

These factors make it problematic to completely reconcile European law with the Anglo-American presumption that employees are external to the firm. Employee interests are often understood to be as central to the firm as the interests of shareholders,

---

86 British unions were traditionally opposed to the idea of codetermination, seeing it as 'a vehicle to dilute union independence and influence … Both sides of industry preferred collective bargaining to be 'free' and voluntarist, and there was resistance to legal framework for industrial relations which was common elsewhere [in Europe] and which would have necessarily embraced the role of labour in the company': Shawn Donnelly, Andrew Gamble, Gregory Jackson and John Parkinson, *The Public Interest and the Company in Britain and Germany* (London: Anglo-German Foundation, 2000) at 28.

87 In Germany firms with more than 5 workers are required to have Works Councils: see Manfred Weiss, 'Individual Employment Rights: Focusing on Job Security in the Federal Republic of Germany' (1988) 67 *Nebraska Law Review* 82–100. The Works Councils, by providing for employee participation at plant level, were introduced in the expectation that they would stem workers' demands for unionization at industrial level. Not surprisingly, these Works Councils were initially strongly opposed by the unions; in the end the stability of the bargaining system was secured by a balance between plant-level negotiation by works council representatives, and national-level collective bargaining by unions. Note also that the scope of the German works councils remains broader than that of the European Works Councils Directive (OJ L 254/64): Sadowski, Junkes and Lindenthal.

88 Köstler; Richardi.

89 Richardi, at 43; see also Manfred Weiss, 'Individual Employment Rights', noting (at 84, note 3) that 'the large majority of works council members are either members or officials of trade unions'.

90 Köstler, at 40; Felix FitzRoy and Kornelius Kraft, 'Co-determination, Efficiency and Productivity' (2005) 43 *British Journal of Industrial Relations* 233–47 at 236.

91 Weiss, 'Individual Employment Rights' at 84.

92 Freedland, 'Employment Law'; Rebérioux.

for instance in Germany where 'Employee interests are distinctly internalized in the governance structure of companies'.[93] The firm is defined not as a *private* institution owned by and accountable to its shareholders, but as a social institution. German law defines the firm as 'a constitutional association ... distinguished by the strong use of non-contractual rights and obligations of its members, rooted in public authority'.[94] The existence of strong information and consultation rights in the context of corporate restructuring ensures that corporate directors are held accountable not only to their shareholders, as in the Anglo-American model, but also to their employees. Some European member states go so far as to require employees' consent before certain proposed restructuring can proceed. Overall the European definition of the proprietary structure of the firm is distinct from the Anglo-American definition, and corporate governance is understood to rest on the three equally important 'legal pillars' of 'financial market regulations, corporate law and labour law'.[95] The success of the European model has often been remarked upon in the Anglo-American context where it has for a long time been argued that the distinction between corporate and labour law is artificial and unhelpful in explaining the employment relationship in the firm.[96]

For these reasons Fannon is correct to state that 'the institutions and policy makers of the European Community have a very broad understanding of what comes within the rubric of social policy and in fact do not really concern themselves with distinctions between say, labour policy and corporate policy at all'.[97] In forging a common market, monetary union and legal harmonization across member states social policy is so tightly bound with economic policy that often there is no attempt to delineate the corporate-labour divide, particularly in the regulation of corporate restructuring. Fannon draws attention to the fact that 'a recurrent and continuing theme underlying the Social Policy is the idea that employee welfare is a fundamental part of a successful economic policy'.[98] Therefore, while growing reference to shareholder value in the European corporate governance debate must

93 '[T]hrough rights to information, consultation and codetermination in works councils, and through representation on the supervisory boards of corporations': Donnelly et al, at 17.

94 Donnelly et al, at 6.

95 Rebérioux, at 126.

96 See Marleen O'Connor, 'Labor's Role in the American Corporate Governance Structure' (2000) 22 *Comparative Labor Law and Policy Journal* 97–133; and O'Connor, 'The Human Capital Era: Reconceptualizing Corporate Law to Facilitate Labor-Management Cooperation' (1993) 78 *Cornell Law Review* 899–965. Blair argues that 'In probing the nature of corporations and corporate governance it is not enough to look only at relationships between shareholders and managers and to assume that employment relationships are a separable topic. The role played by investments in firm-specific human capital and the problems raised by that role suggest that the nature of the employment relationship is central to the nature of the institutional arrangements that are the essence of modern, large corporations': 'Firm-Specific Human Capital' in Blair and Roe, at 80.

97 Fannon, at 30–31.

98 Fannon, at 27.

be acknowledged, it should be understood in context.[99] In advancing the Social Policy Agenda a number of Directives affect corporate governance directly, infringing upon what would be seen in the Anglo-American context as managerial prerogative. As will be seen in Chapter 4 rights of information and consultation restrict or encroach upon managerial prerogative and divert corporate goals away from shareholder value by holding managers accountable to employees. European corporate governance ideology therefore continues to take seriously aims other than maximizing shareholder value.

The 'End of History'?

With continued divergence in governance norms the question may be posed as to which system is most 'efficient'. The emerging consensus appears to be that in the long term, it is difficult to designate any single system as being, overall, superior.[100] In the 1980s German codetermination and Japanese lifetime employment were widely regarded as the more efficient systems because of their booming economies. When they went into recession in the 1990s it was thought that the Anglo-American shareholder primacy model had triumphed after all. There is currently persuasive evidence that 'After decades of intellectual hegemony, conventional shareholder primacy seems poised for decline'.[101] Ultimately the governance choices made in each system reveal more about the political and cultural value placed on employee participation than they do about 'efficiency'. Amir Licht makes this point, arguing that a nation's 'unique set of cultural values' is a highly influential factor in determining its corporate governance mechanisms and the role played by employees.[102] In setting the balance between managerial prerogative and employee autonomy some countries place notions of 'equality, justice and mutual help' above 'ambition, success, wealth and social power'; others prefer to take the converse view, on grounds that wealth

99 Supporting the view that the convergence claims are often overstated Manfred Weiss argues that 'the discussion of the future of workers' participation has to be embedded into a specific context ... Even if it may be possible ... to discover organisational similarities between the systems of different countries, the remaining differences should not be overlooked': 'The Future of Workers' Participation in the EU' in *The Future of Labour Law* at 229–30.

100 Brian R. Cheffins, 'Law, Economics and the UK's System of Corporate Governance: Lessons from History' (2001a) 1 *Journal of Corporate Law Studies* 71–89, referring to this as a 'capitalist beauty contest' (at 75–6). For now the jury is still out: 'Differing corporate governance structures generate differing advantages and disadvantages. Sometimes these net out to zero, sometimes these favour one economy over another when the production task is geared to the type of corporate governance they have. Perhaps one system is overall better and will in the long-run dominate, or perhaps a system that could mix and match would be better overall, by allowing for more variety and competition': Roe, *Political Determinants* at 23.

101 Blair and Stout, 'Specific Investment and Corporate Law' at 2.

102 Amir N. Licht, 'The Mother of all Path Dependencies: Toward a Cross-Cultural Theory of Corporate Governance Systems' (2001) 26 *Delaware Journal of Corporate Law* 147–205 at 150.

maximization is a precondition to pursuing other social values.[103] This does not mean that existing institutions in each jurisdiction are invulnerable to global competition and influence, but it does mean that competing arrangements from one country may be at a disadvantage in another country owing to non-economic factors. In this context no conclusions can be drawn about the inherent value of governance mechanisms in countries which appear to be more economically successful than others at a given time.

Where does this leave the 'end of history' debate? Both sides of the debate have relied on general observations to which there are of course exceptions and counter-examples within all jurisdictions – dwindling job security in Europe on the one hand and stakeholder effects in Britain and the US on the other. It is sometimes said that European economies are drifting, politically, to the right, a factor seen as an important pre-condition for credible commitment to shareholder value.[104] As concerns the UK it is too early to say which approach, if any, will dominate. Britain has proved the hardest case to classify, not least because the political influence of labour rises and falls.[105] The 'Third Way' ideology associated with the New Labour government that came into power in 1997 after two decades of Conservative rule has attempted to steer a middle course between the two 'models of capitalism' – the 'American' model which prioritizes shareholder value and the 'European' model characterized by 'state supported social policies regarding the welfare of employees'.[106] A recent study by the Cambridge Centre for Business Research finds that core institutions of corporate governance in the UK are strongly focused on shareholder interests while at the margins the effect of European worker-participation norms is identifiable.[107] Although European Directives are pulling the UK away from shareholder value towards the stakeholder model this has not gone as far as the European approach of granting employees a central role in decision-making; it is generally limited to what the Cambridge study terms employee 'voice'. In English law employee information and consultation 'do not occupy the central place in management practice and

103 Ibid.

104 Roe, *Political Determinants* at 46. Roe remarks (at 81) that '*No* nation allows unbridled shareholder control of the firm, and the brakes on full control come into play differently … Nevertheless, some nations put the brakes on harder than others' (original emphasis).

105 'The United Kingdom would seem the hardest case for the political theory here, in that by reputation Britain has had a deep securities market for quite some time but has been on both sides of the fence politically': Roe, *Political Determinants* at 98. George Strauss and Eliezer Rosenstein, 'Worker Participation: A Critical View' (1970) 9 *Industrial Relations* 197–214.

106 Fannon, at 4–5. For a statement of New Labour employment policy see the Government's White Paper, *Fairness at Work*, Cm 3968 (Department of Trade and Industry: May 1998).

107 John Armour, Simon Deakin and Suzanne Konzelmann, 'Shareholder Primacy and the Trajectory of UK Corporate Governance' (2002) 41 *British Journal of Industrial Relations* 531–55.

corporate culture that the values associated with shareholder primacy do'.[108] The Cambridge study concludes that the British system cannot be said to have settled conclusively on the shareholder primacy norm in the 'end of history' sense, but neither is Britain likely to *fully* adopt the European stakeholder model. British corporate governance is more accurately viewed as being 'in a state of flux'.[109] The future remains unclear:

> Although the debate has generated an extensive body of theoretical and empirical work, the conclusions remain opaque. There is yet no consensus as to what system of corporate law is the best one and whether legal convergence should be encouraged on a global level. A number of theoretical studies argue that regulatory and institutional convergence of corporate governance practice worldwide is likely, but the studies are in disagreement as to the direction of the convergence. In particular, will the Anglo-American model dominate or will a new hybrid model emerge?[110]

There are no clear answers to this question, and as Deakin argues, trying to make precise predictions about the prospects for convergence may be unhelpful. Instead· he suggests that 'the task is to understand the variety of solutions and the specificity of the local and national conditions which gave rise to them, rather than trying at every point to fit divergent experiences into a single, universal model'.[111] It remains the case that the European worker-participation model of corporate governance retains a form, structure and purpose different in crucial respects from the Anglo-American model, and to this extent remains a valuable comparative reference point in understanding the employment relationship in the Anglo-American firm.

The Efficiency of Employee Ownership

Dismissals for economic reasons are, as noted at the start of this book, generally thought to be justified. So far this chapter has argued that no presumptions can be made about the efficiency of the shareholder primacy norm simply from the fact of its dominance or its association with successful economies. The direction of causality is not clear, and there is no evidence that these economies are successful *because* of, rather than *in spite of* shareholder primacy. It is therefore timely to turn to consider in more detail the efficiency-based arguments for and against employee

108 At 545.

109 At 532: 'what we are likely to see is a period of uncertainty as the corporate governance actors struggle to come to terms with the inevitable contradictions and tensions of the shareholder value norm'.

110 Marc Goergen, Marina Martynova and Luc Renneboog, 'Corporate Governance Convergence: Evidence From Takeover Regulation Reforms in Europe' (March 2005) Utrecht School of Economics Tjalling C. Koopmans Research Institute Discussion Paper Series 05–19 at 2.

111 Simon Deakin, 'The Comparative Evolution of the Employment Relationship' ESRC Centre for Business Research WP317 December 2005b at 2.

claims of ownership in the firm. The efficiency debate is important for a study of job security because efficient firms generate more overall wealth, ensuring that in the long run there are stronger, more vibrant economies and more job opportunities for workers. Anecdotal evidence of economic performance around the globe appears to bear this out, as 'free market' economies seem to have more flexible labour markets and lower unemployment rates than countries where workers enjoy stronger security of tenure. This lends support to the view that a reduced degree of job security is a necessary price to pay in achieving the flexibility and competitiveness associated with successful market economies. However the reality is more complex. Within the stakeholder perspectives the point has often been made that it should not be assumed that whenever firms dismiss thousands of workers in the context of corporate restructuring the reasons for the dismissal are necessarily linked to organizational efficiency. Instead the efficiency claims should be subjected to careful scrutiny. This part of the discussion therefore looks critically at the role played by efficiency-based arguments in determining the role played by employees in the ownership and control of firms.

Advantages of Employee Ownership

Employee participation in the ownership and control of large firms is advocated not only because it seems just and fair, but also because there are efficiency gains to be expected from it. In his study of the ownership of enterprise Hansmann identifies several potential advantages of employee ownership. He then identifies the costs, and weighs these against the benefits to determine why employee ownership is not more widespread in modern free market economies. Hansmann identifies the following potential advantages of employee ownership. The first benefit is that the firm is less likely to lose the acquired knowledge and expertise of its long-term workers; they are less likely to defect to other firms taking with them their specialized knowledge of the firm, its routines, personnel, clients and customers, organizational and production structure, competitors and the broader market in which it operates. This knowledge is vital for the firm's success, and cannot be immediately taught to or learned by replacement hires. There is simply no substitute for time on the job. Employee ownership also allows the firm to avoid the cost of constantly recruiting and training new employees, and running the risk that they will make a bad hire and have to start the whole process over again. Hansmann observes that this can be avoided if the firm ensures that existing workers have incentives to stay with firms in which they have acquired such specialized skills. Employee ownership would also have the advantage of avoiding bargaining strategies such as strikes and lockouts, which raise the transaction costs of bargaining between labour and management. By avoiding the conflict-ridden environment that often results when there is a divergence between the interests of the firm's owners and its workers an open environment of trust and cooperation would result. Management would have fuller information about employee preferences and working conditions, information which is vital in enhancing productivity. Employee ownership would therefore suggest significant efficiency advantages, improved employee productivity, better communication of employee preferences, and reduction in worker alienation.

The case may be made for analyzing German-style employee participation as akin to an ownership stake in the firm, as employees share control with shareholders.[112] There is evidence that codetermination in Germany yields significant economic and social benefits:

> Dissatisfied employees now more often choose to articulate their dissatisfaction ('voice'), rather than choosing the option of leaving the company ('exit'). The resulting drop in the separation rate leads to substantial cost reductions for both parties. For the employer, the expenses for new hiring are reduced, especially the costs of training new employees. The extent of these costs depends primarily on the necessary company-specific knowledge of the affected workplace. In addition to reducing the separation rate and the associated costs, the 'voice' option could also increase work satisfaction and, thus, productivity.[113]

Codetermination therefore appears to be beneficial both for employees as well as for the employer corporations. Hansman and Kraakman have suggested that even within Germany the codetermination model is viewed by some as 'at most, a workable adaptation to local interests and circumstances or, even more modestly, as an experiment of questionable value that would now be politically difficult to undo'.[114] There is certainly pressure within Germany to move away from the codetermination model, prompted as in other jurisdictions by the perceived need to conform to global corporate governance norms and more importantly by the perceived threat of German corporations simply re-incorporating in other European member states which do not have codetermination laws.[115] However there remains overwhelming support in

112 Njoya, 'Employee Ownership and Efficiency'. See Kershaw, at 74, noting that although German firms cannot be said to be 'employee owned', 'the distinction between participation and ownership is not clear cut'.

113 Sadowski, Junkes and Lindenthal, at 41.

114 At 6. Christel Lane supports the view that the German model is drifting away from its traditional structure, arguing that Germany 'is in the process of converging towards the Anglo-American system and that this has fundamentally affected the way strategic decisions are made in firms. Large, internationally oriented companies are particularly affected. But the notion of shareholder value and its many behavioural effects are gradually spreading also to other parts of the economy. Consequently, the distinctive logic, which had underpinned the German variety of capitalism during most of the post-war period, is eroding': 'Changes in Corporate Governance of German Corporations: Convergence to the Anglo-American Model?' (March 2003) ESRC Center for Business Research Working Paper No. 259.

115 On this see Jens C. Dammann: 'German corporate law continues to attach considerable importance to the interests of other stakeholders. Most importantly, German corporate law is designed to serve the interests of employees as well as the interests of shareholders': 'Future of Codetermination after Centros: Will German Corporate Law Move Closer to the U.S. Model?' (2003) *Fordham Journal of Corporate and Financial Law* 607–88 at 608. Donnelly et al note that the German model of codetermination is constantly evolving in response to these pressures, and has recently 'been placed in a new context. The core institutions of the supervisory board and codetermination have been left intact, but the context in which they

Germany for codetermination.[116] In its modern form codetermination continues to ensure political and economic stability, especially through the complementary role of Works Councils as a means of controlling the power of both employers and the unions. The fact that it is subjected to constant scrutiny and reform where necessary does not mean that it lacks support as a valuable industrial tradition. While acknowledging the pressures for Germany to conform to a 'multinational' shareholder-primacy model, a government-appointed non-partisan Codetermination Commission recommended in 1998 that codetermination should be retained.[117] It is fair to say that this decision is sometimes interpreted as a politically pragmatic rather than economically ideal choice: Theodore Baums observes that 'the institution of codetermination is generally accepted in Germany as an effective social compromise' and suggests that the sheer cost of inquiring into and implementing an alternative system seems to have played a dominant role in persuading the Commission to maintain the status quo.[118] However, that is evidence more of the ambiguity of the evidence about the efficiency implications of codetermination, than evidence of disenchantment. Part of the difficulty, in drawing unequivocal conclusions about the benefits of codetermination, lies in finding an appropriate measure by which to quantify these benefits. Baums notes that 'there have been no undisputed econometric studies on the (negative or positive) correlation between co-determination and company performance'.[119] The Codetermination Commission took the same view, appearing to consider it unnecessary to make a decision based entirely on empirical evidence of efficiency as there were both efficiency costs as well as gains: 'in the real world codetermination as an institution generates both efficiency-reducing misallocation and efficiency-raising productivity and cooperative effects. The net impact of these parallel and simultaneous partial effects cannot be determined *a priori*'.[120]

Therefore it is not simply a case of Germany putting up with codetermination because that happens to be the existing system – there is a widespread view that it 'support[s] the competitiveness of German industry by its affinity with a high-skill, high-quality production model in export industries. Large firms have been very successful in adapting codetermination to their competitive needs, and thereby reshaped institutions from having a defensive and status-protecting function towards

---

operate has been changed through the adoption of measures promoting corporate disclosure, market-oriented accounting, performance-oriented executive remuneration, and more flexible use of corporate equity' (at 55).

116 FitzRoy and Kraft.

117 *Bericht der Kommission Mitbestimmung* 1998 (*Co-Determination and New Business Cultures: Conclusions and Perspectives*), discussed in John T. Addison, Lutz Bellmann, Claus Schnabel and Joachim Wagner, 'The Reform of the German Works Constitution Act: A Critical Assessment' (2004) 43 *Industrial Relations* 392–420 at 394.

118 At 185.

119 Ibid.

120 *Kommission Mitbestimmung*, (English translation), par. 27, cited in Addison et al, at 394.

supporting management in the implementation of competitive strategies'.[121] German codetermination may be said to 'provide a means of offering employees a "credible commitment" that their investments in firm-specific human capital will be protected' thereby allowing the firm to reap productivity benefits from the commitment of their workers.[122] On the other side of the debate the claims that the costs would be prohibitive have not been conclusively made out. The question then arises why, in the face of all these potential gains which may well yield superior outcomes to shareholder controlled firms, employee ownership and control does not proliferate. Many answers have been suggested in the literature, but this discussion will focus on three main factors: investment incentives, risk aversion, and transaction costs.

Investment Incentives

One factor which favours allocating ownership and control to shareholders rather than to any other stakeholder is the need to supply shareholders with continued incentives to invest in the firm. The argument is that any other allocation of ownership would constitute an inefficient transfer of wealth from shareholders to employees. If so shareholders would make no further financial investment in the firm. This is linked to the 'protection of private property' arguments addressed in the previous chapter.[123] On the basis that the function of property rights is to guide incentives Alchian and Demsetz emphasize the importance of rewarding those who make inputs into the firm's productivity.[124] Rewards must be matched accurately with inputs. It is important to make 'the payment of rewards in accord with productivity. If rewards were random, and without regard to productive effort, no incentive to productive effort would be provided by the organization; and if rewards were negatively correlated with productivity the organization would be subject to sabotage'.[125] Alchian and Demsetz conclude that the most appropriate incentive is that bundle of rights amounting to the ownership and control of the firm. One important aspect of this bundle of rights is the right to be a residual claimant. The owner also enjoys 'the right to alter membership of the firm: the owner has the right to decide who uses the firm's assets and who doesn't.'[126] This owner they identify as the employer.

The stakeholder response to this is that it is by no means certain that this 'owner' invariably is or should be the shareholders.[127] Rewards and incentives are important in encouraging productivity. However, while there clearly ought to be sufficient incentives for shareholder investment, equally there ought to be sufficient incentives

121 Donnelly et al, at 38.

122 Armour, at 23.

123 The argument is that 'Because it undermines shareholder property rights, stakeholder-oriented management denigrates and discourages equity investment': Alexei M. Marcoux, 'Business Ethics Gone Wrong' (2000) 22 *Cato Policy Report*.

124 Demsetz, at 348.

125 Alchian and Demsetz, at 778.

126 Hart, 'An Economist's Perspective' at 1771; see discussion at 1761.

127 Zingales.

for employees to invest their time, skills and knowledge in their firms. In view of the importance of employees in the modern 'knowledge economy' there is more reason to associate the need to supply incentives with employees than with shareholders. The importance of shareholders, on the other hand, should not be assumed to be invariably self-evident. Marjorie Kelly argues that over the past two decades shareholders' contribution has often proved to be of little use to the company, when a substantial proportion of their financial contribution is not available for the use of the company but 'just goes from one speculator to another':

> I'm not arguing that the interests of shareholders should be completely ignored, and I'm not questioning the motivations of individual investors. I'm just saying that it's wrong to shovel money out to shareholders in ever larger scoops and force other stakeholders to pay the price – with wages held down, tax obligations ducked, suppliers squeezed – all because some investors put in a little money 30 or 50 years ago. Investors do deserve a fair return. But other stakeholders also deserve consideration.[128]

The prospect of a return on their investment is an important incentive for shareholders but, as Zingales argues, there is no reason in principle why they must be rewarded by allowing them the exclusive right to ownership and control of the firm or why they should not, just as stakeholders currently are, be deemed to protect their investment by a more limited contractual means. After all, 'company law says nothing of the level of returns to which shareholders are entitled, nor of the timescale over which their expectations are to be met'.[129] Such reward might consist simply in the right to receive dividends, and not extend to a right to have the directors run the firm exclusively in their interests. The argument that shareholders differ from other stakeholders in the difficulty of specifying their expected return in ex ante contracts is not persuasive as there are similar, if not greater, difficulties of this kind in relation to employees. Further, the shareholders' contribution of finance capital may be easier to replace from alternative sources (such as private capital or loans) than the employees' specialized contribution of their skills and ideas. For this reason there is now a recognized need to reassess the allocation of the residual control in the firm. Human capital investments are often overlooked when it is said that shareholders, as investors, are entitled to a return on their investment in the firm. If one of the economic justifications for the existence of property rights is that they 'furnish incentives to work',[130] then workers' property rights should arise where such rights would supply the strongest incentive to work, that is, where the promise of receipt of wages is, in itself, an insufficient incentive.

---

128 At 18–19.

129 Deakin, 'Workers, Finance and Democracy' at 80–81.

130 A. Mitchell Polinsky and Steven Shavell, 'Economic analysis of Law' in Larry Blume and Steven Durlauf (eds)., '*The New Palgrave Dictionary of Economics and Law* (2nd ed.) (London: Macmillan, 2007) available at ‹www.ssrn.com›.

Workers' Risk Aversion

A similar argument is that shareholders expect rights of ownership and control in return for shouldering the residual risk in the firm. Ownership rights are an important compensation for the party who is prepared to assume the risk of enterprise, and the firm's ownership structure must account for the fact that some parties within it are more risk-averse than others.[131] Again, this much is incontrovertible but the question of identifying this residual risk bearer is more problematic. Shareholders are said to bear the residual risk of enterprise as the return on their investment depends entirely on the firm's profitability. They are said to shoulder the risk of receiving no return on their investment, and therefore by the same token entitled to take the entire profit if the firm should be successful. The claim is that employees' investments of time and effort are not similarly at risk because unlike dividends their wages do not fluctuate with the firm's fortunes. It is also claimed that the return expected by employees in return for any risk they shoulder is much easier to specify fully in advance by contract than that expected by shareholders.

The classical literature on residual risk emphasizes workers' risk aversion. The argument is that workers have limited wealth and prefer to diversify their risk by keeping their income entitlement independent from the firm's fortunes. They are content with, and entitled to no more than, their wages. Taking into account the unavoidable risk which workers already bear, as their jobs and salaries are in any case dependent on the fortunes of the enterprise, the idea is that they would find further entanglement with these firms as owner-controllers particularly undesirable. This approach is based on the ideas of Frank Knight, who depicted the allocation of risk in the firm as one in which 'the confident and venturesome assume the risk or insure the doubtful and timid by guaranteeing to the latter a specified income in return for an assignment of the actual results'.[132] He offered this as the reason behind the specialization of function in the enterprise, with the owner-entrepreneur taking responsibility for decision-making and coordinating the firm's activities, and the worker following directions to work for a fixed remuneration. The shareholder is therefore left to shoulder the risk of enterprise, and is hence entitled to be the firm's owner. Shareholders invest in firms precisely because they are inclined to taking such risks in the expectation of profit should the gamble pay off, or losing their investment should the firm prove unprofitable.

This perception of enterprise risk does not, however, reflect the modern reality that many employees lose everything if the firm for which they work fails. For some employees the solution may be to rely entirely on fixed wages and simply cut their losses and move to another firm and share no part in the risk of enterprise, but this option is not open to all workers. Long-tenured employees may well have no option but to cast their lot with their firm if they are unlikely to ever rebuild their career at

131 Hart, 'Incomplete Contracts'; Hart, 'An Economist's View of Fiduciary Duty' (1993) 43 *University of Toronto Law Journal* 299–313; Zingales.

132 Knight, *Risk, Uncertainty and Profit* at 270, in Putterman and Krozner (eds.).

a new firm.[133] These workers will often bear far more risk than shareholders when layoffs, plant closings, and other forms of corporate restructuring cause them to forfeit their investments in the firm. Hence Blair argues that the 'Knowledge and skills that are specialized to a given enterprise, as well as the effort that has been put forth toward the goals of the enterprise, are "assets" at risk in much the same way that equity capital is at risk once it has been committed to a given enterprise'.[134] It could also be argued that as many institutional investors are pension funds paid into by workers this means that workers ultimately have more to lose from stock market collapse than do shareholders.[135] In any event, as noted above in discussing investment incentives, there is no reason why the risk borne by shareholders must be rewarded by the exclusive right to exercise control. The assumption of company law that shareholders are the firm's residual claimants because they bear the firm's residual risk therefore needs to be reconsidered.[136] If the allocation of ownership and control depends on which of the different groups in the firm bears the residual risk, then the case must be considered for allocating this role to employees.[137]

Transaction Costs

Oliver Hart explains the essence of ownership and control in the firm as the authority to determine those aspects of firm policy which, because of high transaction costs, asymmetric information or unforeseeable contingencies, cannot readily be specified in advance and must therefore be left to the discretion of the owner. The owner decides matters left unspecified by the contract. The crucial issue is how to identify this owner: should it be the shareholders or the employees? It has been seen that Hart advocates careful consideration of the initial allocation of residual rights of control in the firm because it may be too difficult or costly for the parties to redistribute control rights through renegotiation or agreement. The purpose of designating a particular party as 'owner' is to reduce governance costs by avoiding the need for elaborate ex ante contracts or protracted ex post negotiation and agreement, and Hart explains the selection of the shareholder as owner on grounds that shareholder ownership is the solution which incurs the lowest costs.[138]

---

133 Zingales.

134 Blair, 'Firm-Specific Human Capital' in Blair and Roe, at 62.

135 Deakin, 'Workers, Finance and Democracy'.

136 As Deakin and Slinger observe this law relies on a circular argument: 'In the context of the corporation, it is equivalent to arguing that shareholders bear the residual risk *because* company law makes them the residual claimants. It is necessary to go further, and show that shareholders are inherently *more* exposed to risk than other owners of inputs, before the structure of the corporation can be adequately explained on economic efficiency grounds': Deakin and Slinger, 'Hostile Takeovers' at 8.

137 Blair, 'Firm-Specific Human Capital' in Blair and Roe, at 72.

138 Oliver Hart, *Firms, Contracts and Financial Structure* (Oxford: Clarendon Press, 1995).

The main cost taken into account in assigning ownership rights in the firm is the costs of collective governance. On this point Hansmann argues that the 'lowest-cost assignment of ownership', to use Hart's terminology, requires collective governance by shareholders. Hansmann explains this by reference to the homogeneity of shareholders. Shareholder governance is deemed less costly than collective governance by employees because it is thought that their decisions will always be clear and identifiable with certainty in advance – they will always do whatever is necessary to maximize profits. Employee-owned firms are not expected to have such clear unanimity. Instead the expectation is that any benefit derived from employee ownership would be offset by the prohibitive costs of trying to get all the workers to agree in decision-making. The idea is that employees are far more likely than investors to differ among themselves concerning the firm's policies on matters such as relative wages or which plants to keep open and which must be closed. Hansmann argues that these differences increase where there is greater division of labour within the firm. The interests of longer term employees who have disproportionately more invested in the firm diverge from those of new employees. There is a risk of as many opinions as there are workers, which would significantly increase the costs of collective governance. Hansmann suggests that this explains why employee ownership exists only in 'niches' of the economy where employees all do similar work and are of essentially equivalent status within the firm (he cites law firms as a good example), ensuring that there is comparatively little opportunity for conflicts of interest amongst the employee-owners. Hansmann concludes that employee ownership therefore works best where the employee-owners are so homogeneous that any decision made by the firm will affect them roughly equally or where, though the employees differ in ways which cause the burdens and benefits of some decisions to be shared unequally, there is an objective and widely accepted basis for making those decisions. He suggests that this does not apply to most industrial firms, where *full* employee control would introduce serious inefficiencies.

This explanation goes a long way as an analysis of employee ownership in the modern economy, but the distinctions it draws between shareholders and employees in this regard do not controvert the stakeholder proposals. First, it is not proposed that workers would take over ownership of the corporation from the shareholders. Stakeholder theory relies instead on a concept of shared ownership. Hansmann suggests that while in theory shared ownership is possible the costs would still be prohibitive as the co-owners' interests will inevitably diverge. Another possible objection to splitting ownership in this way is the danger of 'fragmentation' of corporate resources, with too many different co-owners having the power to 'clog the title' and to as it were 'impede its alienation' making it difficult or impossible to have a vibrant stock market or an effective market for corporate control.[139] The apprehension is that efficient takeovers would be impeded by a need to consult multiple stakeholders. These objections may be met by a theory of contingent property rights as formulated by Armour and Deakin. The contingent nature of such

139 Merrill and Smith, at 386.

rights would ensure that the principle of shared ownership does not become a fetter on all managerial decision-making, as employee 'ownership' rights would only be triggered by the occurrence of specific events linked to corporate restructuring. Nor would this be a general right available to all employees. These rights would vest in those employees whose skills and knowledge are vital as well as specialized to the firm, so that there would be a real danger of 'expropriation' if they were to lose their jobs during the restructuring. By relying on a contingency theory of ownership the stakeholder theory proposes a way of avoiding the fragmentation of ownership problem. Employees' ownership claims ordinarily lie dormant and only on the occurrence of specified events putting jobs at risk do they take priority over shareholder interests.

More importantly, it is not proposed that workers should be involved in making decisions on everyday corporate governance issues – this would certainly skyrocket governance costs as noted by Hansmann. But so would involving shareholders in everyday decision-making, which is precisely why company law vests this competence in the managers and does not allow shareholders to interfere. In any event the homogeneity of shareholders and the unity of their interest in pursuing profits above saving jobs is a theoretical construct not based on the actual opinions of the people with shares in the firm. Real individual shareholders exhibit the same diversity of opinion as workers.[140] The presumption that workers are united in their interest in job security is no more fanciful, and is in fact much more realistic, than the presumption that shareholders are unanimous in wanting solely to maximize their profits. Stakeholder theory posits that workers are entitled to participate in decision-making when restructuring puts jobs at risk. In this specific situation their interests are no less homogenous than those of shareholders, and their interest in job security is as clear a standard as that of profit maximization.

Employees in the Market for Corporate Control

The hostile takeover represents one of the most dramatic contexts in which attention is drawn to the status of employees in the firm. Crucial questions arise as to whether employee interests should be taken into account in responding to takeover bids, and the implications of resisting a bid on grounds that employee interests would suffer. The extent to which the law allows, or sometimes even requires, employee interests to be considered by the company's directors will be addressed later. This part of the discussion addresses the argument that allowing employee interests to take priority in the regulation of takeover activity runs counter to the efficiency gains associated with the market for corporate control. The market for corporate control is defined as

---

140 Daniel J. H. Greenwood, 'Fictional Shareholders: For Whom Are Corporate Managers Trustees' Revisited' (1996) 69 *Southern California Law Review* 1021–1104: '"Stockholders," as the court uses the term, refers not to the people who own the shares, but to an imaginary creature with no interest but the shares themselves, no plans or desires but maximizing the value of those shares' (at 1045).

'a market in which alternative managerial teams compete for the rights to manage corporate resources'.[141] The emergence of this market in the UK is attributable to a growing perception that many businesses would benefit from being wrested out of the hands of indolent or incompetent managers. Johnston notes that in Britain in the early 1950s takeover bids were regarded as 'a useful stimulus to efficiency. Some managements had become inefficient and slothful … the bidder was regarded as a useful gadfly, stinging sleepy managements into action'.[142]

But while the effect of a hostile takeover on share prices may be positive for many employees it often means large groups of workers being laid off.[143] Even where aggregate gains are reported there is no conclusive evidence linking these gains to previous managerial incompetence.[144] In addition, empirical investigation into the effect of takeovers reveals that there is little evidence of increased efficiency after the acquisition. Although in the US there is evidence of a correlation between the incidence of hostile takeovers and poor managerial performance there is still no certainty that the takeover results in enhanced standards of efficiency. Julian Franks and Colin Mayer's study of the evidence in the UK indicates that hostile takeovers are not directed towards disciplining the management of poorly performing firms. They found that the targets in hostile takeovers tend to be average or slightly below average compared to other companies, and not necessarily the poor performers.[145]

Although this evidence is inconclusive as to efficiency or productivity gains, there is clearer evidence of losses to employees. Shleifer and Summers have argued that takeovers constitute an avenue for managers to renege on implicit agreements with their workers. If incumbent managers prove reluctant to terminate explicit or implicit deals made with their employees with regard to continuing employment, the hostile takeover provides a convenient opportunity for these managers to be replaced with a new managerial team that is less hesitant to dismiss them: 'takeovers are external means of removing managers upholding stakeholder claims'.[146] The result is that 'hostile takeovers facilitate opportunistic behavior at the expense of stakeholders. In

141 Michael C. Jensen and Richard S. Ruback, 'The Market for Corporate Control: The Scientific Evidence' (1983) 11 *Journal of Financial Economics* 5–50.

142 At 10.

143 See Coffee, 'The Uncertain Case for Takeover Reform', for the argument that increases in *share price* following a takeover do not necessarily indicate *efficiency gains* within the firm. Also Deakin and Slinger, 'Hostile Takeovers', who review the economic evidence and note that '[t]his evidence is consistent with a view that hostile bids are effective at raising target shareholder value, and that shareholder-protection measures place the shareholders of companies that receive bids in a particularly strong position. However, it says very little one way or another about the wider proposition that hostile bids are efficiency enhancing' (at 27).

144 Coffee, 'The Uncertain Case for Takeover Reform'.

145 Julian Franks and Colin Mayer, 'Governance as a Source of Managerial Disciplining' (2000) Journal of Applied Corporate Finance' Report for the Company Law Review Committee, <www.dti.gov.uk/cld/franksreport.pdf>

146 At 15.

this way hostile takeovers enable shareholders to transfer wealth from stakeholders to themselves more so than to create it'.[147] Shleifer and Summers argue therefore that 'the disruption costs of at least some hostile takeovers may well exceed their social benefit.'[148] This points to the need for caution in drawing conclusions about efficiency during corporate restructuring, particularly where the resultant job losses involve significant social costs. It also suggests that when employees' firm-specific human capital investments are at risk clear losses to employees should not be justified by, at best, uncertain gains for overall productivity.

Firm-Specific Human Capital

Modern firms are increasingly dependent on their employees, and a large part of the market value of public corporations is now represented by 'intangible assets' including employees' human capital investments. This discussion has referred frequently to the importance of firm-specific human capital (FSHC) and in this part a fuller definition of this concept is offered. Margaret Blair and Thomas Kochan define FSHC as 'the knowledge, skills, ideas, and commitment of the employees' which are critical to the wealth-creating capacity of the firm.[149] The importance of employees' contribution means that it is rational and efficient for firms to promote job security rather than short term profits which come at the expense of retaining valuable workers.[150] When human capital is 'specific' to a particular firm then the workers' skills and knowledge acquired by long service within that firm are by definition of limited value outside that firm and it may become impossible, for all practical purposes, for that employee to leave and establish a comparable new career which means that the years of training investment are lost.[151] Thus both the employees as well as the firm are better off if the employment relationship continues.

In highlighting the importance of FSHC Blair argues that 'the relationships among the people who participate in the productive activity of firms are at the heart of the definition of the firm itself'.[152] The theory of team production which she formulates with Lynn Stout takes into account the importance of stakeholders to the productive process of the firm.[153] Their approach recognizes that employees make an important contribution to the firm's productivity which may on occasions be even more important than the shareholders' investment of finance capital. Proponents of shareholder primacy recognise that employees and other constituencies 'may

147 At 2.

148 At 1.

149 Blair and Kochan, 'Introduction' in Blair and Kochan at 2.

150 Blair and Stout, 'A Team Production Theory' at 250–51.

151 Gary S. Becker, *Human Capital: A Theoretical and Empirical Analysis* (3rd ed.) (London: University of Chicago Press, 1993). Becker distinguishes 'specific training' from 'general training' which will be of use to the employee in alternative workplaces.

152 Blair, 'Firm-Specific Human Capital' in Blair and Roe, at 59. See also Blair, *Ownership and Control*.

153 Blair and Stout, 'A Team Production Theory'.

make formidable investments in the firm (in the sense of irrevocable, specialized commitments of physical or human capital)' but reason that 'all are left to protect themselves through contract'.[154] The difficulty with leaving FSHC investments to be protected by specific contracts is that it is impossible for an employee to ascertain in advance the level of skill and knowledge they will acquire or the value this will add to the firm. There is incomplete information on the employer's side too – the employer cannot specify in advance the likely contribution of its long-term employees. The situation is compounded by the employee's initial gamble that the investment of his or her own time and effort in learning skills useful to the employer, which are not expressly required by the employment contract, will in time be rewarded by increasing levels of remuneration and a reducing likelihood of being laid off. This aspiration is impossible to capture fully by contract.[155] One way of enhancing the protection of these investments is by recognizing the place of employees within the proprietary structure of the firm. Blair concludes that 'Where firm-specific human capital is important, then, arguments about the role played by property rights might in some cases point toward employee control of the enterprise, or at least participation in management, rather than capitalist ownership and control'.[156]

In recognition of the importance of FSHC, and in appreciation of employees' entitlement to share in the firm's profits as a return on this investment, many corporations adopt employee share ownership plans (ESOPs) which give employees a claim on the firm's residual earnings. In the UK this is supported by legislation giving firms incentives to introduce such schemes.[157] A study by Andrew Robinson and Hao Zhang finds that while these schemes constitute an important avenue for the protection of FSHC, participation rates among non-managerial workers are not as high as might be expected.[158] Moreover the effectiveness of ESOPs in safeguarding human capital depends on the existence of complementary support from mechanisms such as 'employee involvement, financial participation, job security and trade unions'.[159] It would therefore be insufficient to rely on share ownership as the sole means of protecting FSHC. In addition these schemes typically retain effective control in the hands of management and non-employee shareholders by ensuring that employee shares carry no voting rights. Even where employee-shareholders do have voting rights, they exercise control in their capacity as shareholders not as employees and so this cannot be deemed to constitute employee-participation per

---

154 Easterbrook and Fischel, at 38.

155 Blair contends that for this reason 'employee investments in firm-specific human capital cannot be well protected by explicit and complete contracts': Blair, 'Firm-Specific Human Capital' in Blair and Roe, at 63.

156 Ibid, at 78.

157 The Employee Share Schemes Act 2002; Finance Act 2003 schedule 22 and Finance Act 2000 schedule 8 entitled 'Employee Share Ownership Plans.'

158 Andrew M. Robinson and Hao Zhang, 'Employee Share Ownership: Safeguarding Investments in Human Capital' (2005) 43 *British Journal of Industrial Relations* 469–88.

159 Robinson and Zhang, at 474–75.

se.[160] Hansmann's review of ESOPs in the United States suggests that they have hardly any impact on employee control in the firm. Only rarely are ESOPs structured to give employees a significant voice in the governance of the firm. In any event approximately 90 percent of all ESOPs in the US are in privately held firms, which makes them of limited relevance to the study of control in the large publicly held company. This picture is similar to that in the UK.[161] Although the ESOP concept was actively promoted when it was introduced in the US in the 1950s, 'it did not become popular until ESOPs were granted substantial federal tax subsidies … and until it was discovered that creation of an ESOP could be a useful defensive tactic for management in an attempted corporate takeover'.[162] In this way ESOPs end up being more about the balance of power between management and shareholders, or increasing the autonomy of managers, than about employee involvement in the firm.[163] It would therefore be preferable to focus on substantive protection of job security rather than employee shareholding. Indeed Robinson and Zhang suggest that where employees have a high expectation of job security there may indeed be no need for the ESOP as a means of protecting FSHC.[164]

The point has been made that not all employment relationships can be defined in terms of property. The ownership claims of employees in stakeholder theory depend on the existence of FSHC which is of value to both the employee and the firm and are at risk of expropriation. This proposal faces two main difficulties. The first difficulty lies in measuring or quantifying the value of FSHC. This aspect is certainly in need of further research.[165] Referring to it as 'human capital', a term which gives the unfortunate impression of appearing to dehumanize work, may be justified in that it has the merit of allowing a more direct comparison with the value of finance capital and thus allowing its importance to be appreciated by those concerned about any

---

160 Dow and Putterman, in Blair and Roe (eds.).

161 Robinson and Zhang: 'not having the expertise or ability to trade/value shares may be barriers precluding non-quoted companies from adopting ESO' (at 479).

162 Hansmann, at 105.

163 Deakin therefore argues that 'employee share ownership in itself is not the answer to the issues raised by the stakeholder debate. Most employee share ownership schemes provide for limited forms of financial participation; these can be a useful mechanism for rewarding employees, but they do not normally confer control of the kind which would provide a mechanism of countervailing power to set against the influence of outside investors': in 'Workers, Finance and Democracy' at 95–6.

164 Robinson and Zhang, at 482.

165 See Laurie J. Bassi, Baruch Lev, Jonathan Low, Daniel P. McMurrer, G. Anthony Siesfeld, 'Measuring Corporate Investments in Human Capital' in Blair and Kochan. Sadowski, Junkes and Lindenthal note that this makes it difficult to quantify the gains (or indeed the costs) of codetermination: 'It is very difficult to use an econometric design to examine the degree to which legally mandated codetermination arrangements promote investment in specific human capital because it is not possible to measure either the initial outlays or the profits of such investment' (at 63). Hence they conclude (at 54) that 'it is not yet possible to make a final theoretical or empirical micro-economic judgment of the codetermination laws'.

potential threat to shareholder value and the firm's overall profitability. While the percentage of the firm's value which is represented by its human capital depends partly on the type of firm as well as its size, financial structure and production methods, the relative value of intangible assets including human capital continues to rise: 'Although we do not have precise estimates of the aggregate value of investments in human capital, it is surely large, and possibly of the same order of magnitude as the aggregate value of equity capital'.[166]

The second difficulty is not specific to stakeholder theory but relates as well to other methods of employment protection, and that is the inevitably complex classification of work relationships. This issue is revisited here to emphasize that no single concept can be found to explain the entirety of those relationships which exhibit themselves in myriad forms in a vibrant labour market. Indeed this is the main ground on which criticism has been levelled at the concept of contract: that it fails to explain certain work relationships and all work relationships go through stages in which it is difficult to explain them in terms of contract. It is certainly the case that with the variety of industries, work contexts and working relationships, there can be no uniform theory that applies to all workers and all employers in all sectors covering the entire duration of the working relationship from establishment to termination and beyond.[167] It must be said that the contractual explanations or statutory regimes do not purport to do so – it is necessary in all these explanations to categorize workers into groups of reasonably homogenous working relationships, and inevitably too many workers and working relationships straddle boundaries or fall between the cracks fitting squarely in no particular group. The same imperative applies to the notion of property. Property rights arise in those employment relationships in which the workers invest firm-specific human capital in the firms for which they work, and where what is at stake is not the existence, viability or profitability of the firm, but profit margins. This method of classification does exclude employees with 'generic' skills, but at least has the potential to enhance job security in the context of economic dismissals for those workers who need it most, that is those least likely to find alternative comparable work and therefore most likely to incur crippling costs of job loss.

Conclusion

This chapter has made the case that the efficiency implications of the shareholder primacy norm are very much open to question. The discussion situated the rise of shareholder primacy in the conditions surrounding the emergence of the takeover market, illustrating that although it is now commonly assumed that efficient firms and shareholder primacy go together in fact the interests of the company have not always been associated with shareholder interests in this way. Shareholder primacy is an institutional response to the need to control managerial power, and there is no

166 Blair, 'Firm-Specific Human Capital' in Blair and Roe, at 67.

167 See Freedland, at 397–8.

reason to suppose that it is necessarily the only efficient solution to this dilemma. Recognizing that shareholder primacy is simply one of a range of potential responses to regulating managerialism allows room to rethink employee ownership and control.

Defining shareholders as *owners*, and not simply as contributors of finance capital, implies that their right to control the firm should be given the same priority accorded to all rights of property. This chapter considered this assertion, and argued that defining shareholders as exclusive owners while assuming that employees are outsiders involved in an arms-length relationship with the firm falls short of the standard required to protect employees' firm-specific investments. This argument was illustrated by reference to takeovers, when firms renege on implicit agreements made to persuade workers to invest their time, skill and effort in the firm. The solution endorsed in this chapter was that if efficiency requires ownership rights to be allocated to the party bearing the residual risk then a measure of these rights should be allocated to employees. This would recognize that owing to the importance of firm-specific human capital employees often have at least as much at stake in the firm as the shareholders. As Blair argues they both, in different ways, have a legitimate claim to ownership of the firm.

This conclusion was stated without going further to prescribe policy outcomes. As Ronald Coase has pointed out in a different context, it is extremely difficult to bridge the distance between understanding the nature of property rights in the firm and making pronouncements about law reform – to do so would require a study of a different kind to that undertaken in this book.[168] Primarily it is crucial to be realistic about the costs of introducing changes to the shareholder primacy norm. The lesson to be learned from the work of Roe and others on path dependence in corporate governance is that once a system settles on a particular path it may well prove costly to deviate from established norms.[169] Despite recognition of the efficiency gains to be derived from protecting firm-specific human capital it may still be feared that the costs of change, including costs associated with 'lock-in' effects, would outweigh the benefits.[170] Such lock-in results primarily from the fact that corporate

168 He suggests that 'The only means available to the government … (apart from exhortation, which is commonly ineffective) is a change in the law or its administration. The forms such changes may take are many. They may amend the rights and duties which people are allowed to acquire or are deemed to possess, or they may make transactions more or less costly by altering the requirements for making a legally binding contract. Or they may change the penalties imposed by the courts when, outside contract, harm is inflicted on others. And, of course, the economist's favourite means, the attaching of taxes and subsidies to the performance of particular actions or governmental regulation prohibiting or requiring the performance of certain actions, may also be employed … Lawyers will no doubt find it easy to add to this list': Coase, *The Firm, the Market, and the Law* at 28.

169 Lucien A. Bebchuk and Mark J. Roe, 'A Theory of Path Dependence in Corporate Ownership and Governance' (1999) 52 *Stanford Law Review* 127–70.

170 Lock-in results from the difficulty of deviating from entrenched legal rules and practices, meaning that in effect a legal system is more or less stuck with, or locked into, the

governance norms are inseparable from other deeply ingrained social and cultural institutions.[171] This book has not made any predictions about the costs of change, but it may be pointed out that so far the opposition to the stakeholder model has been justified purely by reference to productive efficiency and potential costs of collective governance – in other words the substantive costs of employee ownership claims – and not the costs of change. It should also be remembered, as Oona Hathaway points out, that the inflexibility associated with path dependence can lead to inefficiency when legal rules fail to respond to changing underlying conditions meaning that although costly, change may be necessary. This chapter therefore presented the case in favour of allocating a measure of control rights in the firm to the employees, rights triggered when corporate restructuring puts firm-specific human capital investments at risk. Control was defined not as decision-making in the day-to-day affairs of the company, but as the ultimate right to ratify and monitor decisions about restructuring that would place jobs at risk.

As to the claims that corporate governance is converging on the shareholder primacy norm, the assumptions that the Anglo-American 'shareholder primacy norm' has proved triumphant and that the 'employee-participation norm' is waning were found to be largely attributable to overlooking the central role of employees in European firms. Note was made of the continued divergence of labour law and labour relations in different jurisdictions, and the chapter illustrated the significance of employee participation in European corporate law. The next chapter considers this legal framework in more detail, contrasting it with English and American law.

framework of rules to which it has become accustomed over time: Oona Hathaway, 'Path Dependence in the Law: The Course and Pattern of Legal Change in a Common Law System' (2001) 86 *Iowa Law Review* 601–65.

171 Stan J. Leibowitz and Stephen Margolis, 'Path Dependence, Lock-In, and History' (1995) 11 *Journal of Law, Economics and Organization* 205–26.

Chapter 4

The Legal Framework

> It is no good asking the common law how to render void the unjust dismissals of ordinary workers. The answer to that problem must be the one given to the man who asked the way to York: 'You do not start from here'.[1]

Introduction

This book has argued that where the common law, owing to its current emphasis on freedom of contract, offers insufficient conceptual support for enhancing job security, the concept of property in work may provide a better starting point. The purpose of this chapter is to test this argument against the existing legal framework. Resolving conflicting interests in the firm ultimately falls within the preserve of directors acting in their fiduciary capacity. At common law the directors exercise a discretion reinforced by the law's 'business judgment' policy of non-intervention in directors' decisions made in good faith in what they (and not the courts) consider to be the best interests of the company.[2] This chapter contrasts the interpretation of this duty in English and American law. It is often suggested that one way in which the law could protect the interests of long-term employees would be by reformulating the directors' duty to act in the best interests of 'the company' to recognize that employee interests are comparable to those of shareholders. This chapter shows that although there is room within the legal framework for directors to consider stakeholder interests this has not resulted in displacement of the shareholder primacy norm. The chapter then considers whether this position is likely to change owing to the influence of European law. The main reference point is the European Acquired Rights Directive, although mention is made of other Directives granting workers rights of 'information and consultation'. The chapter argues that although these worker-participation Directives tend to be disregarded in the Anglo-American corporate governance debates, they

---

1 Wedderburn of Charlton, 'Labour Law: From Here to Autonomy?' (1987) 16 *Industrial Law Journal* 1–29 at 7.

2 This has been expressed as the court's duty not to substitute its own judgment for that of the directors if the directors' decision can be 'attributed to any rational business purpose': *Sinclair Oil Corp. v Levien,* Del.Supr., 280 A.2d 717 (1971) at 720. For English law see Christopher A. Riley, 'The Company Director's Duty of Care and Skill: The Case for an Onerous but Subjective Standard' (1999) 62 *Modern Law Review* 697–724.

are highly relevant in gauging corporate governance ideology in Europe. The chapter concludes that although these measures have demonstrated potential to drive English law in the direction of worker-participation as a primary benchmark, this potential is unlikely to be realized unless there is a change in the underlying assumptions at common law about the nature of the employment relationship in the firm.

Directors' Duties to Employees

The directors of a firm undergoing restructuring are faced with a crucial choice as to which factors and interests should govern their decisions. More specifically the question is whether they should pay attention purely to the expected impact on shareholder value (whether in the long or short term), or whether they should consider the impact on employee welfare and other stakeholder interests. The law in both the UK and the US generally allows directors to exercise a broad discretion in making this choice, although as shall be seen below it generally allows or requires the directors to consider stakeholder interests without compelling them to actually make decisions which advance those interests.

The discussion begins by examining the directors' duty to act in the best interests of the company. The influence of the shareholder primacy norm on the common law interpretation of this duty was considered in the previous chapter; the interest here is in how this norm is reconciled by law with employee interests. The reference to 'directors duties' is therefore limited to those aspects relating to employee interests. Although the UK and US law regulating directors' duties rests on an identical common law base, both countries have introduced legislative frameworks which resist easy comparison because the US has no federal law similar to the UK's Companies Act. Instead a number of states have passed various statutes governing the companies incorporated within their jurisdiction, the form and content of which varies from state to state. Some have no legislative interventions on this point, leaving directors' duties to be governed by the common law. A complete picture of the American legislation requires a comparison of state laws which this discussion does not attempt.[3] Instead the discussion uses individual state laws to illustrate some of the influences at play in either supporting or derogating from the shareholder primacy norm. Another factor which makes the comparison between British and American law less than straightforward is that unlike the UK's general legislative statement of directors' duties the applicable American statutes were passed during the takeover boom of the 1980s and were specifically designed to regulate takeovers. This means that the American statutes cannot be fully understood without taking into account the broader framework of takeover regulation. A full discussion of takeover regulation is

3 For such a comparative study see Lucian A. Bebchuk and Alma Cohen, 'Firms' Decisions Where To Incorporate' (2003) 46 *Journal of Law and Economics* 383–425; Kathleen Hale, 'Corporate Law and Stakeholders: Moving Beyond Stakeholder Statutes' (2003) 45 *Arizona Law Review* 823–56; Edward S. Adams and John H. Matheson, 'A Statutory Model for Corporate Constituency Concerns' (2000) 49 *Emory Law Journal* 1085–1135.

not attempted here, though reference is made to the role of these statutes in providing a defence to takeovers, particularly in Delaware.[4] The regulation of takeovers in the UK has not offered the same opportunity for recognizing stakeholder interests; as noted in the previous chapter the UK has traditionally been far more inclined to give shareholders the ultimate decision-making power in responding to takeovers. The US by contrast has generally allowed managers much more freedom to reject takeover offers.[5]

The Best Interests of the Company

Directors owe their duties to 'the company' and are required to exercise their discretion bona fide in what they consider to be in 'the interests of the company, and not for any collateral purpose'.[6] The traditional view is illustrated by several well-established cases. In *Greenhalgh v Arderne Cinemas Ltd* Lord Evershed M.R. stated that the phrase 'the company as a whole' does not mean the 'company as distinct from the corporators'.[7] This case was cited with approval in the Australian case of *Kinsela v Russell Kinsela Pty Ltd,* where it was held that 'the proprietary interests of the shareholders entitle them as a general body to be regarded as the company when questions of the duty of directors arise'.[8] In America *Smith v Van Gorkom* held that directors' duties were owed 'to the corporation and its shareholders'.[9] In linking the right to bring a derivative action to the property interest of a stockholder *Simons v Cogan* also reiterated that directors' fiduciary duties are owed only to shareholders and not to other stakeholders.[10] It is not considered necessary, for this purpose, for shareholders to have any *direct* means of ensuring that the directors act in their favour, because directors owe their duty to the company as a whole and not to

---

4 For a full review and discussion see Blair, *The Deal Decade*.

5 Tactics available to American, but not British, managers include the 'poison pill' (a nasty bundle of shareholder rights triggered by tendering a hostile bid), the 'white knight' (a preferred bidder who comes to the rescue of the target company, buying it out to pre-empt the overtures of an unwelcome suitor), sale of the 'crown jewels' in which all the corporation's valuable assets are sold before the acquirer takes over, the 'golden parachute' (expensive compensation packages for the target directors which make the acquisition much more expensive) or the retaliatory 'Pac Man' defence when the target attempts to take over the bidder: Kahan and Rock.

6 *Re Smith and Fawcett Ltd* [1942] Ch. 304 at 306.

7 [1951] Ch. 286 at 291, in context of shareholder voting power in general meeting but applicable to the duty of directors: 'in *Greenhalgh v Arderne Cinemas Ltd* Lord Evershed M.R. said, in a different context, that the benefit of the company meant the benefit of the shareholders as a general body, and in my opinion that is equally true in a case such as the present' (Plowman J, *Parke v Daily News Ltd* [1962] Ch. 927 at 963).

8 (1986) 10 A.C.L.R. 395, CA, NSW, at 401.

9 488 A.2d 858, 872 (Del. 1985). See also *Aronson v Lewis* 473 A.2d 805, 811 (Del. 1984); *Guth v Loft, Inc.* 23 Del.Ch. 255, 5 A.2d 503, 510 (1939).

10 542 A.2d 785 (1987). See Note, 'Creditors' Derivative Suits'.

individual shareholders.[11] Nevertheless the shareholders' predominance arises from the fact that they have the right to elect the board of directors, and these directors are held accountable to the shareholders in general meeting.

This conception of directors' duties is thought to be efficient because it provides a clear beneficiary of the company's interests, that is, shareholders 'both present and future'.[12] This is thought to provide a clear standard against which the directors' conduct can be judged.[13] However, the trouble with conceptualizing the shareholders as the exclusive embodiment of the company's interests is that the benefit of the company and that of the shareholders often diverge, particularly where the best interests of the company are more closely associated with the interests of its employees.[14] Hence the law in both the UK and the US recognizes that acting in the best interests of the company will sometimes mean looking beyond the simple maximization of profits. For instance a number of cases dealing with the interests of creditors have held that shareholders' interests are not invariably predominant. In *Brady v Brady* it was held that 'The interests of the company are to be equated with the interests of the shareholders in general except when the company is insolvent or of doubtful solvency or where the proposed act would be prejudicial to creditors' at which point the interests of the creditors become paramount.[15]

Drawing upon the treatment of creditors' interests there has been comparable recognition that employees' interests may be an appropriate matter of concern for corporate law, both in the UK Companies Act and in the American 'stakeholder statutes' which permit or require directors to take employee interests into account in making decisions. These provisions are reviewed here for two purposes. The first is descriptive and aims to ascertain the extent to which the law promotes stakeholder interests. On this point there is some indication that Anglo-American law in its regulation of directors' duties has introduced some elements of stakeholder protection, but the consensus appears to be that these measures are of little or no effect. The second purpose of the discussion is normative, suggesting that the existing legal framework supports an interpretation of directors' duties which is much more favourable to employees than is currently acknowledged.

---

11 *Percival v Wright* [1902] 2 Ch. 421. Indeed, under the rule in *Foss v Harbottle* (1843) 2 Hare 461 individual shareholders are actually precluded from bringing an action in respect of wrongdoing by directors – the action must be brought by the company. Derivative actions are fraught with difficulty, hence in practice directors' duties are often unenforceable at the instance of the shareholders.

12 *Gaiman v National Association for Mental Health* [1971] Ch. 317 at 330, Megarry J.

13 *Hampson v Price's Patent Candle Co.* (1876) 45 L.J. Ch. 437. Note however that the test is subjective: it is the directors' subjective opinion as to the interests of the company that counts, although their decision may be set aside if it is such that no reasonable man could consider it to be bona fide in the interests of the company: *Re Smith & Fawcett Ltd* [1942] Ch. 304.

14 Janet Dine, 'Private Property and Corporate Governance Part II: Content of Directors' Duties and Remedies' in Patfield (ed.).

15 [1989] A.C. 755 at 758.

Duties to Stakeholders

For a company undergoing restructuring the ability to terminate the existing employment contracts often becomes the single most important issue. In considering directors' duties with regard to employees the primary issue is how far (if at all) directors are accountable to employees. This issue has generally been considered marginal in the discussions on reform of corporate law.[16] The desire to ensure that boards of directors exercise more effective leadership and control over managerial excesses is associated with holding them accountable to their shareholders, and not to other stakeholders.

In Anglo-American law employee interests are readily promoted where doing so will also advance the shareholders' interests. As Bowen J said in *Hutton v West Cork Railway Co*, acting in the interests of the workers 'is for the directors to judge, provided it is a matter which is reasonably incidental to the carrying on of the business of the company', and is to be done only as 'an inducement to them to exert themselves in future, or as an act done reasonably for the purpose of getting the greatest profit from the business'.[17] While the ruling in this case has since been superseded, it illustrates an enduring approach to employee interests. This approach, whereby shareholders' interests are subordinated to broader stakeholder interests for strategic reasons, is reflected in the 'enlightened shareholder value' approach of modern company law. The essence of enlightened shareholder value is that the company's goal of making profits for its shareholders is best arrived at through balancing the interests of the different groups represented within it, so that the long-term maximization of shareholder value is achieved through building long-term relationships with stakeholder groups.[18] The controversial question is how the duty

16 For an overview of this debate see the consultation documents and reports of Law Commissions, *Company Directors: Regulating Conflicts of Interest and Formulating a Statement of Duties* Law Commission Consultation Paper No 153 (London: The Stationery Office, 1998); Department of Trade and Industry, *Modern Company Law For a Competitive Economy: The Strategic Framework* (1999) *Developing the Framework* (2000) *Completing the Structure* (2000), and *Final Report* (2001): Consultation Documents from the Company Law Review Steering Group (London: DTI, 1999–2001). Earlier the 1998 Hampel Committee *Report on Corporate Governance* concluded that: 'to redefine the directors' responsibilities in terms of the stakeholders would mean identifying all the various stakeholder groups; and deciding the nature and extent of the directors' responsibility to each. The result would be that directors were not effectively accountable to anyone since there would be no clear yardstick for judging their performance. This is a recipe neither for good governance nor for corporate success'.

17 (1883) 23 Ch. D. 654 at 666 and 672–3: 'The law does not say that there are to be no cakes and ale, but there are to be no cakes and ale except such as are required for the benefit of the company.'

18 As noted by *The Strategic Framework* (at par. 5.1) and reflected in the *Company Law Reform Bill* (2005) Chapter 2, 'General Duties of Directors'.

of directors to act bona fide in the long-term best interests of the company should be interpreted.[19]

The perspective that the company, as an entity, has its own definable interest, is crucial in this debate. Teubner explains the concept of the 'enterprise-in-itself' as an expression of the enterprise's autonomy, implying that the company's interest does not mean the interests of its resource holders – whether capital or labour – but the interest of the enterprise 'in itself'.[20] If the company is seen as autonomous in this sense then the shareholders and employees, along with all the people and things associated with the company, are seen as part of the environment in which the company exists. In this sense the company is *more* than an association of owners.[21] The reason for formulating this notion of the self-interest of the company is to enable the construction of a corporate environment in which both shareholder and employee interests are accurately perceived and defined. Teubner proposes this as an avenue for transcending both shareholder-orientation and managerialism and favouring decision-making in the interests of the economy as a whole. The corporate interest could then be understood as being broader than the more immediate or specific goals of the individual company.[22]

Leader likewise sees the company as having an interest independent of the interests of any natural person involved in the company. However, recognizing that in practice it is difficult to conceptualize this interest without linking it to the precise constituency affected by the decision he suggests that 'the interest of the company' should be understood as a short-hand way of referring to the best way in which to carry out the function of an artificial person. He suggests that this function would in turn be established by reference to the various interests of natural persons who are affected by the entity, although the interests of the company remain an independent construct. In Leader's formulation the independence of the company's interest does not mean that the company's interest is independent from the interests of natural persons – it means that this interest is independent from any *particular* individual interest or constituency group, so that no stakeholder group will have its interests automatically seen as the best interests of the company in all circumstances. Instead the company will seek to establish a priority between the different groups in the circumstances of each case, and these priorities will shift over time. Leader therefore discerns a difference between the personal and the *derivative* interests of the shareholders: their personal interest is the narrow and selfish interest in profit

19 In the United States the American Law Institute's restatement of the common law duty of care states that directors' should act in 'the best interests of the corporation', in its *Principles of Corporate Governance: Analysis and Recommendations* S 4.01(a) (1985). The same is provided by the *Revised Model Business Corporation Act* S 8.30 (a) 1984.

20 Teubner, 'Company Interest'.

21 Dine observes (at 125) that 'the company is bigger than 100% of the shareholders'. This is in contrast to the nexus of contracts theory which sees the company as something *less* than an association of owners, in the sense that there is nothing there except a network of contracting relations.

22 Teubner, 'Company Interest' at 23–7.

maximization, which may potentially differ from the best interests of the company. Their derivative interest, however, he depicts as identical to the interest of the company, and this interest sometimes gives precedence to shareholder value and sometimes to the value of protecting employee or other constituency interests. Similarly, Janet Dine argues that the company should be seen as a commercial enterprise with purposes of its own, distinct from the narrowly defined interests of its shareholders. In so far as they recognize that the company is something more than the sum of its shareholders the approach of Leader and Dine is consistent with the stakeholder assertion that the company's interests depend on the circumstances and will therefore vary, giving priority sometimes to one group and sometimes to another. The idea that an entity can have interests divorced from those persons who have an interest in it and associated either with its own interest 'in itself' or with an independent 'social interest' is more familiar to the continental European lawyer than to the common lawyer, Lord Wedderburn remarking that the European idea of *Unternehmensinterrese*, *interesse sociale* or *l'intérêt social* is 'to the positivist, English observer an idea that is often a mystery'.[23] There would be no way to assign any definite content to a duty conceived in these terms. Kahn-Freund considered the idea of a 'personless corporation' unsatisfactory in so far as it implies 'that there exists a self-perpetuating entity, the company or enterprise, whose "interests" transcend those of any of its component elements'.[24] Paul Davies and Lord Wedderburn suggest that the 'best interests of the company' is usually defined as 'a short-hand way of referring to the interests of both employees and shareholders', an approach which holds potential for stakeholder theory.[25]

The Companies Act 1985

In the UK Section 309(1) of the Companies Act 1985 provides that 'the matters to which the directors of the company are to have regard in the performance of their functions include the interests of the company's employees in general, as well as the interests of its members'.[26] This introduces employee interests explicitly into the framework of company law. It reverses the common law position as laid down in *Parke v Daily News* where Plowman J held that the decision to make ex gratia payments to employees on the transfer of the company was a breach of the directors' duty to act in the best interests of the company.[27] He appreciated that 'the view that directors, in having regard to the question what is in the best interests of the company, are entitled to take into account the interests of the employees, irrespective of any

---

23 In 'The Future of Company Law' at 36–7. See also Wedderburn, 'Employees, Partnership and Company Law'.

24 Otto Kahn-Freund, 'Industrial Democracy' (1977a) 6 *Industrial Law Journal* 65–84 at 76.

25 Paul Davies and Wedderburn of Charlton, 'The Land of Industrial Democracy' (1977) 6 *Industrial Law Journal* 197–211 at 199, discussing the proposals of the *Bullock Report on Industrial Democracy*.

26 See also 719 of the Companies Act 1985; Section 187 of the Insolvency Act 1986.

27 [1962] Ch. 927.

consequential benefit to the company, is one which may be widely held' but was certain that this view did not represent the law.[28] While it might represent the aspiration of good managers, in law the best interests of the company meant the benefit of the shareholders as a body: 'the defendants were prompted by motives which, however laudable, and however enlightened from the point of view of industrial relations, were such as the law does not recognise as a sufficient justification'.[29] S.309 now ensures that directors will not, simply by taking employee interests into account, be found to be in breach of their duty. But it does not go further. As Parkinson argues, the section is not intended to redefine directors' duties but to confirm that directors who take employee interests into account are not thereby in breach of their fiduciary duty to the company.

Much criticism has been directed at s.309 for failing to provide stronger protection for the interests of employees. In particular it does not provide any mechanism by which employees could take action against directors who do not consider their interests. S.309(2) states explicitly that 'the duty imposed by this section on the directors is owed by them to the company (and the company alone) and is enforceable in the same way as any other fiduciary duty owed to a company by its directors.' Therefore this duty can be enforced only by the directors themselves or by shareholders through a derivative action. Writing before s.309 became law, Davies and Wedderburn noted that although this provision could be said to require directors to exercise their duties in favour of both shareholders and employees as joint stakeholders, making an attempt to balance these interests where they are in conflict, 'the provision operates only so as to specify the interests which the directors are to take into account and not so as to stipulate in any particular situation the weight which a director must attach to either interest'. They argued that this would in theory allow directors 'maximum freedom of action within the context of an enterprise whose existence is seen to depend upon the continued participation of both capital and labour'.[30] However they noted that it could also be interpreted as merely procedural, specifying interests to be taken into account but not requiring anything more than that.

In the event this is precisely what happened. S.309 has been interpreted as merely affording a defence to directors. If a shareholder objects to any decision taken by them it is open to the directors to justify their action on grounds that it benefits the employees or some other stakeholder group. This interpretation is borne out by the case law. For instance in *Re Saul D. Harrison & Sons Plc* the Court of Appeal upheld

28 At 962–3: 'Mr. Leach was cross-examined about that statement: "(Q) One of the matters which affected the conclusion, at least in your mind, as I understand it, was that a company's duty these days must be regarded as one not only to the shareholders, but also to the employees? (A) Yes. I think I said that the prime duty must be to the shareholders; but boards of directors must take into consideration their duties to employees in these days". But no authority to support that proposition as a proposition of law was cited to me; I know of none, and in my judgment such is not the law'.

29 Ibid.

30 At 198. See also Wedderburn, 'Employees, Partnership and Company Law'.

the directors' decision to continue to run the company rather than sell it and realize the assets for the shareholders.[31] The directors' decision was partly based on the fact that they were required to have regard to the interests of their employees, many of whom were unlikely to find alternative employment if the company were sold. Neill L.J. noted that the petitioner, in challenging the directors' decision, was paying 'scant regard to the obligations imposed on the board by s.309 of the 1985 Act to take account of the employees of the company, of whom there are over a hundred.'[32] In *Re Welfab Engineers Ltd* the company was in financial difficulties and the directors, opting for a solution which would allow the company to continue in business, turned down an offer from a purchaser which would have necessitated the winding up of the business.[33] The company was unable to recover and was subsequently wound up. The liquidators claimed that the directors had acted improperly in giving priority to the preservation of the business and the jobs of the employees, including their own jobs as directors, when they ought instead to have sold the business to the highest bidder at the earliest opportunity. The court held that although the directors were not entitled to take action to save their jobs and those of other employees on terms which would clearly leave the creditors in a worse position than on a liquidation, an 'honest attempt to save the business' would not be censured. Hoffman J stated that this was 'particularly so against the background of the pressures which must have been imposed on directors of companies like this by the widespread unemployment and industrial devastation in the Midlands at the time'.[34] In this way s.309 has served to amplify the scope of directorial discretion in decision-making, and the suggestion is often made that the law should be reformed to place emphasis on employment protection by giving employees' enforcement rights under this provision.

Law Reform

Following an extended consultation on the reform of the law governing directors' duties the UK government in 2005 presented to Parliament a new Company Law Reform Bill which is expected to become law in 2007.[35] One of the most controversial points aired during the consultation process was the codification of directors' duties,

31 [1990] B.C.L.C. 14.

32 At 33. This claim was founded on the 'unfair prejudice' remedy in section 459 of the Companies Act and went on appeal to the House of Lords in *O'Neill v Phillips* [1999] 1 W.L.R. 1092.

33 [1990] B.C.L.C. 833.

34 Hoffmann J. at 838. Similar cases are *Fulham Football Club Ltd & Ors v Cabra Estates Plc* (1993) 65 P. & C.R. 284; *Secretary of State for Trade and Industry v Gray* [1995] 1 B.C.L.C. 276.

35 The reform process was launched by the government in March 1998 and finally introduced to the House in the Queen's Speech, 17 May 2005. For a discussion see Allan Wells, 'Company Law Reform – Too Far or Not Far Enough?' (2006) 27 *Business Law Review* 100–101; Julian Harris, 'Law Society Issues Criticisms of Company Law Reform Bill at Second Reading' (2006) *Company Lawyer* 95–6.

and whether they should have a mandatory duty to make decisions in the best interests of both shareholders and employees, and indeed of all stakeholders. In the end this proposal was not adopted. The Bill provides in Clause 156 that 'a director of a company must act in the way he considers, in good faith, would be most likely to promote the success of the company for the benefit of its members as a whole'. Members are defined, as by the present law, as the company's shareholders. Clause 156(3) echoes s.309 in making explicit reference to employee interests: it provides that 'In fulfilling the duty imposed by this section a director must (so far as reasonably practicable) have regard to (a) the likely consequence of any decision in the long term, (b) the interests of the company's employees', and goes on to list the interests of other stakeholder groups such as suppliers, customers, the community and the environment to which directors must have regard. Like s.309 the Bill goes no further than a requirement that directors 'have regard to' these interests. Like the Companies Act it vests the capacity of enforcement in the directors on behalf of the company or the shareholders through a derivative action. The Bill's Explanatory Notes emphasize that Clause 156 is not meant to introduce *new* directors' duties:

> This duty, which codifies the current law, enshrines in statute what is commonly referred to as the principle of 'enlightened shareholder value'. The duty has two elements: a director must act in the way he or she considers, in good faith, would be most likely to promote the success of the company for the benefit of the members as a whole; in doing so, the director must, so far as reasonably practicable, have regard to … wider expectations of responsible business behaviour.[36]

The Bill therefore subjects directors to a test of good faith: 'the decision as to what will promote success, and what constitutes such success, is one for the directors' good faith judgment'.[37] There is, then, no substantive change proposed to the law as interpreted under s.309. Indeed it appears that far from improving the situation or even maintaining the status quo the position of employees would be weakened by the proposed wider list of relationships and interests which are to be considered. Lord Wedderburn argues that 'the employees' interests are now just one of sundry business matters to be considered in so far as they impact upon the company's, i.e. the shareholders', interests'.[38] The ground of his argument is that the language in the Bill has shifted from requiring directors to 'have regard' to employees' 'interests' to asking them to 'take account' of the firm's 'relationship' with its employees among others; and this only where 'relevant' and 'practicable'. But even this modest change from 'shareholder primacy' to 'enlightened shareholder value' has met with opposition. The Law Society has argued that there is a danger that, over time, the list of stakeholder interests in Clause 156(3) may solidify into an inflexible standard,

36 Company Law Reform Bill Part 10 – Company Directors. Chapter 2 – General Duties of Directors at par. 324–25.

37 Company Law Reform Bill par. 324–25.

38 Wedderburn of Charlton, 'The Future of Company Law' at 43.

derogation from which may eventually be assessed by the courts according to objective tests. This would in turn erode the business judgment rule according to which the courts do not second-guess the decisions of business managers.[39]

American Stakeholder Statutes

A similar debate has arisen in the US with regard to the 'corporate constituency statutes', sometimes referred to as 'directors' duty statutes' or stakeholder statutes.[40] A number of states have passed stakeholder statutes mainly to regulate takeovers. Prior to the enactment of these statutes the position in American corporate law was equivalent to English law as laid down by *Parke v Daily News,* associating the company's interests with the shareholders.[41] This is illustrated by *Dodge v Ford Motor Co*, still commonly cited as the classic statement of the rule, where it was held that

> a business corporation is organized and carried on primarily for the profit of the stockholders. The powers of the directors are to be employed for that end. The discretion of directors is to be exercised in the choice of means to attain that end, and does not extend to a change in the end itself, to the reduction of profits, or to the nondistribution of profits among stockholders in order to devote them to other purposes.[42]

As a result the general rule is that although under the business judgment rule the courts will generally not interfere with directors' discretion this must be exercised subject to the duty to promote shareholder interests. As Millon notes this rule came up for reassessment during the takeover boom of the 1980s in the wake of considerable public disenchantment with takeovers, prompting the desire to allow target companies to block hostile bids even where the bid might have been attractive to the shareholders, on grounds that it prejudiced other stakeholder interests.[43] The question was whether the duty to serve shareholders required that directors' response to hostile takeovers had to be determined purely by reference to the potential benefit to the shareholders. The initial response to this query in Delaware was that the directors did have scope, within the exercise of their discretion, to take into account the potential impact of the takeover on all corporate constituencies.[44] As will be seen later this discretion was of great strategic value for directors, and at the same time suggested that the law was in retreat from shareholder primacy. However *Revlon, Inc. v MacAndrews & Forbes Holdings, Inc.* qualified this permission, adding that 'while concern for various corporate constituencies is proper when addressing

39 Harris, 'Law Society Issues Criticisms'.

40 Millon.

41 [1962] Ch. 927.

42 (1919) 170 NW 668 at 684, echoed in *A.P. Smith Manufacturing Co. v Barlow* 98 A.2d 581 (N.J. 1953).

43 At 224–5.

44 *Unocal Corp. v Mesa Petroleum Co.* 493 A.2d 946 (Del. 1985) at 954.

a takeover threat, that principle is limited by the requirement that there be some rationally related benefit accruing to the stockholders'.[45]

In other states, beginning with Pennsylvania and eventually totalling thirty-one states, a legislative solution was adopted. Anti-takeover statutes were passed allowing directors to take non-shareholder constituency interests into account in considering their response to proposed takeovers.[46] Although primarily concerned to increase the scope of managerial discretion in responding to hostile bids the statutes were welcomed by stakeholder proponents.[47] Amongst proponents of shareholder primacy Pennsylvania's enactment of the first anti-takeover statute in 1983 generated considerable disquiet. Even those not opposed to the statutes predicted that Pennsylvania and other states adopting stakeholder statutes would be penalized by local firms choosing to incorporate in other states, to the detriment of both shareholders and the wider state economy.[48] However this prediction did not materialize, and to date there is no evidence that states with stakeholder statutes are at a competitive disadvantage in the market for incorporation. In fact the converse is true: 'states that offer stronger antitakeover protections are substantially more successful both in retaining in-state firms and in attracting out-of state incorporations'.[49] A study by Lucian Bebchuk and Alma Cohen finds that states with no anti-takeover statutes of any kind 'do poorly and retain a relatively small fraction of the companies located in them'.[50] Like the UK Companies Act the stakeholder statutes permit but do not require directors to take stakeholder interests into account. For instance the Pennsylvania statute provides that:

> In discharging the duties of their respective positions, the board of directors, committees of the board, individual directors and individual officers may, in considering the best interests of the corporation, consider the effects of any action upon employees, suppliers and customers of the corporation, communities in which offices or other establishments of the corporation are located, and all other pertinent factors.[51]

---

45 506 A.2d 173 (Del. 1986) at 176.

46 Arizona, Connecticut, Florida, Georgia, Hawaii, Idaho, Illinois, Indiana, Iowa, Kentucky, Louisiana, Maine, Maryland, Massachusetts, Minnesota, Mississippi, Missouri, Nevada, New Jersey, New Mexico, New York, North Dakota, Ohio, Oregon, Pennsylvania, Rhode Island, South Dakota, Tennessee, Vermont, Wisconsin and Wyoming: Grant A. Gartman, *State Antitakeover Laws* (Washington D.C. Investor Responsibility Research Center, 2000), cited in Bebchuk and Cohen.

47 Jonathan D. Springer, 'Corporate Constituency Statutes: Hollow Hopes and False Fears' (1999) *Annual Survey of American Law* 85–124.

48 See Roberta Romano, 'Competition for Corporate Charters and the Lesson of Takeover Statutes' (1993a) 61 *Fordham Law Review* 843–64.

49 Bebchuk and Cohen, at 383.

50 At 387. These states are Alabama, Alaska, Arkansas, California, the District of Columbia, Montana, New Hampshire, and West Virginia.

51 Pa. Cons. Stat. Ann. §§ 511(d),(e),(g) & 1721 (e),(f),(g) (Purdon Supp. 1990).

Only Connecticut provides that directors must consider these interests, using the mandatory 'shall' where Pennsylvania and other states use the permissive 'may'.[52] With regard to clarifying the nature of these interests and how they are to be protected, the statutes do not give priority to any particular constituency. For instance the Minnesota statute allows directors to consider the interests of 'the economy of the state and nation', and 'community and societal considerations'.[53] Some states such as Indiana specify that no single interest may predominate over other interests, and that consideration of constituency interests fits within directors' duty of care, or falls under the protection of the business judgment rule. The Pennsylvania statute specifies that the directors shall not be required to regard any corporate interest or the interests of any particular group as a dominant or controlling interest or factor. The Iowa statute provides that consideration of any or all of the community interest factors is not a violation of the business judgment rule or of any duty of the directors to the shareholders, even if the directors reasonably determine that a community interest factor outweighs the financial benefits to the corporation or its shareholders.[54]

Like s.309 the effect of these statutes is to confirm the centrality of the directors' discretion rather than to vest new rights in stakeholders. Indeed it has been said that their sole purpose is to shield incompetent managers from hostile takeover attempts by allowing them to declare that the takeover would not be in the best interests of employees or other stakeholders. It has been remarked of Indiana's statute that its effect is simply 'to protect stupid decisions' by managers for which some stakeholder interest or other can always be cited in justification.[55] Roe observes that as takeovers were perceived to cause widespread disruption of firms, workers and communities, different interest groups prompted state legislatures to intervene.[56] The stakeholder statutes may well, therefore, reflect an intention to protect incumbent directors rather than stakeholders.[57] Managers have generally upheld the shareholder value norm although 'When their high price jobs were potentially at stake in the takeover wars, [they] sang a different tune. In defending against takeover bids, they pompously intoned that they had a grave responsibility to consider all of the stakeholder interests bundled together in the large modern corporation'.[58] All cases involving constituency

52 Conn. Gen. Stat. Ann. § 33–313(e) (West Supp. 1990); Bebchuk and Cohen.

53 Minn. Stat. Ann. 302A.215(5) (West Supp. 1991).

54 See discussion of these statutes in Bebchuk and Cohen.

55 Douglas M. Branson, 'Corporate Governance "Reform" and the New Corporate Social Responsibility' (2001) 62 *University of Pittsburgh Law Review* 605–47 at 637.

56 For instance in Minnesota, when a hostile bid was made for a company its managers persuaded the state legislature to convene a special session, and 'within hours, the state had a new antitakeover bill': Roe, 'Takeover Politics' at 339.

57 Particularly directors facing the threat of hostile takeover from overseas raiders. Ohio's anti-takeover statute was passed to thwart 'British corporate raider Sir James Goldsmith's pursuit of The Goodyear Tire & Rubber Co. Around the same time, Pennsylvania adopted a strict new standard to help Armstrong Holdings Inc. fend off the Belzberg family of Canada': Roy Harris, 'States of Grace' *CFO Magazine*, July 2002.

58 Branson, at 639.

statutes have (as cases in the UK under s.309) involved corporate directors invoking the statute to defend their decisions. For instance in *Baron v Strawbridge & Clothier* Pennsylvania's constituency statute was relied on in upholding a board's decision to reclassify its stock in response to a threat of a tender offer.[59] In *Amanda Acquisition Corp. v Universal Foods Corp.* the decision turned on the effect of the directors' actions on the value of the company's stock.[60] Wisconsin's constituency statute was cited in upholding the board's decision. In *Keyser v Commonwealth National Finance Corp.* Pennsylvania's statute was applied in scrutinizing the board's response to a hostile offer.[61] This legislation and case law has nevertheless been said to have the incidental effect of detracting from short-term shareholder value. Even Delaware, after some initial hesitation, was eventually influenced by the existence of such legislation in other states to allow directors to reject bids.[62] It therefore imposed limits, albeit modest, on the shareholder primacy norm. Notably this was achieved by allowing a shift of power to the managers, rather than to stakeholders. In view of the major significance of Delaware in shaping corporate law in the US it is worth examining this development in more detail, in order to assess the extent of the derogation from the shareholder primacy norm.

Delaware is well known as the corporate capital of America: 68 percent of publicly traded firms and 58 percent of all firms are incorporated there. This contrasts with 19 percent incorporated in California and about 9 percent each in New York and Texas.[63] Jonathan Macey draws attention to the significant role played by powerful 'interest groups' of corporate managers, lawyers and investment bankers who supply the supporting legal and financial framework for Delaware companies, and who exert significant influence on the direction taken by the law.[64] Macey observes that Delaware introduced anti-takeover provisions towards the end of the 1980s when the possibility emerged that she might lose her dominant hold over the incorporation market, following criticism of the decision of the Delaware Supreme Court in *Smith v Van Gorkom* which indicated that directors could be held liable even for unintentional breaches of their fiduciary duties when considering their response to a takeover bid.[65] There was also criticism of the suggestion made by the Supreme Court in the *Revlon* case that once it was clear that the company would have to be sold the managers no longer had the option of taking defensive action, their proper role being to secure the best price for shareholders. *Revlon* thus cast doubt on the validity of different strategies developed by directors in resisting hostile takeovers, and raised the possibility that many firms would consider reincorporating in a

59 646 F.Supp. 690 (E.D.Pa. 1986).

60 708 F.Supp. 984 (E.D. Wis. 1989).

61 675 F.Supp. 238 (M.D.Pa.1987).

62 Bebchuk and Ferrell.

63 Bebchuk and Cohen.

64 Jonathan R. Macey, '*Smith v. Van Gorkom*: Insights about CEOs, Corporate Law Rules, and the Jurisdictional Competition for Corporate Charters' (2002) 96 *Northwestern University Law Review* 607–29 at 625–26.

65 488 A.2d 858, 872 (Del. 1985).

different state where such defenses were permissible.[66] The significant tax revenues associated with dominance in the state competition for incorporations was an added incentive to create a legal environment which corporate directors would consider attractive, essentially by allowing them as much discretion as possible to respond to takeovers in whichever way they deemed prudent.[67] Delaware responded to the threat of corporate flight by introducing an anti-takeover law, although, significantly, it was not as far-reaching as those in other states which allowed directors to consider stakeholder interests.[68] The Delaware Supreme Court also reaffirmed, in *Paramount Communications Inc. v Time Inc.*, that directors could resist takeovers on grounds of adverse effects for non-shareholder constituencies. The *Paramount* decision was seen as a move to restore confidence in ample scope for directorial discretion after *Revlon*. This case sanctioned the consideration of non-shareholder interests by directors, although it also required the board to show that in coming to their decision they had 'reasonable grounds for believing that a danger to corporate policy and effectiveness existed' and that the actions taken were 'reasonable in relation to the threat posed' by the bid.[69]

Some commentators argue that the effect of the stakeholder statutes is to radically alter the central principle of corporate law, that is, the directors' fiduciary duty to act in the best interests of the company. They depict these statutes as creating a new legal landscape in which directors' duty is not simply to serve shareholders, but also to act in the best interests of other stakeholders.[70] Lawrence Mitchell views this as evidence of increasing 'legal recognition of constituent interests within the corporate structure'.[71] He interprets this law as having significantly altered the frame of reference of the corporation's board of directors and the way it perceives its role. Mitchell suggests that rather than constituting an 'agent' of the shareholders the board is now more accurately viewed as representative of the interests of all participants in the corporation. His

---

66 Michael Kahan and Edward B. Rock, 'How I Learned to Stop Worrying and Love the Pill: Adaptive Responses to Takeover Law' (2002) 69 *University of Chicago Law Review* 871–916. Roe observes that this risk was seen as urgent after a series of memos sent by leading corporate lawyers to their clients in Delaware advising them to consider reincorporation in other states: 'New Jersey, Ohio and Pennsylvania, among others, are far more desirable states for incorporation than Delaware in this takeover era. Perhaps it is time to migrate out of Delaware ...': Roe, 'Takeover Politics' at 341.

67 Kahan and Rock.

68 Bebchuk and Cohen. Although Delaware's anti-takeover law, like that of California and Texas, does not mention stakeholder interests, its significance for the stakeholder case lies in its potential to limit the scope of the shareholder primacy norm.

69 Del.Supr., 571 A.2d 1140 (1989) at 1152.

70 Such as Katherine V.W. Stone, 'Employees as Stakeholders under State Nonshareholder Constituency Statutes' (1991) 21 *Stetson Law Review* 45–72.

71 Lawrence E. Mitchell, 'A Theoretical and Practical Framework for Enforcing Corporate Constituency Statutes' (1992) 70 *Texas Law Review* 579–643 at 585. See more generally Mitchell, *Corporate Irresponsibility: America's Newest Export* (New Haven: Yale University Press, 2001).

argument is derived from a number of decisions, particularly in the context of hostile takeover bids, which uphold the discretion of the board of directors in the face of challenges by shareholders in derivative actions. This suggests that the role of the board has been transformed by the stakeholder statutes into one which is truly independent of any single constituency, including shareholders.

Enlightened Shareholder Value

Like s.309 the stakeholder statutes emphasize that employees and other constituent groups do not have the legal standing to enforce these provisions. The duty to consider stakeholder interests is owed by directors 'solely to the business corporation' and is therefore enforceable only through derivative lawsuits. Even if stakeholders were able to enforce these provisions they would face the additional hurdle presented by the 'business judgment rule' which requires that the courts do not interfere with the directors' decision if they can show that they did at least think about the interests of employees (where the duty to do so is mandatory). The existence or extension of these provisions has been opposed by commentators in both jurisdictions, and on both sides of the stakeholder-shareholder debate. Shareholder supporters apprehend that the provisions will simply serve as a carte blanche for directors, rendering them less accountable to shareholders. Stakeholder supporters such as Kathleen Hale are concerned that such broad director discretion will yield no appreciable benefit for stakeholders and that in the absence of any enforcement mechanism vested in stakeholders it is unlikely that these provisions will make any significant inroads into the shareholder primacy norm. Hale therefore argues that it would be better to scrap them and implement more effective stakeholder-protection proposals.

The opinion of the American Bar Association (ABA) echoes that of the Law Society in the UK. The ABA has interpreted the stakeholder statutes in much the same way as s.309 is understood in the UK, recommending that these statutes should be understood only to 'they confirm what the common law has been: directors may take into account the interests of other constituencies but only as and to the extent that the directors are acting in the best interests, long as well as short term, of the shareholders and the corporation'.[72] This approach is remarkably similar to that adopted in the UK Company Law Reform Bill with its reference to codifying the current law and its statement of the directors' duty as one of promoting the success of the company in the long term. The ABA also recommends that courts should follow the approach of *Unocal Corp. v Mesa Petroleum Co.* where the Delaware Supreme Court stated that directors may consider the impact of a takeover on constituencies other than shareholders subject as always to the duty to act 'in good

72 American Bar Association Committee on Corporate Laws, 'Other Constituencies Statutes: Potential for Confusion' (1990) 45 *Business Lawyer* 2253–71 at 2269. The Report makes specific reference to section 309. See, subsequently, the American Law Institute's *Principles of Corporate Governance: Analysis and Recommendations* (1994).

faith and in the honest belief that the action taken was in the best interests of the company'.[73] The *Paramount* case, like that of *Unocal*, had been seen as an indication that the Delaware courts were inclined to create more room for non-shareholder interests to be given priority by directors.[74] However the decision in *Unocal* is not as wide-ranging as at first thought; it was qualified by the same court in *Revlon,* which related the consideration of non-shareholder interests back to shareholder welfare.[75]

The US courts' decisions taken in the round seem to indicate that other constituencies are only to be considered where doing so is consistent with the best interests of shareholders. For instance in *Shamrock Holdings, Inc. v Polaroid Corp* an action was brought attacking the validity of an employee stock ownership plan (ESOP) on the basis that the ESOP was merely a device to stave off the threat of a hostile takeover, altering the shareholder profile of the company by concentrating shares in hands friendly to management.[76] Although it was conceded by all parties that this strategy would benefit the employees this was not material to the outcome of the case. The issue on which the decision turned was whether or not the ESOP *would increase share earnings in the long run*, benefiting shareholders by raising the stock market value of the company. Thus, Anglo-American law has moved on from *Parke v Daily News* and *Dodge v Ford Motor Co.* in the sense that employee interests are now firmly within the framework of the law governing directors' duties, but it has not gone so far as to endorse the stakeholder perspective. Instead, it has settled on the 'enlightened shareholder value' norm.

The Framework of European Law

In the 1970s the European Economic Community adopted a number of Directives regulating the rights of employees during transfers of undertakings, redundancies and insolvency.[77] These Directives had a clear social aim, which was 'to protect the employees' social expectation of continued employment' when the undertakings for which they worked changed hands or underwent financial difficulty which brought

---

73 493 A.2d 946 (Del. 1985) at 954.

74 It required the board to show that they had 'reasonable grounds for believing that a danger to corporate policy and effectiveness existed' and that the actions taken were 'reasonable in relation to the threat posed': Del.Supr., 571 A.2d 1140 (1989) at 1152.

75 In *Revlon* the court held that 'while concern for various corporate constituencies is proper when addressing a takeover threat, that principle is limited by the requirement that there be some rationally related benefit accruing to the stockholders' (at 176). See also *Mills Acquisition Co. v Macmillan, Inc.* 559 A.2d 1261 (Del. 1989).

76 709 F.Supp. 1311 (1989).

77 The Acquired Rights Directive (Directive 2001/23), the Collective Redundancies Directive (Council Directive 75/129/EEC on the approximation of the laws of the member states relating to collective redundancies as amended by Directive 92/56/EEC and consolidated in Council Directive 98/59/EC) and the Insolvency Directive (Directive 80/987/EEC).

them under new management.[78] The protection and preservation of employee rights has been the predominant concern of the European court in interpreting the scope and effect of the Directives.[79] This reflects the conviction of the EU member states that stimulating economic growth requires the support of social rights and policy.[80] These Directives are now supplemented and extended by the recent Directives on Worker Involvement in the European Company and Information and Consultation of workers.[81]

The Employment Relationship

In keeping with the regulatory approach of European law, the worker-protection Directives do not themselves prescribe sanctions to be imposed on employers for non-compliance; the imposition of such sanctions is left to the jurisdictional competence of individual member states.[82] The nature of such penalties depends largely on how the particular state conceptualizes the employment relationship and the penalties differ significantly between states. The effectiveness of European law in different states is also influenced by the fact that states retain the jurisdiction to define who is an 'employee' and therefore covered by the protective measures of the Directives. For instance the Acquired Rights Directive applies 'without prejudice to national law as regards the definition of contract of employment or employment relationship'.[83] The result is that the extent to which workers can rely on the Directives for employment security depends on the terms on which each member state has implemented the Directive in its domestic law, and there are wide variations.[84] This must be borne in mind when considering the aims of the worker-participation Directives, as there is by no means any guarantee that these aims are perfectly mirrored in domestic law.

Employment protection at the European level has its origin in industrial traditions which conceptualize employment as being founded upon a private law contract, but *also* giving rise to a special relationship regulated by principles of public law which grants workers a form of constitutional entitlement to remain in their jobs

78 Paul Davis, 'Recent Cases: Transfer Regulations' (1988) 17 *Industrial Law Journal* 249–53 at 249.

79 See for example *Schmidt v Spar-* Case 392/92 (1994).

80 Stephen Hardy, 'The Acquired Rights Directive: A Case of Economic and Social Rights at Work' in Hugh Collins, Paul Davies and Ronald Rideout (eds.), *Legal Regulation of the Employment Relation* (London: Kluwer Law International, 2000).

81 Council Directive 2001/86/EC and Council Directive 2002/14/EC.

82 Catherine Barnard, *EC Employment Law* (2nd ed.) (Oxford: Oxford University Press, 2000) at 448.

83 Article 2(2). 'The question whether or not a contract or relationship of employment exists at the date of the transfer must, however, be assessed on the basis of national law': *d'Urso v Ercole Marelli* Case 362/89 (1992) at par. 12.

84 Barnard, *EC Employment Law* at 448.

unless there is just cause for their dismissal.[85] While the employment relationship in the UK is generally governed entirely by the law of contract, governed by the terms of the agreement between the contracting parties, in continental Europe it is generally understood to fall within the realm of 'public' law governed by principles of constitutional law within the sphere of social law and policy. For instance in German law dismissal, even with notice, must be 'socially justified' otherwise it is 'illegal'; selection of employees for redundancy 'must take into account so called "social aspects" [so] that those who suffer the most from the effects of the dismissal should be the last ones to be dismissed ... social justice for each individual case'.[86] In the UK, by contrast, it is trite law that the courts would not take 'social policy' into account in the interpretation of contractual or statutory employment rights, in the absence of express terms requiring them to do so. It is important not to overstate the extent of this divergence, bearing in mind the contractual basis of European law and the statutory framework of employment protection in the UK, but in understanding the implementation of the European Directives in different member states it is nevertheless important to acknowledge divergent approaches to the interpretation of the employment relationship.[87]

These differences in the conceptualization of the employment relationship, and the appropriate scope of social welfare and policy, inevitably affect the implementation of European Directives in different member states. To take the example of the Information and Consultation Directive (ICD), the ICD grants workers rights of 'information and consultation' allowing them to participate in decision-making through meaningful prior consultation. In some states such as Germany and France a decision arrived at without such prior consultation with employee representatives is generally (subject to specified conditions) voidable or even void. The result is that the employment relationship continues.[88] By contrast in the UK the Information and Consultation of Employees Regulations which implement the ICD impose a maximum penalty of £75,000 for failure to consult with workers. This penalty is imposed by way of a fine payable to the Secretary of State, leaving the employees no real remedy

85 For a discussion of French law see Freedland, 'Employment Law'. For German law see Weiss, 'Individual Employment Rights.'

86 Weiss, 'Individual Employment Rights' discussing the Act on Dismissal Protection of 1951 (s.1) at 86 and 88. This law has close parallels with UK unfair dismissal law under the Employment Rights Act 1996. In both countries certain grounds of dismissal enjoy greater protection than the ordinary case, e.g. dismissal of pregnant women; importantly, both countries allow 'economic reasons' to constitute a defence to an unfair dismissal claim.

87 For a more nuanced discussion see Freedland, 'Employment Law' and Wedderburn, 'Labour Law: From Here to Autonomy?'

88 For a fuller discussion see Sylvaine Laulom, 'The European Court of Justice in the Dialogue on Transfers of Undertakings: A Fallible Interlocutor?' in Silvana Sciara (ed.), *Labour Law in the Courts: National Judges and the European Court of Justice* (Oxford: Hart, 2001); and Marlene Frank, 'The Rights of Employees in the Event of the Employer's Insolvency: A Comparative Approach to the Rights of Employees in the United States and Europe' (2005) 1 *New Zealand Postgraduate Law e-Journal* 1–45.

and the employer with what amounts to an incentive to commit an 'efficient breach' of the law if the costs of employee consultation are likely to exceed the maximum fine or, which is equally significant, if consultation costs are unpredictable. While other member states see financial penalties as the exception, in the UK they are the almost invariable rule.[89] Otto Kahn-Freund remarked on this British tendency to 'dilute' European measures which vest substantive rights in workers.[90] Lord Wedderburn describes this as 'the curbing of legislation by the bridle of common law interpretation', observing that 'within the stockade of employment protection in Britain, the erosion of workers' rights by common law orientations in meaning and interpretation is now notorious'.[91] As the law presently stands, the inevitable result of translating these rights into the common law contractual framework is to render these rights subject to the general rule that the breach of contract sounds only in damages. This example illustrates the significance of the current Anglo-American understanding of employment rights as purely contractual. In discussing the differences between the laws of member states regarding the remedies available for breach of European Directives, Lord Slynn of Hadley in *Baxendale v British Fuels* said:

> As I have already said, in English law there would as a general rule be no order for specific performance. The claim would be for damages for wrongful dismissal or for statutory rights including, it is true, reinstatement or re-engagement where applicable. It may be in other countries that an order for specific performance could be obtained under the appropriate domestic law and that on this approach different results would be achieved in different member states. That I do not find surprising or shocking. The Directive is to 'approximate' the laws of the member states … The 'rights' of an employee must depend on national rules of the law of contract or of legislation. There is no Community law of contract common to member states, nor is there a common system of remedies.[92]

If employment rights are understood as proprietary then it becomes easier to explain why some European member states require prior employee *consent* to specified decisions, the absence of which invalidates the decision. This perspective derives support from Guido Calabresi and Douglas Melamed's depiction of property law as a body of rules about entitlements. They defined property rules as rules which protect 'entitlements' by providing that the holder of the entitlement cannot be deprived of it unless she gives advance consent and both parties agree concerning

89 The Employment Rights Act includes remedies of re-engagement and reinstatement, but an employer who refuses to comply with a re-engagement or reinstatement order simply has to pay special damages. In any event these remedies are not much used, and nowhere is the employer's decision declared void.

90 Otto Kahn-Freund, 'On Uses and Misuses of Comparative Law' (1974) 37 *Modern Law Review* 1–27 at 23. This is an example (he cites others) of a tendency for this to occur when law is transplanted from one jurisdiction to another.

91 Wedderburn of Charlton, 'Labour Law: From Here to Autonomy?' at 7.

92 [1999] 2 A.C. 52 at 84.

the appropriate measure of compensation: 'someone who wishes to remove the entitlement from its holder must buy it from him in a voluntary transaction in which the value of the entitlement is agreed upon by the seller'.[93] Calabresi and Melamed distinguish entitlements protected by property rules from 'inalienable' entitlements which law does not allow to be sold (at any price), and entitlements protected by 'liability' rules where there is no requirement for prior consent or negotiation – the holder of the entitlement must be content with whatever compensatory award is determined ex post by the courts.[94] Neither Anglo-American nor European law applies the concept of inalienability to the employment context. Generally speaking the predominant preference in Anglo-American law is for liability rules, so that wrongful dismissal is remedied by damages for breach of contract, while the predominant preference in European law is for property rules, so that wrongful dismissal is declared void (subject, of course, to the court finding that the dismissal in question *was* wrongful).

This suggests that the proprietary perspective of employment rights in the firm offers more generous scope than the contractual framework in promoting job security during corporate restructuring, at least so far as the interpretation of the statutory framework of job security emanating from European law is concerned. This would arguably be more consistent with the European understanding of the employment relationship in the firm. This is not to say that the employment relationship in European law is understood as proprietary, merely that within the Calabresi and Melamed framework it appears more consistent with property rules than with liability rules. European law is not constrained by the need to reconcile employment protection with 'freedom of contract' or, to be more accurate, by the Anglo-American tendency to give greater consideration to freedom of contract than employment protection.[95] More significantly, as Anderman has pointed out, European employment protection law does not rely on the conceptual building blocks of contract and so has not faced the considerable difficulties which result for the UK in trying to squeeze European law into a contractual framework.[96] For those who consider that the European worker participation norms offer a better deal for workers the proprietary framework may

---

93 Calabresi and Melamed, at 1092.

94 'someone may destroy the initial entitlement if he is willing to pay an objectively determined value for it' (at 1092).

95 Freedom of contract is of course an important value in European law (see Richardi), but it is not deemed to be put directly in issue by employment protection in quite the same way. Freedom of contract becomes important where 'in a case of grave misconduct or other urgent reason it was no longer tolerable for either of the two parties to continue the employment relationship' but is not deemed to be incompatible with job security: Weiss, 'Individual Employment Rights' at 84–5.

96 Anderman, 'The Interpretation of Protective Employment Statutes'. He describes the European legislation as a restriction on 'the employer's exclusive right to dispose of his "property" in the job' and therefore, it could be said, effecting a reallocation of property rights in the employment relationship in the firm: 'Termination of Employment' at 106.

offer a useful theoretical framework for assessing the incorporation of similar norms into Anglo-American law.

Regarding prospects for the 'approximation' or harmonization of European law, Manfred Weiss observes that the probable effect of the EU Directives on member states will be to stimulate a more conducive environment for employees: 'countries with a tradition of exclusively adversarial structures have no longer a choice but to restructure their systems towards a concept of partnership and cooperation.'[97] Weiss notes the weaknesses and deficiencies of the various Directives, but also suggests that the very existence of these Directives promotes greater awareness among member states of the value of worker participation. In the UK the Directives have been more warmly welcomed by trade unions than by the Confederation of British Industry (which deemed the worker participation Directives 'extremely unhelpful'[98]), but both sides of industry acknowledge their potential significance for the employment relationship within the firm.[99] Meanwhile, owing to this radically different way of understanding the employment relationship the implementation of the resulting Directives has proved considerably more problematic in the UK than in other member states.

This is best illustrated by reference to the Acquired Rights Directive (ARD) which was introduced to automatically transfer jobs to the new employer during transfers of undertakings. The next part of the discussion compares European and American law governing transfers of undertakings, considering the effect of a transfer on the status of the contract of employment. The focus is on the ARD and the American National Labor Relations Act (NLRA). The discussion then considers the implications of protecting employee interests in situations of insolvency. The interface between the NLRA and the Bankruptcy Code in the US is contrasted with the tension in UK law between the ARD and insolvency practice. The stakeholder model is then used as a theoretical framework in explaining the legislative rights which conceptualize the corporation as a social institution and enhance job security. Some observations are made as to the comparative degree to which the English and American legislative frameworks recognize property rights in work.

The Acquired Rights Directive

A crucial issue that must be settled when the company undergoes a change in its ownership structure is the continuity of the contract of employment. Transfers of undertakings typically involve dismissal of the workers, and the extent to which employers act unilaterally in these situations reveals much about the status of employees within the firm. Regulation in this area may be interpreted as a recognition that the employees' relationship with the firm should not invariably be

97 'The Future of Workers' Participation in the EU' at 249.

98 Lionel Fulton, 'UK' in Simons and Kluge at 131.

99 See for example the Confederation of British Industry report, *Cutting Through Red Tape: the Impact of Employment Legislation* (1999).

governed by the ordinary rules of contract law. The idea that employees have an interest in 'continuity of employment' which ought to be protected during corporate restructuring may be seen as an aspect of property in the firm. The explicit purpose of the ARD as stated in its preamble is 'to provide for the protection of employees in the event of a change of employer, in particular, to ensure that their rights are safeguarded'.[100]

The political impetus behind the ARD was to enlist the cooperation of workers in the project of forging a common market in Europe, a project which was expected to inevitably entail significant corporate restructuring.[101] It was part of the general ethos of European economic policy, that the single market could not be achieved without regard to social policy. The protection and preservation of employee rights has therefore been the predominant concern of the European Court of Justice (ECJ) in interpreting the scope and effect of the ARD.[102] According to the ECJ the aim of the ARD in preserving the pre-existing terms and conditions of the employees affected by a transfer is 'to safeguard the rights of workers … by making it possible for them to continue to work for the new employer on the same conditions as those agreed with the transferor'.[103] The ARD provides that 'the transferor's rights and obligations arising from a contract of employment or from an employment relationship existing on the date of the transfer shall, by reason of such transfer, be transferred to the transferee'.[104] Therefore all the workers employed in the undertaking transferred are automatically transferred to the transferee by the mere fact of the transfer.[105] The transfer 'shall not in itself constitute grounds for dismissal' by either the old or the new employer, except for 'economic, technical or organisational reasons entailing changes in the workforce'.[106] Acquired rights include not just wages and other payments due under the employment contract such as holiday or overtime pay, but also entitlements to statutory compensation for redundancy and unfair dismissal.

The intricacies of the ARD cannot be explored adequately within the confines of this discussion. Instead an overview will be given of its aims, scope and impact.[107]

---

100 Preamble to the Acquired Rights Directive, third recital.

101 Paul Davies, 'Transfers of Undertakings' in Sciara (ed.).

102 See for example *Schmidt*.

103 *d'Urso,* at par. 9.

104 Article 3(1).

105 *d'Urso*, at par 1.

106 Article 4(1).

107 For a comprehensive analysis see John McMullen, 'An Analysis of the Transfer of Undertakings (Protection of Employment) Regulations 2006' (2006) 35 *Industrial Law Journal* 113–39. To avoid the risk of oversimplification it should be noted that the test of a relevant 'transfer' falling within the remit of the ARD depends on the existence of a number of factors but 'all those circumstances are merely single factors in the overall assessment which must be made and cannot, therefore, be considered in isolation': *Spijkers v Gebroeders* Case 24/85 (1986) at par. 13. These factors include 'the type of business, whether or not the tangible assets, such as buildings and movable property are transferred, the value of its intangible assets at the time of the transfer, whether or not the majority of its employees are taken over

Relevant transfers include takeovers, mergers, outsourcing (transfer of service contracts) and asset sales, but do not include acquisitions effected through transfers of shares. Apart from the exception for the sale of shares the ECJ does not make a distinction based on the corporate law nature of the transfer such as whether it was a sale or a merger, as the Directive applies 'regardless of whether or not ownership of the undertaking is transferred'.[108] It covers 'any legal change' including a transfer of operations from one subsidiary to another within the same corporate group.[109] The applicability of the ARD does not depend on the number of workers affected and has been held to apply where only one worker was involved.[110] The Directive applies even when the service contracts transferred involved activities 'merely ancillary' to the business[111] and applies to both 'public and private undertakings engaged in economic activities whether or not they are operating for gain.'[112] It generally does not make a difference whether the transaction involves the sale or transfer of tangible or intangible assets. The crucial factor is whether the undertaking retains its identity.[113]

The reach of the ARD is not easy to escape. Although there is an exception where the dismissal is for economic, technical or organizational reasons the ECJ in the *d'Urso* case rejected the argument that it should adopt an interpretation of the ARD that does not 'curtail freedom to carry on business', holding that 'such a restrictive effect is inherent in the very purpose of the Directive which is to ensure that in the interests of employees the obligations arising under contracts or relationships of employment are transferred to the transferee'.[114] The ARD also grants workers rights to be given information 'in good time' regarding all matters relating to the transfer, including the expected 'legal, economic and social implications … for the employees.' They also have a right to be consulted 'in good time on such measures with a view to reaching an agreement'.[115] The ARD is not hampered by the concept of reciprocity which has impeded the development of similar rights at common law: the automatic transfer binds both parties but the employee, though not the employer, may subsequently object if he or she does not wish to work for the new employer.[116]

---

by the new employer, whether or not its customers are transferred and the degree of similarity between the activities carried on before and after the transfer and the period, if any, for which those activities were suspended' (at par. 12).

108 *Foreningen v Daddy's Dance Hall* Case 324/86 (1988) at par. 9.

109 *Allen v Amalgamated Construction Co.* Case 234/98 (2000).

110 *Schmidt*.

111 Under Article 1(1)(b) 'there is a transfer within the meaning of this Directive where there is a transfer of an economic entity which retains its identity, meaning and organised grouping of resources which has the objective of pursuing an economic activity, whether or not that activity is central or ancillary' (Regulation 3(2) TUPE 2006).

112 Regulation 3(4)(a) of TUPE 2006.

113 *Suzen v Zehnacker* Case 13/95 (1997).

114 *d'Urso*, at par. 15.

115 Article 7(1) and (2).

116 *Katsikas v Konstantinidis* Case 132/91 (1993).

This is in contrast with the common law doctrine of mutuality which generally maintains that 'if the contract of employment be not binding on the employee … then it cannot be binding upon the employer'.[117]

The English courts have been remarkably astute to prevent employers from avoiding the ARD, by adopting a broad interpretation of what constitutes a 'relevant' transfer and a narrow construction of the 'economic, technical or organizational' defence.[118] This may seem surprising in view of the fact that it goes against the common law freedom of contract. Paul Davies observes that while 'the British judiciary might have been expected to be unhappy with [an ECJ] decision which maximised the level of the Directive's interference' with freedom of contract, 'that argument assumes a high level of attachment on the part of the British courts to freedom of contract in the area of social policy'. In fact the British courts have 'paid close attention to the decisions of the ECJ', showing 'how quickly national views on the proper approaches to principles of Community law can develop, even when those principles are new to the domestic system'.[119] Nevertheless, despite the broad reach of the ARD the reciprocity inherent in contract has not been entirely uprooted from English law. It would be injudicious to assume that the ARD and other Directives make it unnecessary to look back at the pre-existing common law rules which are now superseded by European law, because the common law values continue to influence judicial interpretation of the implementing regulations.[120]

Impact of the ARD on English Law

The ARD was for the most part consistent with the existing laws in continental Europe. For instance French law provided that 'if there is a change in the juridical situation of an employer, for example, as a result of succession, sale, or fusion, all contracts of employment existing on the date of the transfer will continue between the new employer and the employees of the enterprise'.[121] On this Freedland comments:

> This conception of the transferability of the acquired rights of the employee provided a significant model for the EC Acquired Rights Directive, so that this Directive, which amounted to a bombshell in British employment law, both because of its conceptual unfamiliarity and its unexpected practical impact, causes very little perturbation in French employment law.[122]

---

117 *Pitcher v United Oil & Gas Syndicate, Inc.* 174 La. 66 (1932) at 69.

118 See *Litster v Forth Dry Dock & Engineering Co.* (1989) I.R.L.R. 161 and *ECM (Vehicle Delivery Service) Ltd v Cox* [1999] I.R.L.R. 559. For a discussion of the courts' approach to TUPE see John McMullen, 'Takeovers, Transfers and Business Re-Organizations' (1992) 21 *Industrial Law Journal* 15–30.

119 Paul Davies, 'Transfers of Undertakings' at 139–40.

120 See Kahn-Freund, 'On Uses and Misuses of Comparative Law'.

121 Barnard, *EC Employment Law* at 446, citing L122–12, al 2 *Code du Travail.*

122 Freedland, 'Employment Law' at 474. He notes that France had 'no need for a major internal measure to implement the Directive' such as the British TUPE, and 'certainly nothing

In France and Italy the role of works councils in employment protection was complemented by the legal enforceability of employment contracts on the transfer of a business since the 1920s (and later in Germany).[123] These laws recognized not only the workers' interest in job security but also the interest of the new employer in receiving, along with the new business, a ready-trained workforce. In contrast English law did not allow these interests to obscure the fact that on a transfer of a business the contractual relationship between the employer and employee simply terminates.[124] As with a contract of service between individuals the contract comes to an end if one of the parties becomes incapable of performing his part of the contract.[125]

The common law rule on the automatic termination of employment contracts when the employer undertaking is transferred is illustrated by *Nokes v Doncaster Amalgamated Collieries, Ltd.* where the House of Lords held that the existing employment contract with the company is automatically terminated on the transfer of the undertaking.[126] Mr Nokes, a coalminer, absented himself from work after he discovered that a new company had taken over ownership of the mines. Coalminers were under a statutory duty not to absent themselves from work while subject to a contract of service, and the new owner sought to make Mr Nokes liable for breach of this duty.[127] The employer argued that contracts of employment were transferred along with the company under the relevant provisions of the Companies Act which provided for the transfer of all the company's property and rights, and that the change in the identity of the employer company was 'a matter of indifference to the employees' so their obligation to work should continue unaffected.[128] The House of Lords rejected this contention, finding instead that the transfer provisions of the Companies Act did not include contracts of employment.[129] At common law there

corresponding to the furore over the effect of those Regulations' (at note 31).

123 Davies, 'Transfers of Undertakings'. James H. Bergeron, 'Global Dynamics of (Un)Fair Employment: Proceedings of the 2000 Annual Meeting of the Association of American Law Schools, Section on Employment Discrimination Law' (2000) 4 *Employee Rights and Employment Policy Journal* 141–64.

124 Damages may however lie for wrongful dismissal; see *Brace v Calder* [1895] 2 Q.B. 253.

125 *Farrow v Wilson* (1869) L.R. 4 C.P. 744, 766: if a contract of service is between individuals and the employer dies, the contract of service is immediately terminated and does not pass to the employer's personal representatives.

126 [1940] A.C.1014.

127 Under s.4 of the Employers and Workmen Act 1875.

128 'If the employer is a company, the servant can have no direct contact with the artificial entity but of necessity deals with and acts under the orders of the company's agents. Moreover, the change involved in a wage earner serving the new company in place of the old is, in normal cases, no greater than the change he would experience when the company which he is serving throughout changes its directors, its shareholders, its managers, its scope of operations, and its name, all of which it may do without losing its identity' (at 1020–21).

129 The Companies Act 1929 provided that: 'Where an application is made to the Court ... the whole or any part of the undertaking or the property of any company concerned in the

is no automatic transfer of contracts of employment when a business changes hands and on the relevant principles of statutory interpretation the Law Lords did not think the wording of the Companies Act would allow such an effect. The outcome in *Nokes* may have been influenced by the fact that it was not an action by a servant seeking to protect his job, but by an employer seeking to impose liability, by way of a fine, on the servant absenting himself from work. The Law Lords considered the liberty of the servant to be at stake, Lord Atkin remarking 'I had fancied that ingrained in the personal status of a citizen under our laws was the right to choose for himself whom he would serve: and that this right of choice constituted the main difference between a servant and a serf'.[130] They therefore favoured a restrictive interpretation of the statute.

The Court of Appeal in *Nokes* had taken a stance more consistent with current law under the ARD, in deciding that allowing a transfer to automatically terminate contracts of employment with no provision for compensation would defeat the common law rights of servants.[131] Sir Wilfrid Greene M.R. observed that excluding contracts of employment from the transfer provisions

> would be remarkable and unfortunate. For the transferee company would start its career without taking over a single employee of the transferor company … The position of the [servants] would be equally unfortunate, since by the dissolution of the transferor company their remedy against it, if any, would have disappeared and all that they could do (and even their right to do this is by no means clear) would be to sue the transferee company for breach of the contract by repudiation on the part of the transferor company – if indeed any such breach could in the circumstances be attributed to that company.[132]

Unlike the House of Lords, the Court of Appeal was not impressed by the argument that the transfer of employment contracts would reduce servants to serfs: 'This is

---

scheme (in this section referred to as "a transferor company") is to be transferred to another company (in this section referred to as "the transferee company"), the Court may [by order] make provision for all or any of the following matters:- (a) the transfer to the transferee company of the whole or any part of the undertaking and of the property or liabilities of any transferor company…In this section the expression "property" includes property, rights and powers of every description, and the expression "liabilities" includes duties' (ss.154 (1) and (4)). The Court of Appeal held that 'when an order of the Court is made under the section transferring to a transferee company the property, rights, powers and liabilities of transferor companies, a written contract of service, entered into between one of the transferor companies and an employee, becomes binding on the transferee company and the employee' (Donoghue v Doncaster Amalgamated Collieries, Ltd. [1939] 2 K.B. 578 at 578).

130 At 1026.

131 At 580.

132 At 584–5. The House of Lords dealt with the first point by saying there was nothing preventing the new employer offering new contracts of employment to the old workers, and the old employer stating to its workers that any who continued working after the transfer would be deemed to have accepted the offer of a new contract with the new employer.

the language of hyperbole and does not, in our opinion, advance the argument'.[133] In reversing the Court of Appeal the House of Lords established that English law did not allow the automatic transfer of employment relationships on the transfer of undertakings. The impact of the ARD on English law was therefore significantly more far-reaching than it was in other member states – hence Anderman's observation that 'the impact of the Acquired Rights Directive … on the "property" rights of UK firms initially produced shocks of a seismic scale'.[134]

The UK has implemented the ARD by means of financial penalties for breach. A worker dismissed by reason of a relevant transfer is treated as having been unfairly dismissed, and is entitled to statutory compensation under the ordinary unfair dismissal legislation.[135] In other member states such as France the effect of dismissing workers in breach of the ARD is to render the employees' dismissal void; the *Cour de Cassation* has held that 'dismissals prior to a transfer of an undertaking were to be treated as null and void'.[136] In the English context the House of Lords declined the invitation in *Baxendale v British Fuels* to take a similar approach. The Law Lords took the view that 'the transferor's liability is to pay damages or to comply with an order under the relevant employment legislation for compensation or reinstatement, but it is not to continue actually to employ the employee he has dismissed'.[137] Too much should not be made of the reinstatement remedy, as it is rarely used and breach of a reinstatement order simply means paying special damages. This interpretation is qualitatively distinct from that of other member states that focus not on damages and compensation but on the continuing employment relationship. It could be said that the European approach is more consistent with the reasoning of the Court Appeal in *Nokes*. It is instructive that in *Baxendale* the House of Lords did not, at an analytical and conceptual level, depart as dramatically from its reasoning in *Nokes* as might have been expected after the intervention of the ARD. That the ARD has not effected a preference for the approach of the Court of Appeal in *Nokes* may be attributed to the fact that the ARD is based on a different conception of the role and status of the employee in the company from that which has hitherto prevailed in the UK.[138] This argument is developed further below.

133 At 585.

134 Anderman, 'Termination of Employment' at 107.

135 Under Regulation 7 of TUPE 2006, applying the Employment Rights Act 1996 Part X.

136 Laulom, at 175, discussing Cass. Soc., 20 Jan. 1998 (1998) *Droit Social* 1023. See Frank.

137 [1998] 3 W.L.R.1070 at 1081.

138 Nigel H.D. Foster, 'Company Law Theory in Comparative Perspective: England and France' (2000) 48 *American Journal of Comparative Law* 573–621.

The TUPE Regulations

The Transfer of Undertakings (Protection of Employment) Regulations (TUPE), were passed to implement the ARD in the UK.[139] They ensure that terms and conditions of employment are not affected by transfers of the employer, and give employees rights of information and consultation before the transfer. Armour and Deakin have highlighted various ways in which the TUPE Regulations limit the power of management to avoid their responsibility towards their employees by restructuring the enterprise, arguing that TUPE limits the company's ability to make decisions with exclusive reference to shareholder interests and allows employee interests to be factored into the decision-making process, thereby often enhancing the survival chances of enterprises undergoing restructuring.[140] TUPE may therefore be understood as an important avenue for recognizing employee rights within the framework of corporate law.

The greatest potential of TUPE lies not just in the automatic transfer of employment contracts or the rights of information and consultation, but also in conferring substantial bargaining power on employee representatives in the restructuring context. As was noted in Chapter 2 bargaining power may be seen as an attribute of ownership when it amounts to genuine decision-making capability. The 'owner' in a theory of the firm is the party who exercises rights of control; the exercise of control rights is in turn determined by the bargaining position or power of the firm's participants. In this sense ownership rights influence decision-making during restructuring, determining the effectiveness with which the parties are able to protect their interests. The best example of this effect is where TUPE acts as a 'governance lever'.[141] The capacity of trade unions, acting on behalf of thousands of workers, to initiate litigation for statutory unfair dismissal and redundancy payments which may run into 'hundreds and hundreds of millions of pounds' guarantees them a place at the bargaining table and a major role in influencing the outcome of the negotiations.[142] If ownership is understood as decision-making authority then TUPE places employees, if they have effective union representation, in this role.

The precise nature of the rights conferred on employees by the TUPE Regulations has inspired much debate. They could be described simply as statutory rights but this still leaves open the question of their underlying conceptual nature. It is not at first easy to understand how the common law of contract might explain what happens to the status of employees when the purchaser is *obliged* by TUPE to take on all existing employees, with the inevitable result that an element of control over

139 Transfer of Undertakings (Protection of Employment) Regulations 2006 (SI 2006 No 246), replacing the initial 1981 Regulations as amended.

140 This is not the invariable outcome: in situations of insolvency TUPE may 'tip the scales against a successful reorganisation': at 460–61.

141 Armour and Deakin, at 458.

142 Armour and Deakin, at 459 discussing the case of *Rover* (above, note 302).

the restructuring process is lost.[143] As will be seen below the comparable American statutory duty to bargain with employee representatives in the context of a transfer obliges the new employer to enter into good faith negotiations with the transferor's employees, but does not impose an obligation to employ them on the same terms and conditions, nor is there statutory liability for breach of these terms and conditions. The notion of statutory 'novation' of the employment contract after the transfer of an undertaking is not easily reconciled with the common law of contract: the House of Lords in *Nokes* said that very clear language would be needed to effect such a result. Although TUPE now supplies the necessary clear terminology of transfer the concept of such automatic novation, creation of a new employment relationship out of the old which is not effected by agreement between the parties, appears at first sight to be conceptually problematic.

Freedland has suggested a clear and helpful way of understanding TUPE within the contractual framework. He explains the effect of TUPE as a statutory 'transformation' of the contract or more precisely a transformation of the parties to the contract.[144] Although the contract is terminated (the contract with the old employer no longer subsists) TUPE allows the employees' rights to subsist in post-employment mode.[145] These rights are then made enforceable against the new employer by the mechanism of a statutory sub-transfer. This is understood from a contractual perspective by reference to the idea of the 'elasticity of the concept of the employing entity'.[146] The implication of Freedland's approach is that under TUPE the contract of employment is not really 'transferred' in 'full employment mode' from one party to another, but merely deemed to continue in existence because the true identity of the employer has not really changed – there has merely been a change in the share ownership of the employing entity or in the ownership of the tangible and intangible assets of the employing entity (a partial transformation of the employing entity). This argument parallels the reasoning of the Court of Appeal in *Nokes* which found that the transfer provisions of the Companies Act could in this way effect a transfer of the employment contracts.[147]

Freedland's interpretation offers a useful way of understanding the view taken by the House of Lords in *Baxendale v British Fuels*.[148] This case is authority for

143 For the potential scope for 'avoiding' or 'contracting out of' TUPE see McMullen.

144 Freedland, *The Personal Employment Contract* at 408–9 and 506–14; either a 'full' or a 'partial transformation' of the parties: 491–515.

145 At 108: 'a personal employment contract should be regarded as continuing to exist, but in post-employment mode, after a period of contractual employment has ended and after there have ceased to be any mutual obligations regarding the resumptions of employment'.

146 At 492. He notes at 499: 'thus an actual transformation of the employing party may be permitted, contrary to general doctrine, partly on the basis that it seems to be similar to, or little more than, an internal change of management, and partly on the basis that it seems to be similar to, or little more than, a partial transformation rather than a complete one'.

147 As Freedland argues, 'the logic of [*Nokes*] might be regarded as excluding total novation but permitting partial novation': at 498.

148 [1998] 3 W.L.R.1070.

the proposition that a dismissal rendered *unfair* by regulation 7 of TUPE (2006) is nevertheless *effective*. All TUPE does is allow the dismissed employee to seek damages for unfair dismissal against the transferee. *Baxendale* established that TUPE does not confer a substantive right to continue in actual employment with the transferee. While a transfer of an undertaking does not automatically extinguish an employee's relationship with the firm, but automatically transfers it to the new 'owner', an actual dismissal is not void and the employee cannot compel the transferee to employ him on the same terms and conditions as he had previously enjoyed, or indeed at all. This suggests that the contract of employment has in fact not been transferred; it is the *remedy* for breach that has been made available as against the transferee. Freedland explains this by saying that the effect of the dismissal is to shift the employment contract into 'post-employment mode'. In post-employment mode some of the employee's contractual claims (actual employment) have been extinguished while others (compensation) subsist. TUPE effects a 'contractual sub-transfer' of the subsisting post-employment rights and obligations. Freedland's analysis thus translates the effect of the ARD into contractual language allowing it to be better understood.

However in understanding the purpose and function of TUPE and trying to reconcile its underlying ideology with that of the ARD as interpreted by the ECJ a different focus may be required. By saying that the employment relationship is not itself transferred, but only some of the post-employment rights such as a claim for damages for unfair dismissal are transferred, *Baxendale* diverts attention from the ECJ's emphasis on 'making it possible for [employees] to continue to work for the new employer on the same conditions as those agreed with the transferor.'[149] In this sense *Baxendale* does not meet the aim of the ARD which, as described by Paul Davies, is to ensure that the transferee takes on the employees of the company it acquires, thereby protecting the employees' 'social expectation of continued employment'.[150] In falling short of ensuring continued employment *Baxendale* illustrates that it is quite problematic to choose the framework of contract as the best mechanism through which to implement the ARD. In *d'Urso* the ECJ reaches a result which is more consistent with the ARD, emphasizing the irrelevance of the parties' agreement even when arrived at after voluntary collective bargaining:

> the rules of the Directive had to be considered to be mandatory, so that it was not possible to derogate from them in a manner unfavourable to employees. The implementation of the rights conferred on employees by the Directive may not therefore be made subject to the consent of either the transferor or the transferee nor the consent of the employees' representatives or the employees themselves, with the sole reservation, as regards the workers themselves, that, following a decision freely taken by them, they are at liberty, after the transfer, not to continue the employment relationship with the new employer.[151]

---

149 *d'Urso*, at par. 9.

150 Davies, 'Recent Cases: Transfer Regulations' at 249.

151 *d'Urso*, at par. 11. For a discussion of this point of law see Laulom and McMullen.

In previous cases which, like *d'Urso*, involved employees who did not want their employment contracts to transfer, the court held that an 'employee cannot waive the rights conferred upon him by the mandatory provisions' of the ARD, and that the contract of employment was transferred 'even if the workers employed in the undertaking did not consent or if they object'.[152] The ARD asserts that although a transfer has taken place, it is not effective to terminate the rights of employees of the old employing entity, and goes further, on the reasoning in these cases, to provide that the parties are not at liberty to agree otherwise. The court in *d'Urso* added that 'it follows that in the event of the transfer of an undertaking, the contract of employment or employment relationship between the staff employed by the undertaking transferred may not be maintained with the transferor' (the old employer), not even by agreement between the parties.[153] This impedes the contractual freedom of both employer and employee: 'the rules of the Directive apply to all parties, including the employees' trade union representatives, who may not derogate from them by means of agreements concluded with the transferee or the transferor'.[154] In *d'Urso* the Italian government argued that such an interpretation of the ARD 'would curtail freedom to carry on business' and 'would call in question agreements made with trade-union organizations concerning the detailed transfer arrangements and the number of employees to be transferred'. As mentioned earlier the ECJ rejected this argument holding that 'such a restrictive effect is inherent in the very purpose of the Directive which is to ensure that in the interests of employees the obligations arising under contracts or relationships of employment are transferred to the transferee'.[155] The ECJ therefore emphasizes the transfer of the employment relationship, rather than the transfer of certain contractual rights and obligations, holding that dismissal contrary to the ARD is ineffective so that the employees 'must be regarded as still in the employ of the undertaking'.[156] It could therefore be said that the intention of the ARD as it affects English law is not merely to introduce 'implied terms', favourable to employees, into their employment contracts, but to create an entirely new framework of rights independent of contract.

152 In *Daddy's Dance Hall*, and *Berg v Ivo Martin* Case 144/87 (1988) respectively. The ECJ stated in *Daddy's Dance Hall* that both parties can agree to vary terms and conditions of employment affected by a transfer of undertaking, 'provided that the transfer of the undertaking itself may never constitute the reason for that amendment' (at par. 17), which goes against the ethos of contract.

153 *d'Urso*, at par. 12. The case is different where part only of an undertaking is transferred, in which case the transferor may retain employees who are not working within the transferred part: *Botzen v Rotterdamsche Droogdok* Case 186/83 (1986).

154 *d'Urso*, at par. 17.

155 *d'Urso*, at par. 15.

156 *Bork v Foreningen* Case 101/87 (1989).

TUPE Rights as Property Rights

The foregoing principle is implemented in UK law by the rule in TUPE that 'any purported variation of the contract shall be void if the sole or principle reason for the variation is (a) the transfer itself; or (b) a reason connected with the transfer'.[157] Armour and Deakin contend that by ensuring that workers' interests cannot be abrogated without their consent TUPE superimposes onto the common law a new framework of rights which is recognizably proprietary, ensuring that the employees' terms and conditions of employment become binding on the transferor and cannot be altered to the employees' detriment or indeed at all. One of the ways in which a distinction is made between contract and property is that contractual rights are personal (the doctrine of privity ensures that they do not ordinarily bind third parties) while property rights bind the entire world. This may be framed as the distinction between rights *in personam* and rights *in rem*. If the relationship between employees and the firm is understood as proprietary it at once becomes clear why and how the employees' rights and status in the firm should bind the firm's successor. Under TUPE existing or 'acquired' rights arising from employment automatically bind the purchaser of the undertaking; more signficantly, the 'liabilities – actual and potential – to employees … run with the assets of the enterprise'.[158] In this way TUPE adopts property rules to achieve an effect which would be 'impossibly costly to replicate by contract'.[159] The Regulations provide the type of protection afforded by property rules (in the Calabresi and Melamed sense) by ensuring that corporate decisions which affect employees adversely are not taken without their consent, and that the firm's successor is obliged to observe the employees' accrued rights in the firm.

The explanation of Armour and Deakin is elegant and persuasive in so far as it makes use of the well-understood terminology of property thereby avoiding the need to create new concepts to explain what TUPE does and how it achieves this effect. The only potential objection to a proprietary analysis is that it appears inconsistent with flexibility, and so appears at first sight less attractive than the reasoning of the House of Lords in *Baxendale* that TUPE rights sound only in damages. In the interests of flexibility the solution proposed by Armour and Deakin is to view the TUPE rights as 'contingent claims'. This proposal was discussed in Chapter 3 in defining the stakeholder interest. The point of note here is that understanding property rights as contingent claims explains TUPE's conferral of rights to information and consultation triggered in situations where employees' firm-specific interests are threatened by the transfer of the business. In this sense TUPE rights, by being activated only on the occurrence of certain contingencies, do not operate to automatically obstruct all organizational changes in the firm. The proprietary nature of TUPE rights is therefore qualified in an important aspect. As

157 Regulation 4(4), discussed in McMullen, 'The Transfer of Undertakings' at 127.

158 Armour and Deakin, at 452.

159 At 453.

explained earlier this does not impede the characterization of employees' rights as proprietary. It remains the case that the Regulations make it more difficult for an employer to unilaterally vary the terms and conditions of employment, and offer a significant measure of protection for employees. The Regulations also recognize, as Armour and Deakin point out, that employees have a claim not only to their contractual benefits, but also have a claim on the specific enterprise for which they work and to which their firm-specific human capital is bound. In this way TUPE may be seen as legal recognition that, as Anderman puts it, the property rights of employers are not absolute. Underlying the TUPE regime is an explicit acceptance of the link identified by Meyers between employees and their jobs, hence employees are granted a claim to retain their jobs when the undertaking is sold. This is one area where a proprietary stakeholder model of the firm may provide an alternative framework for understanding the employment relationship as well as for safeguarding employees' interests.

American Regulation of Transfers

In American law the primary statute governing the corporation's duty to its workers in the context of takeovers, mergers and transfers or sales is the National Labor Relations Act 1935 (NLRA).[160] This is expressed as a 'duty to bargain' with the relevant union; its significance therefore depends on whether the workers are unionized or whether there is a collective bargaining agreement in force. This duty to bargain is regulated by the five-member National Labor Relations Board under the doctrine of 'unfair labor practices'. Section 8 of the NLRA makes it an unfair labour practice for an employer or union to refuse to bargain collectively with the employees' authorized representative. The parties must 'meet at reasonable times and confer in good faith' but they do not have to come to an agreement. In a parallel to the ARD's 'economic, technical, organizational' defence the NLRA allows the employer to introduce unilateral changes without bargaining with the workers on grounds of 'business necessity'.[161]

The NLRA duty to bargain does not impose a statutory duty to hire the transferor's workers. According to Edward Rock and Michael Wachter, depending on how the transfer of the undertaking is structured in corporate law terms an employer may be able to avoid any obligation to the employees. In *Fall River*

160 29 U.S.C. §§ 151–69 (the Wagner Act, 1935), substantially amended by the Labor Management Relations Act 1947 (LMRA) 29 U.S.C. §§ 141–97 (the Taft-Hartley Act, 1947). The Worker Adjustment and Retraining Notification (WARN) Act provides that an employer with over 100 employees must give workers sixty days' notice of layoffs: 29 U.S.C. § 2101–09 (1988). The WARN Act has no provision for severance pay and according to Summers US employers prefer, as do their counterparts in the UK, to give their workers the required pay in lieu of notice. Also of interest is the duty to notify State 'dislocated worker rapid response units' under the job training legislation. A number of states also have legislation specifically intended to regulate redundancies and plant closures, discussed in Gould.

161 Chicoine.

Dyeing the US Supreme court held that when substantial continuity exists between the business of the asset seller (predecessor) and purchaser (successor), the successor has a duty to bargain with the workers' union if it takes the business together with the majority of the predecessor's employees; if over 50 percent of the existing workforce is retained then the duty to bargain is triggered. Crucially, because the successor has no duty to retain any workers the Court concluded that triggering the duty to bargain 'rests in the hands of the successor'.[162] It emerges from the analysis of this and other cases by Rock and Wachter that under the NLRA, as is the case under the ARD, it generally does not make a difference whether any assets have been acquired from the predecessor along with the workers; hiring the majority of workers will suffice.[163] Under the ARD the reverse is also true, that asset purchase by itself may be sufficient to trigger the ARD even if there is no intention to take on any workers.[164] This is not the case under the NLRA. A firm which merely purchases the assets of another, even if it purchases those assets in their entirety, does not automatically come under a duty to bargain with that firm's employees.[165] However, falling back on a contractual interpretation, such a duty may arise if there is evidence of actual or constructive agreement to assume the liabilities of the predecessor under an existing collective bargaining agreement (CBA). Similarly outsourcing and taking over out-contracted work is covered by the ARD but not by the NLRA – under the NLRA the new contractor has no obligation to the employees unless it has agreed to observe the terms of an existing CBA. Except in the case of mergers an employer can avoid the duty to bargain simply by not hiring a majority of the workers previously employed by the predecessor, an escape avenue expressly prohibited by the ARD.

The basis of the American approach, as described by Rock and Wachter, is that under the ordinary rules of contract law the purchaser of a business is free to take on an individual employment contract, but unless he does so he is not deemed to be automatically bound by it. The US Supreme Court therefore held in *Howard Johnson* that the successor employer is free not to hire the predecessors' employees,

---

162 *Fall River Dyeing & Finishing Corp. v NLRB* 482 U.S. 27 (1987) at 41. See discussion in Edward B. Rock and Michael L. Wachter, 'Labor Law Successorship: A Corporate Law Approach' (1993–94) 92 *Michigan Law Review* 203–60.

163 *NLRB v. Burns Int'l Security Servs., Inc.*, 406 U.S. 272, 288 (1972). Under the ARD the case may be different where tangible assets are central to the undertaking (*Oy Liikenne AB v Liskojarvi* Case 172/99 (2001)), but in *The Scottish Coal Company v McCormack* it has been doubted whether the distinction between 'labour intensive' and 'asset reliant' undertakings is crucial ([2005] C.S.I.H. 68) discussed in McMullen, 'The Transfer of Undertakings' at 121.

164 *ECM (Vehicle Delivery Service) Ltd v Cox* [1999] I.R.L.R. 559 (even more so if the reason no workers are taken on is to avoid the ARD). This may be different where the undertaking is labour-intensive: in that case it seems the transferee may avoid the ARD by not taking on the majority of the workers (*Betts v Brintel Helicopters Ltd* [1997] I.R.L.R. 361) but see *The Scottish Coal Company v McCormack* (ibid).

165 *Howard Johnson Co. v Detroit Local Joint Executive Board* 417 U.S. 249, 260–62, 264 (1974).

and free to offer employment on terms entirely different from those provided by the predecessor. Moreover if there is no express contractual provision to the contrary the predecessor employer has no duty to obtain the successor's undertaking to assume the existing contracts and retain the employees.[166] This law is therefore very similar to that in England before the ARD came into force. The law governing CBAs is similar to that governing individual employment contracts. Unless the successor company voluntarily assumes the CBA it is free to disregard it, even if the successor was aware of a contractual promise, by the predecessor to the union, to require assumption of the agreement by any successor. The union's remedies for such breach run only against the predecessor employer.[167] This remedy makes current American law more protective than English common law prior to the ARD when the position would have been governed by the common law rule that CBAs do not generally constitute legally binding contracts. However TUPE now provides that 'a collective agreement made by or on behalf of the transferor with a [recognized] trade union [shall] have effect as if made by or on behalf of the transferee with that trade union … as if the transferee were a party to the agreement'. This automatic transfer of CBAs results in a position substantially better for unionized workers in the UK than in the US.[168]

A brief glimmer of hope for greater employee protection in the US seemed to be offered by the US Supreme Court decision in *John Wiley & Sons v Livingstone* that an arbitration clause may survive the transfer, so that a successor employer may be required to submit to arbitration the question which contractual obligations of the predecessor, if any, survived the sale and remained binding on the successor.[169] The court ruled that 'the disappearance by merger of a corporate employer which has entered into a collective bargaining agreement with a union does not automatically terminate all rights of the employees covered by the agreement'.[170] This ruling implied that in such circumstances, the CBA itself would survive the transfer. It was recognized that employee interests are in need of protection because employees do not usually participate in decisions leading to a change in corporate ownership or any change in corporate structure, and their interests will rarely be considered in these negotiations despite the fact that they may be vitally affected. It was therefore held that 'the objectives of national labor policy, reflected in established principles of federal law, require that the rightful prerogative of owners independently to arrange their businesses and even eliminate themselves as employers be balanced by some protection to the employees from a sudden change in the employment relationship'.[171] This case appeared to limit employer prerogatives where employee interests were at stake. However *John Wiley* was not followed in later cases. In *NLRB v Burns Int'l*

166 *Howard Johnson*; and see *NLRB v Burns*.

167 *Howard Johnson*, at 258 note 3.

168 Regulation 5.

169 376 U.S. 543 (1964).

170 At 548.

171 At 549.

Security Services, Inc the Court faced with essentially similar facts went to great lengths to distinguish *Wiley* out of concern that

> a potential employer might be willing to take over a moribund business only if he can make changes in corporate structure, composition of the labor force, work location, task assignment, and nature of supervision. Saddling such an employer with the terms and conditions of employment contained in the old collective bargaining contract may make these changes impossible and may discourage and inhibit the transfer of capital.[172]

Similarly in *Textile Workers Union v Darlington Manufacturing Co*. the Supreme Court upheld the managerial prerogative to close a business without consulting the employees.[173] The trend has therefore been to ensure that CBAs do not impede corporate restructuring. The decision in *Wiley* which sought to balance 'the rightful prerogative of owners' with protection of employees, has been explained on the narrow grounds that the court was concerned to give judicial support to arbitration as the best means of solving industrial disputes, rather than motivated by a desire to enhance employment protection.[174] This would explain why it has been distinguished in subsequent cases where the duty to arbitrate was not in issue. It is also significant, as Rock and Wachter point out, that the organizational restructuring in *Wiley* involved a merger, not a sale. At the level of corporate law there was no change in the identity of the firm, and therefore the 'new' firm was subject to all liabilities under corporate law as the 'old' firm. Viewed in this light it is easier to see why the court in *Wiley* found that the firm was, in the same way, subject to all the same labour law rights and obligations as existed before the merger. As a result it remains the case, under the rule in *Wiley*, that a merger has no effect on existing obligations under a valid CBA. The situation is otherwise where the restructuring involves the creation of a new firm – the limited scope of *Wiley* means it would not then apply.

James Atleson observes of the NLRA that despite its reliance on collective representation, which is a real problem in the context of a long and steady decline in the numbers of US workers represented by unions (12 percent in 2003, compared to 29 percent in the UK[175]), nevertheless the NLRA does provide an important measure of protection where unions exist. Atleson makes the important point that by imposing a duty to bargain collectively the NLRA recognizes a legal claim to the interests of the corporation by a party other than the shareholders. Although a union cannot compel the exercise of a managerial duty it does have the privilege of refusing to work except upon its own terms. In some circumstances the protective framework

172 406 U.S. 272 (1972) at 287–88. *Wiley* was similarly distinguished in *Howard Johnson*.

173 380 U.S. 263 (1965).

174 James B. Atleson, *Values and Assumptions in American Labor Law* (Amherst: University of Massachusetts Press, 1983).

175 David G. Blanchflower, 'A Cross Country Study of Union Membership' IZA Discussion Paper Series, DP No. 2016 March 2006; Heidi Grainger, *Trade Union Membership 2005* (London: Department of Trade and Industry, 2005).

of the NLRA may even approximate the effect of ARD in limiting the employer's freedom to dismiss employees without prior information and consultation. For instance in *NLRB v Fibreboard Paper Products* the employer subcontracted its employees' work to an independent firm in order to save money, and did so without bargaining with its employees.[176] The Supreme Court ruled that the employer was in breach of its obligation to bargain with the union, and upheld the order made by the NLRB that the employer must reinstate all its employees with a substantial back-pay award. This case recognized a certain measure of job tenure for the employees, circumscribing the ability of management to make unilateral changes without consulting the employees. However, the decision in *Fibreboard* has not been as influential as it might have been, and has tended to be distinguished.

The more influential presumption is that while employee rights derive entirely from the terms of the contract, managerial rights and powers are deemed to be inherent, and are fully reserved and maintained 'in the absence of restrictions in isolated collective bargaining agreements or under the labor relations laws'.[177] More importantly, as Atleson emphasizes, the duty to bargain does not extend to decisions which lie at 'the core of managerial authority' or what the courts have termed 'managerial prerogatives',[178] such as the employer's right to close all or part of its business for any reason.[179] Instead the duty to bargain is limited to 'rates of pay, wages, hours of employment or other conditions of employment'.[180] Non-mandatory bargaining topics such as job security and worker participation are 'found in a third of agreements or fewer'.[181] In *Fibreboard* Justice Stewart stated that certain decisions are excluded from the scope of collective bargaining because they are 'fundamental to the basic direction of a corporate enterprise'.[182] Justice Blackmun in *First National Maintenance Corporation v NLRB* stated that in passing the NLRA 'Congress had no expectation that the elected union representative would become an equal partner in the running of the business enterprise in which the union's members are employed', and that 'management must be free from the constraints of the bargaining process to the extent essential for the running of a profitable business'.[183] The NLRA therefore does not do much to enable employees to influence core decision-making processes.

---

176 379 U.S. 203 (1964).

177 Phillip I. Blumberg, 'The Protection of Workers' Rights in the Event of Insolvency and Business Reorganization: United States Report' (1989) 5 *Connecticut Journal of International Law* 7–46 at 8.

178 *NLRB v Burnup & Sims,* 379 U.S. 21 at 24 (1964).

179 *Textile Workers Union v Darlington Manufacturing Co*. 380 U.S. 263 (1965) where the court upheld the company's decision to close a mill despite the fact that the closure was a reprisal against the employees' decision to join the union.

180 Section 8 NLRA, and see *General Motors Corp. v NLRB*, 191 NLRB 951, 952 (1971).

181 Joel Cutcher-Gershenfeld and Thomas Kochan 'Taking Stock: Collective Bargaining at the Turn of the Century' (2004) 58 *Industrial & Labor Relations Review* 3–26 at 10.

182 At 223.

183 452 U.S. 666, at 676 (1981).

As will be seen later European rights of information and consultation go much further.

Transfers and Insolvency

Both the ARD and the NLRA are at variance with the regulation of insolvent firms. Where a firm is on the verge of insolvency it would usually be better for all parties for the firm to be sold as a going concern than to be wound up. Insolvency regulation therefore facilitates the recovery of the firm with winding up viewed as a last resort. The apprehension, as stated in *NLRB v Burns*, is that potential purchasers would be dissuaded from making offers by the risk of acquiring obligations to the existing workforce, in which case employment protection would indirectly cause the firm to be wound up leaving all parties worse off. Insolvency law in the UK is subject to the European Insolvency Directive, which provides for payment of employees' outstanding pay claims on insolvency.[184] This Directive was prompted by concern that there was insufficient protection for employees at risk of losing their jobs, or who had actually lost their jobs, by reason of the employer's insolvency. It was amended in 2002 'to take further account of its social aims' by extending the scope of its applicability.[185] Member states may set a ceiling on the amount of compensation payable to employees in cases of insolvency, but must inform the Commission of the method used to calculate this ceiling, and the ceiling 'must not fall below a level which is socially compatible with the social objective of [the] Directive'.[186]

It could therefore be said that insolvency law in the UK already has inbuilt recognition of the interests of employees. The question is whether further protection in the form of the ARD is helpful. If the firm is sold as a going concern jobs would be preserved by the ARD making the purchaser subject to pay potentially unlimited compensation to employees rather than the limited payment under the insolvency law.[187] This is a matter of concern to creditors as the ARD gives priority to employeeswhich those employees would not have in insolvency. Moreover the obligatory transfer of workers to the purchaser might deter prospective purchases altogether, either in order to avoid taking on the company's existing work-force or to avoid incurring

184 Council Directive 80/987/EEC on the approximation of laws relating to the protection of employees on the insolvency of the employer.

185 Insolvency Protection Directive Council Directive 2002/74/EC on the protection of employees in the event of the insolvency of their employer.

186 Malcolm Sargeant, 'Protecting Employees with Insolvent Employers' (2003) 32 *Industrial Law Journal* 53–9 at 55.

187 Armour and Deakin; Sandra Frisby, 'TUPE or not TUPE? Employee Protection, Corporate Rescue and "One Unholy Mess"' (2000) *Company, Financial and Insolvency Law Review* 249–71; Paul Davies, 'Employee Claims in Insolvency: Corporate Rescues and Preferential Claims' (1994) 23 *Industrial Law Journal* 141–51; Hugh Collins, 'Transfers of Undertakings and Insolvency' (1989) 18 *Industrial Law Journal* 144–58; Wanjiru Njoya, 'The Interface Between Redundancy and TUPE Transfers' (2003) 32 *Industrial Law Journal* 123–8.

liability for their outstanding claims against their employer.[188] Drawing attention to this double-edged effect Sandra Frisby argues that in such a scenario the ARD represents more of a threat than a route to job security. Amendments to the ARD in 1998 addressed this concern, allowing partial derogation from the ARD during 'insolvency proceedings which have been instituted with a view to the liquidation of the assets of the transferor' where the employer and employee representatives come to an agreement 'designed to safeguard employment opportunities by ensuring the survival of the undertaking'.[189] The TUPE regulations now provide that employment protection under the ARD does not extend to transferors undergoing bankruptcy proceedings, where employees' claims are covered by existing compensation awards under insolvency legislation. The transferor however remains liable for claims extending beyond the scope of compensation available under insolvency law. In this way a balance is sought to be achieved between the interests of creditors and those of employees.[190]

In the US there is a similar conflict between the aims of the NLRA and the Bankruptcy Code.[191] According to Phillip Blumberg the aim of the NLRA in situations of insolvency is to ensure 'the continued effectiveness of a pre-existing collective-bargaining agreement' where the bankrupt employer continues in business under Chapter 11 of the Bankruptcy Code.[192] As Blumberg explains, in this situation it is an 'unfair labor practice' under the NLRA for the employer to renege on promises made to the workers under a CBA. The NLRA provides that a bankrupt employer wishing to modify the CBA must enter into good faith negotiations with the union to agree suitable alternative terms.[193] However, this tends to defeat the objectives of the Bankruptcy Code, which under section 365 allows the court to give leave for the bankruptcy trustee to reject any executory contract of the debtor, including CBAs. The rationale of s.365 is that claims arising under executory contracts should not allow an avenue for further dissipation of the debtor's assets. An important limitation on the courts' s.365 jurisdiction was introduced by s.1113 of the Code, which sets out the conditions which must be satisfied before a court will approve a trustee's proposed rejection of a CBA.[194] These requirements generally relate to consultations

---

188 It has been argued that this liability includes the protective award in respect of the transferor's failure to consult: *Kerry Foods Ltd v Creber* (2000) I.R.L.R. 10; *TGWU v James McKinnon Jr* [2001] I.R.L.R. 597.

189 Article 5. Between its introduction in 1998 and repeal in 2006 Article 4 of TUPE allowed the transferee of an insolvent company to avoid its ARD obligations (see Davis, 'Recent Cases: Transfer Regulations' and McMullen, 'The Transfer of Undertakings' for a discussion).

190 TUPE Regulation 8, discussed in McMullen, 'The Transfer of Undertakings' at 133.

191 Gary M. Roberts, 'Bankruptcy and the Union's Bargain: Equitable Treatment of Collective Bargaining Agreements' (1987) 39 *Stanford Law Review* 1015–56.

192 11 U.S.C. §§ 101–1330 (2002); Blumberg, at 15.

193 Ibid.

194 Amendment introduced by Congress in reaction to the Supreme Court decision in *NLRB v Bildisco & Bildisco*, 465 U.S. 513 (1984) which made it easy for firms to avoid

with the unions and duties to provide the unions with relevant information. Despite the protective provisions of s.1113 the general tendency of the bankruptcy courts is to give effect to the employers' right to reject CBAs.[195] Therefore although the Bankruptcy Code in theory works together with the NLRA to protect workers' interests during liquidation or reorganization in practice effective employee protection relies not on the statutory framework but on the industrial strength of their union, which may for instance decide to take strike action if the CBA is rejected.[196]

The import of s.1113 is similar to European rights of information and consultation under the ARD, except that while the general tendency under the ARD is to *preserve* the existing employee rights subject to certain exceptions, s.1113 goes the other way. It *allows* the termination of the collective bargaining agreement subject to certain exceptions. The European Court usually favours a restrictive interpretation of the ARD, leaning against finding exceptions to the ARD on 'economic, technical or organisational' grounds, while the American courts favour a much broader interpretation of s.1113 and are generally inclined to approve rejections of CBAs.[197] The difference in treatment of employee claims in the company in the two countries can therefore be said to extend to insolvency situations.

Collective Representation

Notions of job property become especially relevant where, in a unionized workplace, the union is able to secure the employees' position through bargaining over matters which would ordinarily be deemed to fall within the managerial prerogative. This is only possible where collective bargaining goes beyond the purely 'labour' topics of wages, hours of work and terms and conditions of employment. To varying degrees both UK and US law recognize the important role of collective representation in regulating economic dismissals. This generally takes the form of giving employee representatives rights to prior information and consultation before large-scale dismissals. The significance of these measures must however be viewed in the light of declining recourse to collective representation by both British and American

---

executory CBAs by showing only that 'the equities' were in their favour and that negotiations were unlikely 'to produce a prompt and satisfactory conclusion' (at 525–26, discussed in Blumberg).

195Roberts.

196 Blumberg.

197 Donald C. Dowling Jr., 'The Intersection Between U.S. Bankruptcy And Employment Law' (1994) 10 *Labor Lawyer* 57–72 at 66. For the ECJ approach see the decision of the Advocate General in *d'Urso*: 'I do not share the view that the directive allows any kind of dismissal on economic, technical or organizational grounds. The directive expressly prohibits such dismissals where they occur as a result of the transfer of the undertaking. It is only where the dismissals have already taken place, for example if they had already been decided on before the question of any transfer of the undertaking arose, that they come under that derogation (at 34). Article 4 of the directive cannot therefore be used as an argument to dismiss some of the employees on account of the transfer of the undertaking' (at par. 35).

workers. This makes it questionable whether this approach is as effective in the Anglo-American context as it could be, relying as it does on systems of collective worker representation which may be few and far between.

In English law before the European Directives came into force collective bargaining depended not on the legal framework but on the industrial power of the unions – collective *laissez faire*. Until 1999 there was no statutory duty to bargain, except for a brief period in the 1970s.[198] Collective agreements were not, and are still generally not, legally binding on either the employer or the union.[199] The picture is substantially redrawn by European law. The European Charter of Fundamental Rights mentions the worker's right to information and consultation (Article 27), now implemented by the Information and Consultation Directive. In supplementing the framework of other employment protection Directives the ICD aims to enhance and extend employee rights of information and consultation, and thereby to further support employee participation in corporate governance, by facilitating employee participation in decision-making. Effectively the ICD had significant impact only in the UK and Ireland (and, for different reasons, the new member states) and it is instructive that a Downing Street advisor described this Directive as 'an "asteroid" about to hit Britain'.[200] As mentioned when discussing the ARD, other member states already had mechanisms in place to facilitate and guarantee the exercise of information and consultation rights. Under the British 'single channel' model of collective representation the only mechanism in place for consulting workers was the trade union. This left non-unionized workers unable to benefit from rights of information and consultation granted by European law. In addition with no general framework for consultation workers only had such rights under the specific terms laid down by the ARD and other directives, mainly the European Works Councils (EWC) Directive and the Collective Redundancies Directive (CRD). As the ARD has been discussed above it only remains to give a brief explanation of the EWC and the CRD.

198 Under the Industrial Relations Act 1971 the employer had to recognize a registered union which represented the majority of its workers, under the jurisdiction of the National Industrial Relations Court. This was abolished by the Trade Union and Labour Relations Act 1974, reintroduced by the Employment Protection Act 1975 and abolished again by the Employment Act 1980. It has now been reintroduced by the 1999 amendments to the Trade Union and Labour Relations (Consolidation) Act 1992 and governed by Schedule A1 of the 1992 Act (as amended).

199 *Ford Motor Co. Ltd v AEU* [1969] 2 Q.B. 303. Under the Industrial Relations Act 1971 s.34 there was a presumption that collective agreements were intended to create legal relations. This remained the case until it reverted to the common law position by virtue of s.18 of the Trade Union and Labour Relations Act 1974. The current position is contained in s.179 of the Trade Union and Labour Relations (Consolidation) Act 1992: agreements are not legally binding unless they comply with s.179.

200 Cited in Mark Hall, 'Assessing the Information and Consultation of Employees Regulations' (2005) 34 *Industrial Law Journal* 103–26 at 103.

The EWC provides an institutional framework at the transnational level for 'works councils' to be involved in training workers with new skills to enhance their 'employability' and thereby reduce the social effects of lay-offs.[201] At the moment this only applies to corporations with operations in more than one member state, although there have for a long time been proposals that French and German-style works councils should be implemented generally across the European Union. Works councils are set up in the firm to give employees a role in designing the corporation's training programmes and ensuring that their skills will be of use in the external labour market. In some member states such as France the central government and local authorities also play a role in the implementation of training programmes for 'lifelong learning'. This contrasts with the Anglo-American model in which this responsibility rests primarily with the individual worker and less on the state and in which 'employability' is not generally seen as the duty of the corporation to be implemented through formal mechanisms within the corporation itself.[202] Rights of information and consultation under the EWC require employers to consult with workers at least once a year on a specified range of issues. In 2003 the Commission announced a long-awaited process of review of this Directive to 'reinforce the right to information and consultation'.[203] Matters over which workers have information and consultation rights under the EWC include the firm's 'structure, economic and financial situation, the probable development of the business and of production and sales … investments and substantial changes concerning organization … [and] transfers of production, mergers, cut-backs or closures of undertakings, establishments or important parts thereof'.[204] The broad reach of these rights extends beyond the fringes of labour regulation into the core of managerial prerogative.

The paramount aim of the CRD's redundancy protection is to maintain the employee's position, and not simply to facilitate his or her search for alternative employment. The redundancy procedure protects the rights of incumbent employees (usually on the basis of how long they have been with the firm) by preventing the employer from unfairly selecting which employees will be laid off. The CRD is designed to give early warning and relevant information about proposed redundancies to employee representatives.[205] The aim is for these representatives to be consulted

201 Council Directive 94/45/EC, implemented in the UK by the Transnational Information and Consultation of Employees Regulations 1999.

202 'In the critical area of job training and the acquisition of skills, U.S. employers rely heavily on the external skills market and educational preparation prior to employment … although U.S. Bureau of Labor Statistics surveys have shown that U.S. firms provided more training in the 1990s than they had before, the training gap is still significant': Christopherson, at 4–5.

203 Pascale Lorber, 'Reviewing the European Works Council Directive: European Progress and United Kingdom Perspective' (2004) 33 *Industrial Law Journal* 191–99 at 191.

204 Article 12, European Works Council Directive.

205 Implemented in the UK by Part IV of the Trade Union and Labour Relations (Consolidation) Act 1992. In UK law employers must notify the Secretary of State when they are proposing to dismiss as redundant twenty or more employees at one establishment

at an early stage, giving them time to formulate suggestions and alternatives so that workers are laid off only as a last resort, and regulations govern the amount and quality of information that must be given. Employees may make a complaint against an employer who does not comply; the penalty in the UK is a fine of up to £5000 payable to the court (not the affected employees).

The effect of these Directives, read together with the transfer and insolvency laws, is that the information and consultation obligation goes considerably further than the American 'duty to bargain' in two important ways. It differs from the obligation imposed on employers and unions by the NLRA in that it extends to non-unionized workers through representatives selected according to the statutory framework. UK workers were for some time unable to fully enjoy this protection because there was often no union to exercise the rights granted to workers' representatives. The UK was found to be in breach of its obligations under European law for lacking a framework for the consultation of non-unionized workers (or members of an unrecognized union) under the CRD and the ARD, and was obliged to introduce new European-style mechanisms to allow non-unionized workers to participate effectively.[206] Another important difference is that unlike the NLRA duty to bargain and the scope of collective bargaining in English law, both of which are limited to wages, hours and terms and conditions of work, the European rights of information and consultation extend to such matters as the firm's organizational structure. These are matters which would fall within the scope of managerial prerogative in Anglo-American law and on which directors would hold themselves accountable exclusively to their shareholders. Although employee rights of information and consultation still do not extend as far in the UK as they do in Europe they are now a significant source of protection for workers.[207]

Codetermination

Codetermination involves two-tier boards of directors: a managing board responsible for day-to-day management and a supervisory board which appoints and supervises the managing board and sets managerial remuneration and overall corporate strategy.[208] Worker representatives sit on the supervisory board. Several EU member states have

---

within a period of ninety days. For 100 or more employees, the notification must be given at least ninety days before the first of the redundancies takes effect and where twenty to ninety-nine redundancies are proposed at least thirty days before the first of the redundancies takes effect.

206 *Commission v UK*, Cases C–382/92 and C–383/92 (1994).

207 'Information and consultation rights do not provide employees with a veto over a restructuring; nor will the English courts nullify a commercial transaction entered into by an employer simply because it is in breach of employee information and consultation laws. But the effect of such a breach on the employer's part can nevertheless be substantial': Deakin, 'Workers, Finance and Democracy' at 97.

208 Gary Gorton and Frank Schmid, 'Class Struggle Inside the Firm: A Study of German Codetermination' (2000) *National Bureau of Economic Research* Working Paper No W7945.

legislation providing for varying degrees of codetermination, though none of these is as far-reaching as the German system.[209] In Germany all private corporations (GmbHs) with over 500 employees must have a management board (*Vorstand*) as well as a supervisory board (*Aufischtsrat*), with employees constituting a third of the supervisory board. In stock corporations (AGs, the equivalent of the publicly traded corporations in the UK and US) with over 2000 employees half the board comprises employee representatives.[210] Under the Codetermination Act 1976 the supervisory board of stock corporations with over 2000 workers is split equally between shareholder and employee representatives. The potential for an impasse in decision-making is avoided by giving the shareholders an ultimate casting vote – the board appoints a chairman who has the deciding vote if the board is split, and if the board is unable to agree on this appointment the chairman is elected by the shareholders. In this way the German model recognizes that the effective involvement of worker participation in decision-making requires a degree of flexibility and compromise. In any case the worker and shareholder representatives work together on the board in a spirit of cooperation rather than conflict, as Germany has 'a long history of thinking in terms of reforming the capitalist system by restricting management's unilateral powers'.[211] This means it does not often become necessary to use the casting vote.[212] Although there are difficulties in the flow of information from the management to the supervisory board which render the supervisory board less powerful or influential than it might otherwise be, nevertheless 'codetermination does empower employees' who are able to 'change the objective function of the firm' by exercising their power to approve or veto important decisions made by managers.[213]

Although it depends partly on trade unions for its effectiveness, German codetermination is institutionalized entirely within a legislative framework from which it derives legitimacy and support. This is significant as contrasted with the Anglo-American model of worker participation in decision-making which depends, in so far as it exists, almost entirely on the existence and industrial strength of the unions in a particular workplace or industry with very little reliance on supportive

---

209 These are Austria, the Czech Republic, Denmark, Finland, France, Greece, Hungary, the Republic of Ireland, Luxembourg, Malta, the Netherlands, Poland, Portugal, the Slovak Republic, Slovenia, Spain and Sweden: <www.seeurope-nctwork.org> updated 15th May 2006.

210 The Gesellschaften mit beschrankter Haftung (GmbH) and Aktiengesellschaften (AG); under the Industrial Constitution Act of 1952 and the Codetermination Act 1976.

211 Manfred Weiss, 'Worker Participation in the EU' in Paul Davies, Antoine Lyon-Caen, Silvana Sciarra and Spiros Simitis, *European Community Labour Law: Principles and Perspectives: Liber Amicorum Lord Wedderburn* (Oxford: Clarendon Press, 1996) at 213.

212 Gorton and Schmid, at 19.

213 Gorton and Schmid, at 6.

legislation.[214] Reflecting the German approach the Takeover Directive (TOD)[215] and the European Company Statute (ECS)[216] both allow, although they do not mandate, corporate structures which include employee representatives on the board of directors. A brief overview of these statutes will now be given, highlighting the degree to which they recognize employees' right to participate in decision-making.

The ECS was introduced to allow companies to be incorporated as European companies and is supplemented by a Directive on Worker Involvement in the European Company (WID) to which it makes specific reference.[217] During the extended European debate over the TOD and the ECS (the TOD was eventually passed 27 years after the original proposal; the ECS after 31 years of debate), one of the most controversial matters which prevented its acceptance by all member states was that of worker participation in decision-making and control of enterprise. Germany was opposed to the TOD on grounds that it 'fail[ed] to accommodate any responsibility of directors to non-shareholder stakeholders'.[218] On the role of employees, the TOD confers rights of information and consultation on worker representatives of both the bidder and target companies in the context of a hostile bid.[219] The TOD also requires a statement of intention concerning jobs. In Britain this statement is an insignificant formality but in France a promise not to lay workers off is sometimes expected.[220] The case regarding the ECS was similar, as a lack of

---

214 Britain is famous for its voluntarist collective bargaining tradition: Davies and Freedland, *Labour Legislation and Public Policy* (Oxford: Oxford University Press, 1993); similarly trade unions in the US do not generally rely on the NLRA to assert their voice: Ellen Dannin, 'The NLRA at Seventy: A Union Movement for the New Century' (2005) 8 *Journal of Labor and Society* 489–99; Blumberg notes, in the context of insolvency, that 'employee protection – where it exists at all – is found almost entirely in union representation and union collective bargaining agreements rather than in statutory or administrative regulation' (at 1).

215 Directive 2004/25/EC on Takeover bids which was formally adopted on 21 April, 2004, implemented in the UK on 20 May 2006 by amendments to the Takeover Code and by the Takeover Directive (Interim Implementation) Regulations 2006. The interim regulations await the Companies Bill which is expected to become law in 2007.

216 Council Regulation 2157/2001, Statute for a European Company (*Societas Europaea*).

217 Council Directive 2001/86/EC.

218 Christian Kirchner and Richard W. Painter, 'Takeover Defenses Under Delaware Law, the Proposed Thirteeth EU Directive and the New German Takeover Law: Comparisons and Recommendations for Reform' (2002) 50 *American Journal of Comparative Law* 451–76 at 458. In 2002 Germany passed its own takeover law allowing the supervisory board (on which employees sit) more power to resist hostile takeover attempts, a move strongly supported by trade unions.

219 Article 8 (disclosure of the bid and relevant documents), Article 9(5) (board duty to give opinion on bid to employee representatives and publicize their response) and Article 14 (preserves rights of information and consultation conferred by other Directives or domestic laws).

220 On the UK, see Deakin and Slinger, 'Company Law' at 15–16: the statement 'says nothing more than that the bidder company will respect the company's prior legal obligations

agreement on the role of worker participation impeded consensus: 'While it [proved difficult] for Germany to "export" its employee-oriented model to Europe, due in no small part to British opposition, Germany [was] central to blocking any version of the Societas Europaea that would undermine the existing pluralistic approach to the company domestically'.[221]

That these recent Directives succeeded, despite the extreme difficulties they faced, in being adopted supplies crucial evidence of continued support for codetermination within the European framework, suggesting that the claims about declining support for codetermination may be exaggerated. It is clear that codetermination yields efficiency benefits in parts of the European Union where it applies, and the question may be posed why there is still no realistic prospect of the extension of this model to the UK.[222] Paul Davies has observed that the UK may adapt its own functional equivalents of the two-tier board structure, through the role of non-executive directors in monitoring executive directors. However he points out that this can only go so far, as the role of directors in the two systems differs in important respects. The German supervisory board plays an important role in establishing and maintaining relationships with stakeholders, particularly employees, which the UK or US non-executive directors do not.[223] In addition much depends on whether the company is closely held or publicly traded. According to Roe codetermination works best in the context of the strong employee-participation norms associated with the closely-held firms which dominate continental European economies. These norms are partly responsible for 'inducing concentrated ownership' as shareholders respond by keeping shares within the family or other close private groups. Therefore Roe suggests that the kind of social democracy which supports an important political and economic role for worker participation on boards of directors 'mixes badly with the public firm' favoured by the Anglo-American economy.[224] From the perspective of agency theory it increases the costs of aligning the interests of managers with those of shareholders by providing powerful incentives for managers to align themselves publicly with the employees' interests. The result is that 'the internal structure of public firms must necessarily be weaker for shareholders' and the shareholder primacy norm takes second place to employee participation.[225] However the continued support

---

to its employees'; on France see Roe, *Political Determinants* at 44.

221 Donnelly et al, at 32.

222 As proposed, unsuccessfully, by the *Report of the Committee of Inquiry on Industrial Democracy* (the Bullock Report) Cmnd. 6706, 1977.

223 Paul Davies, 'Board Structure in the UK and Germany: Convergence or Continuing Divergence?' (2000) 2 *International Comparative and Corporate Law Journal* 435–56.

224 Roe, *Political Determinants* at 33.

225 At 24. There is support for this view in the European literature. In terms of the separation of ownership and control, 'The European Commission tried to establish a global level-playing field for a takeover market. However, the adoption of such a unified takeover code by countries with different initial settings may disperse ownership in some of them, but may further consolidate the blockholder-based system in others': Goergen et al, at 10; they observe (at 3) that 'although the shareholder-centred view of corporate governance is

for worker participation in the European Directives will inevitably have an impact on the normative framework of English law in the long run, by keeping worker participation norms on the agenda of the corporate governance debates.

Corporate Governance Effects

In upholding the constitutionality of the NLRA in *NLRB v Jones & Laughlin Steel Corp.*, the US Supreme Court took account of the fact that a management team selected by and accountable to the shareholder-owners of the firm would be expected to exclusively defend the shareholders' position, therefore employees needed union representation to defend their interests, creating the need for legislative protection for employee representation.[226] Accordingly the NLRA, unlike codetermination in European law, is not predicated upon the institutionalization of employee participation within the firm. Instead employees' interests are viewed as entirely distinct from the interests of the company, as represented by management, thereby requiring an independent framework for protection of these interests. Collective bargaining is seen not as a mechanism of employee participation in enterprise but simply as the best means to bridge the gap between employees, as outsiders, and the corporation. Managers are often resistant to collective bargaining and aggressively undertake 'union-busting' strategies to avoid employee organization or union action.[227] This is in contrast to the European perception of workers as part of the social fabric of the corporation. European employee participation in corporate governance, particularly as implemented through rights of information and consultation, codetermination and works councils is based on cooperation rather than conflict, best exemplified by German law which provides that the employer and the works council shall 'co-operate on the basis of mutual trust'.[228] This approach is the outcome of a radically different understanding of the nature of the firm. As Anderman puts it

> [In the] European concept of shared power in an enterprise … [t]he shareholders are acknowledged as the owners of the shares of the enterprise but this is not equated with all ownership rights of the enterprise. Instead, the bundle of rights and responsibilities that is associated with ownership of the firm is viewed in less absolute terms. Owing to the legal integration of employee representatives in the organs of company decision-making and Works Councils in some form of consultation or co-decision process, it is difficult for judges or legislators to view the company as owned solely by the employer. This concept of significant limitations on the exclusive property rights of employers may help

---

receiving widespread recognition, some economies seem to opt for the blockholder-based system'.

226 301 U.S. 1(1937); see discussion in Paul C. Weiler, *Governing the Workplace: The Future of Labor and Employment Law* (Massachusetts: Harvard University Press, 1990).

227 For a study of this issue see Pencavel; Robert J. Flanagan, 'Has Management Strangled U.S. Unions?' (2005) 26 *Journal of Labor Research* 33–63.

228 Works Constitution Act s.74. For a discussion see Kahn-Freund, 'Industrial Democracy'.

to explain the stronger substantive norms and remedial robustness of European standards of unfair dismissal.[229]

Of relevance in this context is the distinction drawn between corporate law and labour law, mentioned in Chapter 3. It was noted there that workers' rights under American law are not considered significant in assessing the dominance of the shareholder value norm in American corporate law and corporate governance.[230] Fannon observes that American labour legislation such as the NLRA adds 'very little to the obligations of management or companies' and is not directly concerned with employee participation in decision-making.[231] Although unionized employees are in a stronger position where a CBA exists covering successorship and assigning the employer's obligations to the new owner, it has been noted that relatively few employees are unionized. The problem is particularly acute in the private sector, where the number of US employees covered by CBAs now falls below 9 percent.[232] Even where a CBA exists it is unusual for its terms to 'restrict employer discretion' with regard to employee protection.[233] Outside the unionized workplace employees have no effective job protection when the employer corporation undergoes a change in its ownership structure. These factors ensure that collective representation and collective bargaining in the US do not generally encroach upon the corporate law domain. This is a significant difference between European (and to some extent English) law and the comparable American law.

Therefore the employee-participation Directives form part and parcel of the corporate governance framework of European law, reflecting strong worker participation norms which in certain situations override the shareholder primacy norm. The significance of this for the UK, subject as it is to European law, is somewhat muted by the fact that UK employment protection statutes are generally interpreted so as to keep their reach firmly within the bounds of labour law. This limits the extent to which they affect the allocation of ownership and control in the firm. Therefore although in theory these Directives have the potential to induce a shift towards worker participation as the overriding concern during corporate restructuring in the UK, the overall effect of this protective framework is not as strong as the European equivalents. This means that the overall effect of the Directives on UK law, from a corporate governance perspective, should not be over-emphasized. The ARD may be an exception in that although *Baxendale* allows TUPE to be seen as just one more

229 Anderman, 'Termination of Employment' at 125. This is well illustrated in the *Recommendations of the Committee on Corporate Governance* chaired by Marc Vienot (Association Française Des Entreprises Privées and Mouvement des Entreprises de France, July 1999).

230 Although see Rock and Wachter for an analysis of the conceptual overlap between corporate and labour law; see, arguing for a rethink of the corporate-labour divide, O'Connor, 'The Human Capital Era'.

231 Fannon at 42–3. See also O'Connor, 'Labor's Role'.

232 Cutcher-Gershenfeld and Kochan.

233 Blumberg, at 7.

cost to be factored into corporate restructuring rather than a substantive enforcement of continuity of employment, these costs incurred by TUPE liability are not subject to a statutory cap. Liability under TUPE is indeed potentially unlimited, as it includes not just employees' contractual claims against the transferor such as back wages and holiday pay, but also statutory claims such as unfair dismissal compensation, and damages in respect of claims in tort such as liability in negligence for injuries at work.[234] Furthermore, the automatic transfer of these liabilities to the transferor may scupper the entire deal, and therefore the trade union is placed in a powerful position by being able to offer not to enforce any of these outstanding claims. This gives the employer a compelling reason to negotiate the terms of the transfer with the union.[235] In practice, therefore, TUPE ensures that restructuring may not proceed without the consent of the unions. In this context TUPE rights operate as property rights. However, this is not possible unless the workers are unionized, and must be read in light of declining levels of unionization in the UK. Moreover, the same effect cannot be achieved in the case of other worker-protection Directives where the costs of non-compliance are limited to a very affordable fixed statutory maximum.

Conclusion

An important element in the idea of an employee's property right in a job is 'freedom from arbitrary dismissal'.[236] This idea is reflected to some extent in both Europe and America, where rights of consultation and bargaining, and in some instances the employer's inability to proceed without the consent of employee representatives, qualify the common law assumptions of the employers' prerogatives as owner of the enterprise, and involve a sharing of this ownership interest with the employees. However there has so far not been a radical change in the underlying common law model. This is partly due to the dominant conceptual role of contract, which in English law has caused the European protective measures to be translated from the envisaged property-like entitlement to remain in one's job enjoyed in other member states, into a contractual claim for damages. Another explanation may lie in differences in the proprietary structure of firms. The level of support for employee participation in the European tradition is said to be incompatible with the publicly-held fragmented shareholding which is typical of the Anglo-American corporate structure. A third explanation is the difference in collective bargaining traditions. Unionization is increasingly insignificant in the Anglo-American workplace, while trade unions remain much more active in Europe. Unions, works councils, and other forms of worker representation play a vital supportive role in the European framework. Without this institutional support, and 'diluted' by contract, the judicial interpretation of European statutes in the UK remains much closer in spirit and

234 Robert Upex, Richard Benny and Stephen Hardy, *Labour Law* (Oxford: Oxford University Press, 2004) at par. 9.41.

235 Armour and Deakin.

236 Selznick, at 68.

effect to the American labour legislation than it does to the Directives. Because collective bargaining in the UK is more similar to the US 'gap bridging' model than the European unitary approach, the result is that despite the potential proprietary effect of TUPE, English law on the whole remains closer to America's 'duty to bargain' than it does to the European idea of substantive protection of the continuing employment relationship.

It is possible, although it is still too early to tell, that as European law becomes more deeply embedded in English law this will have an effect on the current dominance of the shareholder primacy norm in the UK. The courts' robust application of TUPE demonstrates the potential for this to occur. However, while recent European statutes have the potential to institutionalize property rights in work in the UK this cannot be realized without support from the underlying common law conceptual structure. Statutory employment protection is not free-standing. Judicial interpretation of this legislation looks to the common law for guiding principles and values. As long as the common law ideology is associated predominantly with notions of individual liberty and equality highlighted by the law of contract, rather than the less dominant motif of employee protection which is also displayed in judicial dicta, the new framework of European law will not be as influential as the traditional common law definition of 'the best interests of the company'.

Conclusion: Corporations, Workers and Property

This study has proposed a different starting point in thinking about workers' rights in the modern large publicly-held corporation, arguing that organizational restructuring aimed purely at boosting share value, and the attendant economic dismissals, encroach upon workers' property rights in their jobs. Whether the concept of property in work has any application outside this context, and whether it would prove equally promising in addressing other problems relating to the employment relationship, is a matter for future research. Its potential capacity to enhance job security in the context explored in this book suggests that the idea may well be worth further investigation.

In this study the concepts of ownership and property have been understood not in the general sense in which one might assert rights to items of personal property, but in the sense proposed by stakeholder theory. Critics of property rights perspectives often fail to appreciate the sophistication and flexibility of property, yet it is precisely these qualities that make property such a valuable conceptual tool in analyzing the allocation of control and decision-making rights in the firm. It is customary to explain the network of relationships in the firm solely by reference to contract. This is a useful reference point but there is no reason why the analysis of these legal relations should be restricted to this single conceptual perspective. It is certainly not argued that the proprietary approach should henceforth become the sole benchmark in ascertaining the conceptual nature of workers' rights. The study merely takes cognizance of the limits of contract in protecting employees' legitimate expectation of continued employment and the frequent calls for solutions that lie 'beyond contract', and suggests that describing workers' rights as proprietary offers an additional conceptual framework for analyzing protective employment legislation in the context of corporate restructuring. This broader perspective suggests new ways of striking a more socially desirable balance between job security and economic efficiency.

The book has argued that employees' property in their work entitles them to participate in corporate governance on the same basis as shareholders' property in their shares. There were two main obstacles to be tackled in constructing this argument. First, the claim that there are sufficient mechanisms for protecting employee interests *outside* the framework of corporate law, primarily through contract and employment regulation. This claim relies on a 'bright line' divide between labour law and corporate law. Second, even if it were to be accepted that there is a case for viewing employees as members of the firm along with shareholders, there remained the obstacle of identifying a suitable theoretical framework for the definition and delineation of their rights. The book has presented some ways in which the stakeholder theory of the firm can address both concerns. Stakeholder theory addresses the first concern by maintaining that ownership of the firm is shared between shareholders and employees in circumstances where firm-specific human capital is just as valuable to the firm as finance capital. This value should not, it has been suggested, be obscured by doctrinal boundaries, hence the interdisciplinary method of this study. The second concern, for an appropriate theoretical framework, is met by grounding stakeholder theory in a pluralist and evolving concept of property. As was conceded at the outset much work remains to be done in developing and refining this theory. But its starting point, which turns attention back to the controversial question who owns the firm, is surely sound. It is axiomatic that the owner of property has the right to make decisions about its use and disposition, and there are compelling reasons of justice and efficiency why this should be so. What is less clear is whether it remains appropriate, in the modern firm, to assign the role and status of 'owner' exclusively to shareholders. Avoiding the terminology of ownership altogether does not eradicate the problem, but instead allows exclusive notions of shareholder-ownership to become more deeply entrenched with adverse consequences for workers. Ownership is a powerful idea and should be harnessed rather than disregarded. This book therefore joins in the efforts to face this question squarely.

In the Anglo-American corporate governance debates the idea of exclusive shareholder ownership is defended on two influential grounds. First that shared shareholder-stakeholder ownership would have a deleterious effect on efficiency, and second that it goes against the fundamental values of the common law tradition. It is hoped that this study has gone some way towards allaying those fears by showing first that efficiency does not point unambiguously in the direction of shareholder primacy and second that the common law tradition does not give unequivocal support to the dominant assumptions of exclusive shareholder property rights in the firm and the relegation of workers' rights to contract. In developing this argument the book expressed reservations about the capacity of European law, *in itself*, to constitute the most effective vindication of employment rights in the UK. The European Directives have lent crucial support to worker involvement in decision-making but this study has suggested that they are unlikely to seduce English law away from its ingrained Anglo-American approach to the nature of the employment relationship in the firm. The inherent difficulties in legal transplantation highlighted by Kahn-Freund were adverted to. A close scrutiny of the interpretation of legislation implementing European law reveals that despite the rule of statutory interpretation requiring the meaning of the law to be derived from the intention of parliament as expressed in the words of the statute itself, the process is not entirely scientific and draws implicitly on the conceptual understanding and value judgments of the broader legal, cultural and philosophical tradition. The statutory framework by itself can only go so far, and a more feasible solution for those who accept that workers' rights are not exhaustively defined by employment contracts may well lie, therefore, within the common law itself.

In this light the corporate governance debate should review its implicit assumptions from a perspective open to different ideas that have emerged in centuries of deliberation about the nature of the employment relationship and the respective roles of capital and labour, and not limit itself to solutions which appear to have triumphed in recent history. Given that the process of market evolution is chaotic and adaptive rather than linear and unidirectional, too much reliance should not be placed on prevailing institutional rules and structures. The idea of workers' property rights, suitably refined and adapted to the modern economy, continues to offer a cogent conceptual framework for job security. The property-rights view of work is not about absolute immunity from dismissal, but encompasses the right to participate in decision-making when jobs are at risk. This is not to say that property in work is totally devoid of the power traditionally associated with property rights. This more radical element is still discernible in the claim that decision-making should extend beyond the reach of pure 'labour law' issues and extend to issues traditionally deemed to lie within the core of 'managerial prerogative'. Property may indeed venture where contract has hitherto feared to tread. Reexamining the allocation of property rights in the firm in light of modern theories of firm-specific human capital investments and team production in the new economy makes it possible to embrace employees within the firm's legal structure. The result is a theory of the firm, and of corporate law, which takes into account the contribution made by employees in corporate enterprise and accords them the measure of job security to which they are entitled in return.

The idea of property in work, despite its deep roots in the Anglo-American legal tradition, has not received the consideration it deserves. In tracing the development of this idea this study has explored various implications of thinking about the employment relationship in the firm from a property rights perspective, bringing together a broad range of perspectives. If the result has been to raise more questions about property in work than have been answered, and if the book thereby helps to promote deeper understanding of, and wider debate about, property in work, it will have served its purpose.

Bibliography

Adams, Edward S. and Matheson, John H., 'A Statutory Model for Corporate Constituency Concerns' (2000) 49 *Emory Law Journal* 1085–1135.

Addison, John T., Bellmann, Lutz, Schnabel, Claus and Wagner, Joachim, 'The Reform of the German Works Constitution Act: A Critical Assessment' (2004) 43 *Industrial Relations* 392–420.

Alchian, Armen A., 'Uncertainty, Evolution and Economic Theory' (1950) 58 *Journal of Political Econoy* 211–21.

Alchian, Armen and Demsetz, Harold, 'Production, Information Costs, and Economic Organization' (1972) 62 *American Economic Review* 777–95.

Anderman, Steven, 'The Interpretation of Protective Employment Statutes and Contracts of Employment' (2000) 29 *Industrial Law Journal* 223–42.

Armour, John, 'Who Should Make Corporate Law? EC Legislation Versus Regulatory Competition' ESRC Centre for Business Research, University of Cambridge, Working Paper No. 307 June 2005.

Armour, John and Deakin, Simon, 'Insolvency and Employment Protection: the Mixed Effects of the Acquired Rights Directive' (2003) 22 *International Review of Law and Economics* 443–63.

Armour, John, Deakin, Simon and Konzelmann, Suzanne, 'Shareholder Primacy and the Trajectory of UK Corporate Governance' (2003) 41 *British Journal of Industrial Relations* 531–55.

Atleson, James B., *Values and Assumptions in American Labor Law* (Amherst: University of Massachusetts Press, 1983).

Ballam, Deborah A., 'The True Origins of the Employment-at-Will Doctrine' (1996) 17 *Berkeley Journal of Employment and Labor Law* 91–130.

Barmes, Lizzie, 'The Continuing Conceptual Crisis in the Common Law of the Contract of Employment' (2004) 67 *Modern Law Review* 435–64.

Barnard, Catherine, *EC Employment Law* (2nd ed.) (Oxford: Oxford University Press, 2000).

Barnard, Catherine, Deakin, Simon and Morris, Gillian (eds.), *The Future of Labour Law: Liber Amicorum Sir Bob Hepple QC* (Oxford: Hart Publishing, 2004).

Bassanini, Andrea and Duval, Romain, 'Employment Patterns in OECD Countries: Reassessing the Role of Policies and Institutions' OECD Social, Employment and Migration Working Paper, No. 35, and OECD Economics Department Working Paper, No. 486 (Paris: OECD, 2006).

Baums, Theodore, 'Company Law Reform in Germany' (2003) 3 *Journal of Corporate Law Studies* 181–89.

Bebchuk, Lucian A. and Cohen, Alma, 'Firms' Decisions Where to Incorporate'

(2003) 46 *Journal of Law and Economics* 383–425.

Bebchuk, Lucian A. and Ferrell, Allen, 'Federalism and Takeover Law: The Race to Protect Managers from Takeovers' (1999) 99 *Columbia Law Review* 1168–99.

Bebchuk, Lucian A. and Roe, Mark J., 'A Theory of Path Dependence in Corporate Ownership and Governance' (1999) 52 *Stanford Law Review* 127–70.

Becker, Gary S., *Human Capital: A Theoretical and Empirical Analysis* (3rd ed.) (London: University of Chicago Press, 1993).

Beermann, Jack M. and Singer, Joseph W., 'Baseline Questions in Legal Reasoning: The Example of Property in Jobs' (1989) 23 *Georgia Law Review* 911–95.

Bell, John, Boyron, Sophie and Whittaker, Simon, *Principles of French Law* (Oxford: Oxford University Press, 1998).

Bennett, Michael, 'Montana's Employment Protection: A Comparative Critique of Montana's Wrongful Discharge from Employment Act in Light of the United Kingdom's Unfair Dismissal Law' (1996) 57 *Montana Law Review* 115–41.

Bergeron, James H., 'Global Dynamics of (Un)Fair Employment: Proceedings of the 2000 Annual Meeting of the Association of American Law Schools, Section on Employment Discrimination Law' (2000) 4 *Employee Rights and Employment Policy Journal* 141–64.

Berle, Adolf A., 'Corporate Powers as Powers in Trust' (1931) 44 *Harvard Law Review* 1049–74.

Berle, Adolf A., 'For Whom Corporate Managers Are Trustees: A Note' (1932) 45 *Harvard Law Review* 1365–72.

Berle, Adolf A. and Means, Gardiner C., *The Modern Corporation and Private Property* (New York: Harcourt, Brace & World, 1932).

Black, Bernard and Coffee, John, 'Hail Britannia?: Institutional Investor Behavior Under Limited Regulation' (1994) 92 *Michigan Law Review* 1997–2087.

Blades, Lawrence E., 'Employment at Will vs. Individual Freedom: On Limiting the Abusive Exercise of Employer Power' 67 *Columbia Law Review* 1404–35.

Blair, Margaret M. (ed.), *The Deal Decade: What Takeovers and Leveraged Buyouts Mean for Corporate Governance* (Washington D.C.: The Brookings Institution, 1993).

Blair, Margaret M., *Ownership and Control: Rethinking Corporate Governance for the Twenty-First Century* (Washington D.C.: Brookings Institute, 1995).

Blair, Margaret M., 'Closing the Theory Gap: How the Economic Theory of Property Rights Can Help Bring "Stakeholders" Back into Theories of the Firm' (2005) 9 *Journal of Management and Governance* 33–9.

Blair, Margaret M. and Kochan, Thomas (eds.), *The New Relationship: Human Capital in the American Corporation* (Washington D.C.: Brookings Institution Press, 2000).

Blair, Margaret M. and Roe, Mark (eds.), *Employees and Corporate Governance* (Washington D.C.: Brookings Institution Press, 1999).

Blair, Margaret M. and Stout, Lynn, 'A Team Production Theory of Corporate Law' (1999) 85 *Virginia Law Review* 247–328.

Blair, Margaret M. and Stout, Lynn A., 'Specific Investment and Corporate Law'

(2006) 7 *European Business Organization Law Review*.

Blanchflower, David G., 'A Cross Country Study of Union Membership' IZA Discussion Paper Series, DP No. 2016 March 2006.

Blumberg, Phillip I., 'The Protection of Workers' Rights in the Event of Insolvency and Business Reorganization: United States Report' (1989) 5 *Connecticut Journal of International Law* 7–41.

Blume, Larry and Durlauf, Steven (eds.), *The New Palgrave Dictionary of Economics and Law* (2nd ed.) (London: Macmillan, forthcoming 2007).

Branson, Douglas M., 'Corporate Governance "Reform" and the New Corporate Social Responsibility' (2001) 62 *University of Pittsburgh Law Review* 605–47.

Brown, Elizabeth G., 'Poor Relief in a Wisconsin County, 1846–1866: Administration and Recipients' (1976) 20 *American Journal of Legal History* 79–117.

Cabot, Walter M., 'The Free Market Promotes Long-Term Efficiency that Benefits All Stakeholders' (1991) 21 *Stetson Law Review* 245–52.

Calabresi, Guido and Melamed, Douglas A., 'Property Rules, Liability Rules, and Inalienability: One View of the Cathedral' (1972) 85 *Harvard Law Review* 1089–1128.

Carby-Hall, Jo, 'Redundancy' (2000) 42 *Managerial Law* 1–127.

Cheffins, Brian R., 'Law, Economics and the UK's System of Corporate Governance: Lessons from History' (2001a) 1 *Journal of Corporate Law Studies* 71–89.

Cheffins, Brian R., 'Does Law Matter? The Separation of Ownership and Control in the United Kingdom' (2001b) 30 *Journal of Legal Studies* 459–84.

Chicoine, Jeffrey, 'The Business Necessity Defense to Unilateral Changes in Working Conditions Under the Duty to Bargain in Good Faith' (1992) 8 *Labor Lawyer* 297–312.

Christopherson, Susan, 'Why Do National Labor Market Practices Continue to Diverge in the Global Economy? The "Missing Link" of Investment Rules' (2002) 78 *Economic Geography* 1–20.

Clark, Robert, 'The Interdisciplinary Study of Legal Evolution' (1981) 90 *Yale Law Journal* 1238–74.

Coase, Ronald, 'The Nature of the Firm' (1937) 4 *Economica* 386–405.

Coase, Ronald, *The Firm, the Market, and the Law* (Chicago: University of Chicago Press, 1988).

Cochran, Thomas and Miller, William, *The Age of Enterprise* (New York: Harper and Row, 1961).

Coffee, John C., 'The Uncertain Case for Takeover Reform: An Essay on Stockholders, Stakeholders and Bust-ups' (1988) *Wisconsin Law Review* 435–65.

Coffee, John C., 'Unstable Coalitions: Corporate Governance as a Multi-Player Game' (1990) 78 *Georgetown Law Journal* 1495–1549.

Coffee, John C., 'The Rise of Dispersed Ownership: The Roles of Law and the State in the Separation of Ownership and Control' (2001) 111 *Yale Law Journal* 1–82.

Collins, Hugh, 'Market Power, Bureaucratic Power, and the Contract of Employment' (1986) 15 *Industrial Law Journal* 1–15.

Collins, Hugh, 'Transfers of Undertakings and Insolvency' (1989) 18 *Industrial Law*

Journal 144–58.
Collins, Hugh, 'Independent Contractors and the Challenge of Vertical Disintegration to Employment Protection Laws' (1990) 10 *Oxford Journal of Legal Studies* 353–80.
Collins, Hugh, 'The Meaning of Job Security' (1991) 20 *Industrial Law Journal* 227–39.
Collins, Hugh, *Justice in Dismissal: The Law of Termination of Employment* (Oxford: Clarendon Press, 1992).
Collins, Hugh, *Employment Law* (Oxford: Oxford University Press, 2003).
Collins, Hugh, Davies, Paul and Rideout, Ronald (eds.), *Legal Regulation of the Employment Relation* (London: Kluwer Law International, 2000).
Cook, Jacqueline and Deakin, Simon, 'Stakeholding and Corporate Governance: Theory and Evidence on Economic Performance' ESRC Centre for Business Research, University of Cambridge (July 1999).
Coope, Christopher M., 'Justice and Jobs: Three Sceptical Thoughts about Rights in Employment' (1994) 11 *Journal of Applied Philosophy* 71–7.
Cooter, Robert and Kornhauser, Lewis, 'Can Litigation Improve the Law Without the Help of Judges?' (1980) 9 *Journal of Legal Studies* 139–63.
Craig, Paul and Harlow, Carol (eds.), *Lawmaking in the European Union* (Dordrecht: Kluwer, 1998).
Cutcher-Gershenfeld, Joel and Kochan, Thomas, 'Taking Stock: Collective Bargaining at the Turn of the Century' (2004) 58 *Industrial & Labor Relations Review* 3–26.
Cutforth, Arthur E., *Methods of Amalgamation and the Valuation of Businesses for Amalgamation and Other Purposes* (1982 edition) (New York: Garland Publishers, 1926).
Dammann, Jens C., 'Future of Codetermination after Centros: Will German Corporate Law Move Closer to the U.S. Model?' (2003) *Fordham Journal of Corporate and Financial Law* 607–88.
Dannin, Ellen, 'The NLRA at Seventy: A Union Movement for the New Century' (2005) 8 *Journal of Labor and Society* 489–99.
Dau-Schmidt, Kenneth G., 'Labor Law and Industrial Peace: A Comparative Analysis of the United States, the United Kingdom, Germany, and Japan under the Bargaining Model' (2000) 8 *Tulane Journal of International and Comparative Law* 117–46.
Davies, Anne, *Perspectives on Labour Law* (Cambridge: Cambridge University Press, 2004).
Davies, Paul, 'Recent Cases: Transfer Regulations' (1988) 17 *Industrial Law Journal* 249–53.
Davies, Paul, 'Employee Claims in Insolvency: Corporate Rescues and Preferential Claims' (1994) 23 *Industrial Law Journal* 141–51.
Davies, Paul, *Gower's Principles of Modern Company Law* (6th ed.) (London: Sweet and Maxwell, 1997).
Davies, Paul, 'European Developments: Amendments to the Acquired Rights

Directive' (1998) 27 *Industrial Law Journal* 365–73.

Davies, Paul, 'Board Structure in the UK and Germany: Convergence or Continuing Divergence?' (2000) 2 *International Comparative and Corporate Law Journal* 435–56.

Davies, Paul and Freedland, Mark, *Labour Law: Texts and Materials* (2nd ed.) (London: Weidenfeld and Nicolson, 1984).

Davies, Paul and Freedland, Mark, *Labour Legislation and Public Policy* (Oxford: Oxford University Press, 1993).

Davies, Paul and Wedderburn of Charlton, 'The Land of Industrial Democracy' (1977) 6 *Industrial Law Journal* 197–211.

Davies, Paul, Lyon-Caen, Antoine, Sciarra, Silvana and Simitis, Spiros, *European Community Labour Law: Principles and Perspectives. Liber Amicorum Lord Wedderburn* (Oxford: Clarendon Press, 1996).

Deakin, Simon, *Contract, Labour Law and the Developing Employment Relationship* (PhD Thesis: University of Cambridge, 1989).

Deakin, Simon, 'The Changing Concept of the Employer in Labour Law' (2001a) 30 *Industrial Law Journal* 72–84.

Deakin, Simon, 'The Contract of Employment: A Study in Legal Evolution' (2001b) 11 *Historical Studies in Industrial Relations* 1–36.

Deakin, Simon, 'Evolution for our Time: A Theory of Legal Memetics' (2002) 55 *Current Legal Problems*1–42.

Deakin, Simon, 'The Coming Transformation of Shareholder Value' (2005a) 13 *Corporate Governance* 11–18.

Deakin, Simon, 'The Comparative Evolution of the Employment Relationship' ESRC Centre for Business Research Working Paper No. 317 December 2005b.

Deakin, Simon and Morris, Gillian, *Labour Law* (4th ed.) (Oxford: Hart Publishing, 2005).

Deakin, Simon and Slinger, Giles, 'Hostile Takeovers, Corporate Law and the Theory of the Firm' (1997) 24 *Journal of Legal Studies* 124–51.

Deakin, Simon and Slinger, Giles, 'Company Law as an Instrument for Inclusion: Regulating Stakeholder Relations in the Context of Takeovers' ESRC Centre for Business Research, University of Cambridge Working Paper No. 145 September 1999.

Deakin, Simon and Wilkinson, Frank, *The Law of the Labour Market* (Oxford: Oxford University Press, 2005).

Deakin, Simon, Hobbs, Richard, Konzelmann, Sue and Wilkinson, Frank,'Anglo-American Corporate Governance and the Employment Relationship: A Case to Answer?' ESRC Centre for Business Research, University of Cambridge Working Paper No. 308 June 2005.

Demsetz, Harold, 'Toward a Theory of Property Rights' (1967) 57 *American Economic Review* 347–59.

Dennett, Daniel C., *Darwin's Dangerous Idea: Evolution and the Meanings of Life* (London: Simon & Schuster, 1995).

Dodd, E. Merrick, 'For Whom Are Corporate Managers Trustees?' (1932) 45

Harvard Law Review 1145–63.

Donaldson, Thomas and Preston, Lee, 'The Stakeholder Theory of the Corporation: Concepts, Evidence, and Implications' (1995) 20 *Academy of Management Review* 65–91.

Donnelly, Shawn, Gamble, Andrew, Jackson, Gregory and Parkinson, John, *The Public Interest and the Company in Britain and Germany* (London: Anglo-German Foundation, 2000).

Dowling Jr.,Donald C., 'The Intersection Between U.S. Bankruptcy And Employment Law' (1994) 10 *Labor Lawyer* 57–72.

Easterbrook, Frank H. and Fischel, Daniel R., *The Economic Structure of Corporate Law* (Cambridge, Massachusetts: Harvard University Press, 1991).

Eisenberg, Melvin, 'Relational Contracts' in Jack Beatson and Daniel Friedmann (eds.), *Good Faith and Fault in Contract Law* (Oxford: Clarendon Press, 1995).

Eisenberg, Melvin A., 'The Corporation as a Nexus of Contracts and the Dual Nature of the Firm' (1999) 24 *Journal of Corporate Law* 1253–92.

Epstein, Richard A., 'In Defense of the Contract at Will' (1984) 51 *University of Chicago Law Review* 947–82.

Fama, Eugene, 'Agency Problems and the Theory of the Firm' (1980) 88 *Journal of Political Economy* 288–307.

Fama, Eugene F. and Jensen, Michael C. 'Separation of Ownership and Control' (1983) 26 *Journal of Law and Economics* 301–25.

Fannon, Irene Lynch, *Working Within Two Kinds of Capitalism: Corporate Governance and Employee Stakeholding US and EC Perspectives* (Oxford: Hart Publishing, 2003).

FitzRoy, Felix and Kraft, Kornelius, 'Co-determination, Efficiency and Productivity' (2005) 43 *British Journal of Industrial Relations* 233–47.

Feinman, Jay M., 'The Development of the Employment at Will Rule' (1976) 20 *American Journal of Legal History* 118–135.

Flanagan, Robert J., 'Has Management Strangled U.S. Unions?' (2005) 26 *Journal of Labor Research* 33–63.

Foster, Nigel H.D., 'Company Law Theory in Comparative Perspective: England and France' (2000) 48 *American Journal of Comparative Law* 573–621.

Fox, Alan, *Beyond Contract: Work, Power and Trust Relations* (London: Faber, 1974).

Frank, Marlene, 'The Rights of Employees in the Event of the Employer's Insolvency: A Comparative Approach to the Rights of Employees in the United States and Europe' (2005) 1 *New Zealand Postgraduate Law e-Journal* 1–45.

Franks, Julian and Mayer, Colin 'Governance as a Source of Managerial Disciplining' (2000) Journal of Applied Corporate Finance' Report for the Company Law Review Committee <www.dti.gov.uk/cld/franksreport.pdf>

Fredman, Sandra, 'Women at Work: The Broken Promise of Flexicurity' (2004) 33 *Industrial Law Journal* 299–319.

Fredman, Sandra, 'Labour Law in Flux: The Changing Composition of the Workforce'

(1997) 26 *Industrial Law Journal* 337–52.

Freedland, Mark, *The Personal Employment Contract* (Oxford: Oxford University Press, 2003).

Freeman, Edward, 'Business Ethics at the Millennium' (2000) 10 *Business Ethics Quarterly* 169–80.

Friedman, Milton, 'The Methodology of Positive Economics' In *Essays in Positive Economics* (Chicago: University of Chicago Press, 1953).

Frisby, Sandra, 'TUPE or not TUPE? Employee Protection, Corporate Rescue and "One Unholy Mess"' (2000) *Company, Financial and Insolvency Law Review* 249–71.

Ghilarducci, Teresa, Hawley, James and Williams, Andrew, 'Labour's Paradoxical Interests and the Evolution of Corporate Governance' (1997) 24 *Journal of Law and Society* 26–43.

Goergen, Marc, Martynova, Marina and Renneboog, Luc, 'Corporate Governance Convergence: Evidence From Takeover Regulation Reforms in Europe' (March 2005) Utrecht School of Economics Tjalling C. Koopmans Research Institute Discussion Paper Series 05–19.

Gordon, Jeffrey and Roe, Mark, (eds.), *Convergence and Persistence in Corporate Governance* (Cambridge University Press, New York, 2004).

Gorton, Gary and Schmid, Frank, 'Class Struggle Inside the Firm: A Study of German Codetermination' (2000) *National Bureau of Economic Research* Working Paper No. W7945.

Gould, William B. IV, 'The Idea of the Job as Property in Contemporary America: The Legal and Collective Bargaining Framework' (1986) *Brigham Young University Law Review* 885–918.

Gould, William B. IV, 'Job Security in the United States: Some Reflections on Unfair Dismissal and Plant Closure from a Comparative Perspective' (1988) 67 *Nebraska Law Review* 28–55.

Grainger, Heidi, *Trade Union Membership 2005* (London: Department of Trade and Industry, 2005).

Grantham, Ross, 'The Doctrinal Basis of the Rights of Company Shareholders' (1998) 57 *Cambridge Law Journal* 554–88.

Gray, Kevin J., 'Property in Thin Air' (1991) 50 *Cambridge Law Journal* 252–307.

Gray, Kevin and Gray, Susan F., *Elements of Land Law* (4th ed.) (Oxford: Oxford University Press, 2005).

Green, Francis and McIntosh, Steve, 'Union Power, Cost of Job Loss and Workers' Effort' (1998) 51 *Industrial & Labor Relations Review* 363–83.

Greenwood, Daniel J.H., 'Fictional Shareholders: For Whom Are Corporate Managers Trustees' Revisited' (1996) 69 *Southern California Law Review* 1021–1104.

Grossman, Sanford and Hart, Oliver, 'The Costs and Benefits of Ownership: A Theory of Vertical and Lateral Integration' (1986) 94 *Journal of Political Economy* 691–719.

Hale, Kathleen, 'Corporate Law and Stakeholders: Moving Beyond Stakeholder

Statutes' (2003) 45 *Arizona Law Review* 823–56.

Hall, Mark, 'Assessing the Information and Consultation of Employees Regulations' (2005) 34 *Industrial Law Journal* 103–26.

Hall, Peter A. and Soskice, David (eds.), *Varieties of Capitalism: The Institutional Foundations of Comparative Advantage* (Oxford: Oxford University Press, 2001).

Hannah, Leslie, 'Takeover Bids in Britain Before 1950: An Exercise in Business "Pre-History"' (1974) 16 *Business History* 65–77.

Hannah, Leslie, *The Rise of the Corporate Economy* (London: Methuen, 1983).

Hansmann, Henry, *The Ownership of Enterprise* (London: Belknap Press, 1996).

Hansmann, Henry and Kraakman, Reinier, 'The End of History for Corporate Law' (2001) 89 *Georgetown Law Journal* 439–68.

Harris, James W., *Property and Justice* (Oxford: Oxford University Press, 1996).

Harris, Julian, 'Law Society Issues Criticisms of Company Law Reform Bill at Second Reading' (2006) *Company Lawyer* 95–6.

Hart, Oliver, 'An Economist's Perspective on the Theory of the Firm' (1989) 89 *Columbia Law Review* 1757–74.

Hart, Oliver, 'An Economist's View of Fiduciary Duty' (1993) 43 *University of Toronto Law Journal* 299–313.

Hart, Oliver, *Firms, Contracts and Financial Structure* (Oxford: Clarendon Press, 1995).

Hart, Oliver and Moore, John, 'Property Rights and the Nature of the Firm' (1990) 98 *Journal of Political Economy* 1119–58.

Hathaway, Oona, 'Path Dependence in the Law: The Course and Pattern of Legal Change in a Common Law System' (2001) 86 *Iowa Law Review* 601–65.

Hepple, Bob, 'The Right to Work' (1981) 10 *Industrial Law Journal* 65–83.

Hepple, Bob, 'Restructuring Employment Rights' (1986) 15 *Industrial Law Journal* 69–83.

Hepple, Bob, *Rights At Work: Global, European and British Perspectives* (London: Sweet & Maxwell, 2005).

Hepple, Bob and Morris, Gillian, 'The Employment Act 2002 and the Crisis of Individual Employment Rights' (2002) 31 *Industrial Law Journal* 245–69.

Hermann, Donald H.J. and Sor, Yvonne S., 'Property Rights in One's Job: The Case for Limiting Employment-At-Will' (1982) 24 *Arizona Law Review* 763–820.

Honoré, Tony, *The Quest For Security: Employees, Tenants, Wives,* The Hamlyn Lectures (London: Stevens & Sons, 1982).

Hovenkamp, Herbert, *Enterprise and American Law: 1836–1937* (Cambridge: Harvard University Press, 1991).

Ireland, Paddy, 'Capitalism Without the Capitalist: The Joint Stock Company Share and the Emergence of the Modern Doctrine of Separate Corporate Personality' (1996a) 17 *Legal History* 40–72.

Ireland, Paddy 'Corporate Governance, Stakeholding, and the Company: Towards a Less Degenerate Capitalism?' (1996b) 23 *Journal of Law and Society* 287–320.

Ireland, Paddy, 'Company Law and the Myth of Shareholder Ownership' (1999) 62

Modern Law Review 32–57.

Jacoby, Sanford, 'The Duration of Indefinite Employment Contracts in The United States and England: A Historical Analysis' (1982) 5 *Comparative Labor Law* 85–128.

Jarrell, George A. and Bradley, Michael, 'The Wealth Effects of Litigation by Targets: Do Interests Diverge in a Merge?' (1980) 28 *Journal of Law and Economics* 151–77.

Jensen, Michael C. and Ruback, Richard S., 'The Market for Corporate Control: The Scientific Evidence' (1983) 11 *Journal of Financial Economics* 5–50.

Johnston, Alexander, *The City Takeover Code* (Oxford: Oxford University Press, 1980).

Kahan, Marcel and Klausner, Michael, 'Path Dependence in Corporate Contracting: Increasing Returns, Herd Behavior and Cognitive Biases' (1996) 74 *Washington University Law Quarterly* 347–66.

Kahan, Michael and Rock, Edward B., 'How I Learned to Stop Worrying and Love the Pill: Adaptive Responses to Takeover Law' (2002) 69 *University of Chicago Law Review* 871–916.

Kahn-Freund, Otto, 'A Note on Status and Contract in Modern Labour Law' (1967) 30 *Modern Law Review* 635–44.

Kahn-Freund, Otto, 'On Uses and Misuses of Comparative Law' (1974) 37 *Modern Law Review* 1–27.

Kahn-Freund, Otto, 'Industrial Democracy' (1977a) 6 *Industrial Law Journal* 65–84.

Kahn-Freund, Otto, 'Blackstone's Neglected Child: the Contract of Employment' (1977b) 93 *Law Quarterly Review* 508–28.

Katz, Avery, 'Taking Private Ordering Seriously' (1996) 144 *University of Pennsylvania Law Review* 1745–63.

Kay, John and Silberston, Aubrey, 'Corporate Governance' (1995) 153 *National Institute Economic Review* 84–95.

Kelly, Gavin and Parkinson, John, 'The Conceptual Foundations of the Company: A Pluralist Approach' (1988) 2 *Company Financial and Insolvency Law Review* 174–97.

Kelly, Marjorie, 'The Incredibly Unproductive Shareholder' (2000) 80 *Harvard Business Review* 18–19.

Kershaw, David, 'No End in Sight for the History of Corporate Law: The Case of Employee Participation in Corporate Governance' (2002) 2 *Journal of Corporate Law Studies* 34–81.

Kim, Pauline T., 'Bargaining with Imperfect Information: A Study of Worker Perceptions of Legal Protection in an At-will World' (1997) 83 *Cornell Law Review* 105–60.

Kirchner, Christian and Painter, Richard W., 'Takeover Defenses Under Delaware Law, the Proposed Thirteeth EU Directive and the New German Takeover Law: Comparisons and Recommendations for Reform' (2002) 50 *American Journal of*

Comparative Law 451–76.

Klein, Benjamin, Crawford, Robert G. and Alchian, Armen A., 'Vertical Integration, Appropriate Rents and the Competitive Contracting Process' (1981) 89 *Journal of Political Economy* 615–41.

La Porta, Rafael, Lopez-de-Silanes, Florencio and Shleifer, Andrei, 'Corporate Ownership Around the World' (1999) 54 *Journal of Finance* 471–517.

Lane, Christel, 'Changes in Corporate Governance of German Corporations: Convergence to the Anglo-American Model?' (March 2003) ESRC Center for Business Research Working Paper No. 259.

Leibowitz, Stan J. and Margolis, Stephen, 'Path Dependence, Lock-In, and History' (1995) 11 *Journal of Law, Economics and Organization* 205–26.

Licht, Amir N., 'The Mother of all Path Dependencies: Toward a Cross-Cultural Theory of Corporate Governance Systems' (2001) 26 *Delaware Journal of Corporate Law* 147–205.

Lorber, Pascale, 'Reviewing the European Works Council Directive: European Progress and United Kingdom Perspective' (2004) 33 *Industrial Law Journal* 191–99.

Macey, Jonathan R., '*Smith v. Van Gorkom*: Insights about CEOs, Corporate Law Rules, and the Jurisdictional Competition for Corporate Charters' (2002) 96 *Northwestern University Law Review* 607–29.

McGee, John, (2006) 122 *Law Quarterly Review* 525–28.

McMullen, John, 'Takeovers, Transfers and Business Re-Organizations' (1992) 21 *Industrial Law Journal* 15–30.

Manne, Henry, 'Mergers and the Market for Corporate Control' (1965) 73 *Journal of Political Economy* 110–21.

March, James G., *Decisions and Organizations* (New York: Basil Blackwell, 1998).

Mattei, Ugo, *Comparative Law and Economics* (Ann Arbor: University of Michigan Press, 1997).

Merrill, Thomas and Smith, Henry, 'What Happened to Property in Law and Economics?' (2001) 111 *Yale Law Journal* 357–98.

Meyers, Frederic, *Ownership of Jobs: A Comparative Study* (Los Angeles: University of California, 1964).

Michie, Jonathan and Oughton, Christine, 'Employee Participation and Ownership Rights' (2002) 2 *Journal of Corporate Law Studies* 143–59.

Millon, David, 'Redefining Corporate Law' (1991) 24 *Indiana Law Review* 223–77.

Mitchell, Lawrence, E., 'A Theoretical and Practical Framework for Enforcing Corporate Constituency Statutes' (1992) 70 *Texas Law Review* 579–643.

Mitchell, Richard, O'Donnell, Anthony and Ramsay, Ian, *Shareholder Value and Employee Interests: Intersections Between Corporate Governance, Corporate Law and Labour Law* (Melbourne: University of Melbourne, 2005).

Morrison, Wayne (ed.), *Blackstone's Commentaries on the Laws of England* (London:

Cavendish Publishing, 2001).

Morriss, Andrew P., 'Exploding Myths: An Empirical and Economic Reassessment of the Rise of Employment at-Will' (1994) 59 *Missouri Law Review* 679–774.

Moss, Scott A., 'Where There's At-Will, There are Many Ways: Redressing the Increasing Incoherence of Employment At-Will' (2006) 67 *Pittsburgh Law Review*.

Mossoff, Adam, 'Locke's Labor Lost' (2002) 9 *University of Chicago Law School Roundtable* 155–64.

Munzer, Stephen, *A Theory of Property* (Cambridge: Cambridge University Press, 1990).

Njoya, Wanjiru,. 'The Interface Between Redundancy and TUPE Transfers' (2003) 32 *Industrial Law Journal* 123–8.

Njoya, Wanjiru, 'Employee Ownership and Efficiency: An Evolutionary Perspective' (2004) *Industrial Law Journal* 211–41.

Njoya, Wanjiru, 'Employment, Implicit Contracts and the Duty of Care' (2005) 121 *Law Quarterly Review* 33–8.

Njoya, Wanjiru, (2006) 17 *Kings College Law Journal* 182–88.

O'Connor, Marleen A., 'The Human Capital Era: Reconceptualizing Corporate Law to Facilitate Labor-Management Cooperation' (1993) 78 *Cornell Law Review* 899–965.

O'Connor, Marleen A., 'Organized Labor as Shareholder Activist: Building Coalitions to Promote Worker Capitalism' (1997) 31 *University of Richmond Law Review* 1345–98.

O'Connor, Marleen, 'Labor's Role in the American Corporate Governance Structure' (2000) 22 *Comparative Labor Law and Policy Journal* 97–133.

Parkinson, John, *Corporate Power and Responsibility: Issues in the Theory of Company Law* (Oxford: Clarendon Press, 1993).

Patfield, Fiona (ed.), *Perspectives on Company Law: I* (London: Kluwer Law International, 1995).

Pencavel, John, 'Unionism Viewed Internationally' (2005) 26 *Journal of Labor Research* 65–97.

Pennington, Robert R., 'Can Shares in Companies be defined?' (1989) 10 *Company Lawyer* 140–44.

Posner, Richard A., 'A Reply to Some Recent Criticisms of the Efficiency Theory of the Common Law' (1980-81) 9 *Hofstra Law Review* 775–94.

Prentice, Dan D. and Holland, Peter R.J. (eds.), *Contemporary Issues in Corporate Governance* (Oxford: Clarendon Press, 1993).

Pretto-Sakmann, Arianna, *Shares and Sub-Shares: The Boundaries of Personal Property* (Oxford: Hart Publishing, 2005).

Putterman, Louis and Krozner, Randall (eds.), *The Economic Nature of the Firm: A Reader* (Cambridge: Cambridge University Press, 1996).

Radin, Max, 'The Endless Problem of Corporate Personality' (1932) 32 *Columbia Law Review* 643–67.

Ramsay, Ian (ed.), *Gambotto v WCP Limited: Its Implications for Corporate*

Regulation (Melbourne: Centre for Corporate Law & Securities Regulation, 1996).

Rebérioux, Antoine, 'European Style of Corporate Governance at the Crossroads: The Role of Worker Involvement' (2002) 40 *Journal of Common Market Studies* 111–34.

Reich, Charles A., 'The New Property' (1964) 73 *Yale Law Journal* 734–87.

Ribstein, Larry E. and Alces, Kelli, 'Directors' Duties in Failing Firms' (2006) Illinois Law and Economics Working Papers Series, Working Paper No. LE06-004 (January 2006).

Richardi, Rheinhard, 'Worker Participation in Decisions Within Undertakings in the Federal Republic of Germany' (1982) 5 *Comparative Labor Law* 23–50.

Riley, Christopher A., 'The Company Director's Duty of Care and Skill: The Case for an Onerous but Subjective Standard' (1999) 62 *Modern Law Review* 697–724.

Roberts, Gary M. 'Bankruptcy and the Union's Bargain: Equitable Treatment of Collective Bargaining Agreements' (1987) 39 *Stanford Law Review* 1015–56.

Robinson, Andrew M. and Zhang, Hao, 'Employee Share Ownership: Safeguarding Investments in Human Capital' (2005) 43 *British Journal of Industrial Relations* 469–88.

Rock, Edward B. and Wachter, Michael L., 'Labor Law Successorship: A Corporate Law Approach' (1993-94) 92 *Michigan Law Review* 203–60.

Roe, Mark, 'Chaos and Evolution in Law and Economics' (1996) 109 *Harvard Law Review* 641–68.

Roe, Mark, *Political Determinants of Corporate Governance* (Oxford: Oxford University Press, 2003).

Rogowski, Ralf and Wilthagen, Ton (eds.), *Reflexive Labour Law* (Deventer: Kluwer, 1994).

Romano, Roberta, 'Competition for Corporate Charters and the Lesson of Takeover Statutes' (1993a) 61 *Fordham Law Review* 843–64.

Romano, Roberta, 'Corporate Governance as Ideology' (1993b) 102 *Yale Law Journal* 2021–37.

Rottenburg, Simon, 'Property in Work' (1961–62) 15 *Industrial & Labor Relations Review* 402–5.

St. Antoine, Theodore J., 'You're Fired!' (1982) 10 *Human Rights* 32–7; 53–4.

Sadowski, Dieter, Junkes, Joachim and Lindenthal, Sabine, 'The German Model of Corporate and Labor Governance' (2000) 22 *Comparative Labor Law and Policy Journal* 33–66.

Samuel, Horace B., *Shareholders' Money: An Analysis of Certain Defects in Company Legislation with Proposals for their Reform* (London: Sir Isaac Pitman & Sons Ltd, 1933).

Sargeant, Malcolm, 'Protecting Employees with Insolvent Employers' (2003) 32 *Industrial Law Journal* 53–9.

Sayre, Francis B., *Cases on Labor Law* (Cambridge: Harvard University Press, 1922).

Sciara, Silvana (ed.), *Labour Law in the Courts: National Judges and the European*

Court of Justice (Oxford: Hart, 2001).

Sealy, Leonard S., *Cases and Materials in Company Law* (7th ed.) (London: Butterworths, 2001).

Selznick, Philip, *Law, Society and Industrial Justice* (New York: Russel Sage Foundation, 1969).

Sheikh, Saleem and Rees, William (eds.), *Corporate Governance and Control* (London: Cavendish, 1995).

Shleifer, Andrei and Summers, Lawrence, 'Breach of Trust in Hostile Takeovers' *National Bureau of Economic Research Working Paper No. W2342* (May 1989). Published in Alan J. Auerbach (ed.), *Corporate Takeovers: Causes and Consequences* (Chicago: University of Chicago Press, 1988).

Simons, Rolf and Kluge, Norbert (eds.), *Workers' Participation at Board Level in the EU-15 Countries: Reports on the National Systems and Practices* (Brussels: Hans Böckler Foundation and European Trade Union Institute, 2004).

Simpson, Derek, 'Manufacturing: What We Want From Warwick' (2005) 55 *Federation News* 28–9.

Singer, Joseph W., 'The Reliance Interest in Property' (1988) 40 *Stanford Law Review* 611–750.

Singer, Joseph W., 'Jobs and Justice: Rethinking the Stakeholder Debate' (1993) 43 *University of Toronto Law Journal* 475–731.

Slinger, Giles, 'Spanning the Gap: The Theoretical Principles That Connect Stakeholder Policies to Business Performance' (1998) University of Cambridge: ESRC Centre for Business Research Working Paper Series (WP 11).

Smith, Gordon D., 'The Shareholder Primacy Norm' (1998) 23 *Journal of Corporation Law* 277–323.

Springer, Jonathan D., 'Corporate Constituency Statutes: Hollow Hopes and False Fears' (1999) *Annual Survey of American Law* 85–124.

Steinfeld, Robert J., *The Invention of Free Labor: The Employment Relation in English and American Law and Culture, 1350-1870* (Chapel Hill: University of North Carolina Press, 1991).

Steinmetz, William (ed.), *Private Law and Social Inequality in the Industrial Age: Comparing Legal Cultures in Britain, France, Germany, and the United States* (Oxford: Oxford University Press, 2000).

Sternberg, Elaine, 'The Defects of Stakeholder Theory' (1997) 5 *Corporate Governance* 3–10.

Stone, Katherine V.W., 'Employees as Stakeholders under State Nonshareholder Constituency Statutes' (1991) 21 *Stetson Law Review* 45–72.

Stone, Katherine V.W., 'Knowledge at Work: Disputes Over the Ownership of Human Capital in the Changing Workplace' (2002) 34 *University of Connecticut Law Review* 721–64.

Strauss, George and Rosenstein, Eliezer, 'Worker Participation: A Critical View' (1970) 9 *Industrial Relations* 197–214.

Summers, Clyde W., 'Worker Dislocation: Who Bears the Burden? A Comparative Study of Social Values in Five Countries' (1995) 70 *Notre Dame Law Review*

1030–78.

Teubner, Gunther, *Law as An Autopoietic System* (Oxford: Blackwell Publishers, 1993).

Teubner, Gunther and Hopt, Klaus J. (eds.), *Corporate Governance and Directors' Liabilities* (Berlin: Walter de Gruyter, 1985).

Thelen, Kathleen, *Union of Parts: Labor Politics in Postwar Germany* (Ithaca: Cornell University Press, 1991).

Tomlins, Christopher L., *Law, Labor and Ideology in the Early American Republic* (Cambridge: Cambridge University Press, 1993).

Topel, Robert, 'Specific Capital and Unemployment: Measuring the Costs and Consequences of Job Loss' in Allan Meltzer and Charles Plosser (ed.s) *Studies in Labor Economics in Honor of Walter Oi* (Amsterdam: Elsevier, 1990).

Upex, Robert, Benny, Richard and Hardy, Stephen, *Labour Law* (Oxford: Oxford University Press, 2004).

Van der Weide, Mark E., 'Against Fiduciary Duties to Corporate Stakeholders' (1996) 21 *Delaware Journal of Corporate Law* 27–86.

Vitols, Sigurt and Englehardt, Lutz, 'National Institutions and High Tech Industries: A Varieties of Capitalism Perspective on the Failure of Germany's "Neuer Markt"' Social Science Research Center Berlin February 2005, <www.ssrn.com>.

Waldron, Jeremy, *The Right to Private Property* (Oxford: Clarendon Press, 1988).

Webb, Sidney and Webb, Beatrice, *Industrial Democracy* (Edinburgh: R & R Clark Limited, 1898).

Wedderburn of Charlton, *Company Law Reform*, Fabian Tract 363 (London: Fabian Society, 1965).

Wedderburn of Charlton, *Labour Law: Old Traditions and New Developments* (Toronto: Clarke, Irwin & Co, 1968).

Wedderburn of Charlton, 'The Social Responsibility of Companies' (1985) 15 *Melbourne University Law Review* 4–30.

Wedderburn of Charlton, 'Labour Law: From Here to Autonomy?' (1987) 16 *Industrial Law Journal* 1–29.

Wedderburn of Charlton, 'Employees, Partnership and Company Law' (2002) 31 *Industrial Law Journal* 99–111.

Wedderburn of Charlton, *The Future of Company Law: Fat Cats, Corporate Governance and Workers* (London: Institute of Employment Rights, 2004).

Weiler, Paul C., *Governing the Workplace: The Future of Labor and Employment Law* (Massachusetts: Harvard University Press, 1990).

Weinrib, Ernest J., *The Idea of Private Law* (London: Harvard University Press, 1995).

Weiss, Manfred, 'Individual Employment Rights: Focusing on Job Security in the Federal Republic of Germany' (1988) 67 *Nebraska Law Review* 82–100.

Weiss, Marley S., 'The Impact of the European Economic Community on Labor Law: A Comparative American Commentary' (1993) 68 *Chicago-Kent Law Review* 1427–68.

Wells, Alan, 'Company Law Reform – Too Far or Not Far Enough?' (2006) 27

Business Law Review 100–101.

Wheeler, Sally (ed.), *A Reader on the Law of the Business Enterprise* (Oxford: Oxford University Press, 1994).

Whincop, Michael, *An Economic And Jurisprudential Genealogy Of Corporate Law* (Aldershot: Ashgate/Dartmouth, 2001).

White, Phil J., 'Unfair Dismissal Legislation and Property Rights: Some Reflections' (1985) 16 *Industrial Relations Journal* 98–105.

Williams, Joan, 'The Rhetoric of Property' (1998) 83 *Iowa Law Review* 277–361.

Williamson, Oliver E. and Winter, Sidney G. (eds.), *The Nature of the Firm: Origins, Evolution and Development* (Oxford: Oxford University Press, 1993).

Winkler, Adam, 'Corporate Law or the Law of Business? Stakeholders and Corporate Governance at the End of History' (2004) 67 *Journal of Law and Contemporary Problems* 109–33.

Wood, Horace G., *A Treatise on the Law of Master and Servant* (2nd ed.) (Albany: John D. Parsons, 1877) (original ed. 1886).

Worthington, Sarah, 'Shares and Shareholders: Property, Power and Entitlement' (2001) 22 *The Company Lawyer* 258–66; 307–14.

Yale Law Journal, Note, 'Creditors' Derivative Suits on Behalf of Solvent Corporations' (1979) 88 *Yale Law Journal* 1299–318.

Zingales, Luigi,'Corporate Governance' in Peter Newman (ed.), *The New Palgrave Dictionary of Economics and the Law* (London and Basingstoke: Macmillan, 1998).

Index